Are You Ready for Cooking?

by

H. Win

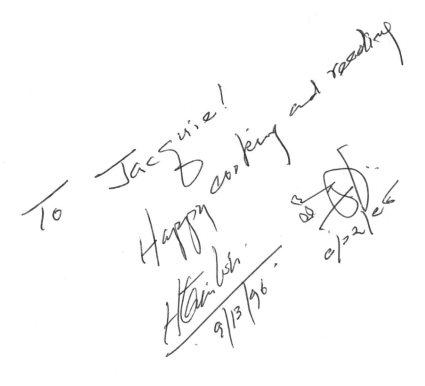

This cookbook is dedicated in the memory of our first son John Htain Win, my wife Susan's parents William Russell McEnroe Jr. and Jane VanDusen McEnroe and my father, Oo Nyo and mother Daw Kyawt Yin.

CONTENTS

2. Preparing and Cooking Techniques, 158

iv

3. The Art of Recipe Variation, 183

4. Simmer-Saute, 216

5. Techniques versus Flavor, 242

Index, 277

List of Diagrams

List of Tables

Introduction

"When you are in a hurry, follow the old roads you know" is an old Burmese saying. Thus, when you are exhausted and lack enthusiasm for cooking, you resort to your old familiar favorite dishes to play it safe. Hence, some 207 traditional, popular, and simple American and Asian recipes are featured. Among which 38 vegetable and 17 egg recipes are included for the vegetarians.

Current trend in Western cooking is expanding into the use of, among others, Asian seasoning ingredients, such as cilantro, chutney, curry, fenugreek, ginger, mango, papaya, turmeric, and so forth. One reason would be to use more of the ingredients that are low in fat and cholesterol, alternative herbal ingredients, in cooking. The Asian ingredients also provide exciting flavor dimension, robustness, and crisp spiciness, contrasting the usual mild and blended Western flavor. This trend is the beginning of a dietary paradigm shift in the Western culinary art. The Asian recipes included in this cookbook will lead you to a different panorama of flavors. I might also add that the Indian vegetarian recipes included are among the most exciting in aroma, flavor, and taste that any ethnic cooking has to offer without resorting to milk, eggs, cheese, etc. Most recipes are primarily intended for weekday cooking for the busy people who must prepare their casual but healthful, satisfying, and inexpensive meals. Cooking skill requirements for the recipes are minimal. However, non-recipe texts on The Art of Recipe Variations, Simmer-Saute, and Techniques Versus Flavor are included to provide basic skill for the casual cooking and quench some culinary artistic thirsts.

Recipes are reproducible, safe, and simple. Condensed instructions for cooking and ingredients preparations are used in the recipes. But their detailed mechanics are described in a modular format with their safety precautions in a separate chapter, Chapter 2, for use as reference. The recipes are healthful without emphasizing either abstention from harmful but essential foods (cholesterol, fats, saturated fats, and so forth) or managing of the caloric intake and the dietary supplements (amino acids, antioxidants, trace metals, vitamins, etc.). Hence, my understanding of the wellness is not focussed to dieting, counting calories, and so forth if a person's general health is good and has no specific medical condition that requires dietary or nutritional regimentation. This doesn't mean that I am not interested in longevity of life. On the contrary, my desire for the longevity is no less than anyone who is fanatic about a healthful longer life.

The recipes employ most kinds of ingredients, but in moderation. The keyword here is "moderation". This magic word may be trivial but its implications are biologically significant, at least to my big picture of the wellness. The human body system is a wonderful organization of cells. It self-manages the production of biochemical necessities (enzymes, hormones, proteins, etc.) and destruction of excesses and harmful substances. Thus, it self-regulates, self-repairs, self-replicates, and self-services for its own survival. Although the life and health sciences are making progress in exponential proportions they are still many light years away from complete understanding of the system at the molecular level. Therefore, the scientific imperatives of the human system are largely unknown and will remain so for a long time.

Although no human being understands the reaction mechanisms of the system completely, most scientists can imagine, using their knowledge, experience, and intuition, a chemical scenario that fits their own big picture. An oversimplified chemical scenario that fits my imagination would consist of a series of biochemical reactions that are neatly packed in our body, synthesizing and metabolizing the biochemical necessities from what we breath, drink, and eat. They function perpetually during their life span. To produce and manage the biochemical activities within such a small and compact body, most of these reactions could be assuming more than one task (multi-task capabilities). Furthermore, they could also be interdependent of each other in establishing their reactions equilibria (in balances). When these equilibria are thrown out of balance by our emotional stress, overeating, overdrinking, etc., the system must immediately reestablish the balances for its survival. The equilibria orchestrate their efforts to produce the needed biochemical and destroy the excesses that are causing the problem. But, these efforts to restore the balances could impose extra burden on the reactions that are performing their routine housekeeping chores. Therefore, sustaining such detours could lead to illnesses, diseases, and so forth.

In order for the system to survive, every equilibrium must have a certain capacity to tolerate the upsets. When the equilibria are thrown out of balances they immediately express the imbalances to us via pain, indigestion, hunger, etc. Other kinds of equilibria upsets are not communicated to us immediately. Instead, the excesses are metabolized into fats, plaques, stones, etc. and are deposited in certain parts of the body or vital organs. Thus, the repeated upsets could eventually lead to diseases, illnesses, and so forth. I believe our system allows us to eat,

2

drink, and enjoy our favorite foods, but in moderate amounts and frequencies. As long as the equilibria are disturbed within their tolerance limits along with our stress management and regular exercises, our system can maintain our wellness for us. Thus, we need to listen to our system signals and help them to help us. Hence, consumption in moderation is a keyword to help maintain the equilibria within their tolerance capacities. Overindulgence in our favorite foods is our common weakness. Strict dieting, counting calories, and resorting to dietary supplements and artificial food substitutes are our self-deceptive solutions. The real solution is in educating ourselves to learn to manage our emotional stress, physical fitness, and eating and drinking in moderation.

There is many more exciting and interesting info installed for your enjoyment in the chapters ahead.

I am especially grateful to my beloved wife Susan and my friend and colleague Keith C. Atkinson, who have given me unlimited access to their knowledge, patience, and wisdom during the entire time of writing this book. I also would like to extend my gratitude for sharing/reviewing part of the manuscript to a number of friends, colleagues, and neighbors, including Mrs. Barbara Carroll, Professor John A. Kaczynski Jr., Oo Kyaw Myint (Johnny), Joshua Salary Jr., and Dr. Mahm Thet San (Stanley). My special gratitude to Mrs. Vicky Manohar Singh for her efforts towards researching valuable botanical names of some Burmese herbs and spices. I am also very much grateful to the management and the staff of the Herald House Publishing for their competent and dedicated efforts in all phases of the production and the production of the complimentary promotional flyers for this cookbook

Finally, I never could have completed this book without emotional support and help from the remaining family. To my brother Lt. Col. Htain Lin (Retired) for his critical discussion and experienced advice; to my daughter Tracey for her creative art work of this cookbook cover and the drawings in the book; to my daughter Lydia for her assistance in marketing; and to my 6-year old granddaughter Eshee (Alicia) for taking some time from her busy schedule (playing) to pose for the cover picture of this cookbook. Finally, my unending gratitude to my son Patrick for his critical advice and sponsoring publication of this cookbook.

Htain Win   May 15, 1996

1.
RECIPES

Bell Pepper (Sweet Pepper),
Capsicum grossum

Abbreviations

It is essential to introduce the acronyms used throughout this cookbook at the outset. The abbreviations are used because the words they compress are so basic in cooking jargons that one cannot talk about the cooking or the recipes without encountering them repeatedly. Thus, the acronym usage is intended to expedite reading and conserve valuable print space.

AF - aroma and flavor;
AFT - aroma, flavor, and taste;
AFTT - aroma, flavor, taste, and texture;
AFs - aromas and flavors;
AFTs - aromas, flavors, and tastes;
AFTTs - aromas, flavors, tastes, and textures;
CIs - core ingredients; **F** - degrees Fahrenheit;
GIs - garnishing ingredients; **in** - inch or inches;
MIs - main ingredients; **MSG** - monosodium glutamate;
oz - ounce or ounces; **SIs** - secondary ingredients.

About Recipes

Format. The recipes are presented in a format. The elements of the format are:

Numbering: The format consists of recipe serial number preceding the recipe title. They are arranged in order of increasing Arabic numeral beginning with the first recipe, **"1   Beef with Pickled Tofu"**. The recipe is assigned number 1.

Head notes: Some recipes are shown with some interesting notes about the recipe and they are presented in the Head Notes which appears immediately below the recipe title.

Grouping: Ingredients are listed in groups following the Head Notes, if the notes are used. To simplify the cooking the ingredients used at the same point in the cooking are grouped together in the recipes. The groups are numbered with Arabic numerals in the sequences of their uses in the instructions. Thus, Group 1 ingredients are used before Group 2, the Group 2 ingredients are used before the Group 3, and so forth. However, it is customary in all ethnic cooking to prepare the ingredients (culling, cutting, trimming, washing, etc.) before the cooking begins. They are to be prepared and set aside before using unless specified otherwise. The ingredients listed in the same group may be prepared and

5

set aside in any order. They may also be put in the pot in any order as long as they are used at the specified point of the cooking sequence. However, when water or broth is listed as the first ingredient in a group, it should be added to the cooking before the other members to make the mixing easier.

Cooking: The techniques are described in the last section of the format. Essential cooking steps are described in short brief sentences. They contain sufficient info to prepare the dish. References to their detailed descriptions are indicated when the techniques are critical or lengthy (baking casseroles, cooking rice, grilling kabob, etc.). For instance, preparing corn starch mixture is described in the recipes as "combine Group 2 and set aside (see section 2)." Since the descriptions are included only in Chapter 2 the chapter number is excluded to shorten the reference. Most recipes employ simmer-saute technique to save over-the-stove time and simplify sauteing of seasoning ingredients. The technique is self explanatory. Its detailed mechanics are described in section 25. Chapter 4 is dedicated to the technique.

Ingredients. Special effort was made to keep the use of potentially unhealthful ingredients, such as butter, butter flavor, hard margarine, animal fats, heavy cream, coconut products, and other ingredients with high saturated fats and cholesterol contents to moderation in the recipes. Exotic, expensive, and rare ingredients are avoided. Those used are inexpensive and readily available in your neighborhood supermarkets. Some Asian recipes employ only the ingredients that are readily available in the supermarkets (such as cardamon seeds and powder, cilantro, cinnamon sticks, coriander powder, cumin seeds and powder, Madras curry powder, soy sauce, fresh ginger, etc.). Asian ingredients that are not commonly available in the supermarkets such as fish sauce, shrimp paste, dried fermented soybean, pickled tofu in rice wine, etc. are readily available in Asian grocery stores. Most Asian ingredients are relatively inexpensive, with the exception of saffron ($30 per ounce), and they range from US $0.99 to $5 for 20 servings or more. Most items, including the saffron, are used sparingly in cooking, and their shelf-life is three years or more under proper storage.

Listing. Most users look for the recipes in cookbooks by the type of a MI they have an appetite for, such as beef, chicken, vegetable, etc. Thus, all beef recipes are grouped together under Beef title. The group titles are arranged in alphabetical order.

Measurements. Ingredients are measured in one of the following units (whole or fractional): cups, inches, ounces, quarts, tablespoons, and teaspoons. Some vegetable amounts are expressed in physical counts or sizes (small, medium or large). Upper case T is used in all tablespoon measurements (such as 2 Tablespoons) to avoid inadvertent confusion with the teaspoon measurements. The abbreviated units (oz and in) are used without their periods. The measurements are intended for use with the fresh and pure ingredients. Old herbs and spices should be replaced. Otherwise, the impure or old ingredients (paprika, coriander, cumin, curry powder, etc.), may require to use 25 to 50 percent more than the amounts specified in the recipes to obtain their intended AFTs.

Pot Size. To prepare 2 1/2 to 3 quarts of food for four servings use 4- to 5-quart size pot for cooking. The cooking requires room for boiling, food expansion, mixing, and so forth in the pot. Thus, all cooking in the recipes are done in a 5-quart pot with cover, unless specified otherwise.

Servings. Each recipe will serve four people generously, unless specified otherwise. The intent is to make each recipe enough for the busy people who wish to prepare only one dish for their meals. Thus, you can use most any recipe as a main dish served on steamed rice, noodles, pasta, baked and mashed potatoes, biscuits, bread, salad, etc. Most of our family meals consist of only one-main-dish meals served on steamed rice and some side dishes such as mango chutney or fresh vegetables and occasionally with a vegetable soup. Such one-main-dish meals are ideal for busy people. The recipes are quite flexible. You may cut the ingredient proportions into halves for two servings or prepare a recipe for four servings and package the leftovers for three individual servings and freeze them, if you are living alone. You can also use the recipes to prepare for eight servings by using twice the proportions of the ingrrdients given in the recipes. After cooking, the food is served in a 3-quart serving bowl unless specified otherwise.

Substitutions. Most American dishes are much milder in flavors than the Asian dishes. However, there are a few which are spicy and/or hot, such as Cajun, Mexican, and Italian foods. The Asian dishes also have a wide range of mildness and spiciness. Several hot and/or spicy recipes are included. They are identified with asterisks at the end of the titles of the dishes. One asterisk (*), two asterisks (**), and three asterisks (***) for three-fire alarm (hot). Fresh cayenne, jalapeno, and bell peppers are used

7

either in whole, fractional, or diced. The cayenne, jalapeno, and red peppers are interchangeable in any recipe. The amount of hot peppers used in the recipes may be increased, decreased or omitted. It is important to indicate that the uses of fresh lemon juice in the recipes, especially in the marinating and cooking, are intended only for the freshly squeezed juice, to avoid the residual bitter tastes on the foods after they are simmered, grilled, baked, or fried.

If any of the ingredients used in the recipes (peppers, MSG, salt, and so forth) are unsuitable for your health conditions, such as allergy, diabetes, high blood pressure, etc., you may substitute with appropriate medically approved ingredients or avoid using the recipe altogether. Otherwise, substitution and variation of the proportions of the ingredients should be kept to a minimum, with the exception of the hot peppers, to experience their intended AFTT at least at your initial use of the recipes. Substitutions of alternate cooking techniques, such as using boiling for steaming, baking for simmering or steaming, etc. are less critical to the flavors than substituting the ingredients (see Chapter 5, "Techniques versus Flavor").

Cooking Time

If you ask someone casually, How long will it take a person to make a soup from a precooked soup can? That someone would answer, "five minutes". But in reality it will take at least 15 minutes. This time includes getting cooking utensils, the soup can, opening the soup can, transferring the soup mix into the pot, adding water, dispersing the soup mix in water, and heating it on the stove with occasional mixing. In addition, it will take about 5 more minutes to do the dishes after enjoying your soup. This all add up to about 20 minutes just to prepare a simple soup from the precooked soup mix. It just shows you that any cooking will take more than 20 minutes.

There are eight types of dishes included in this book: casserole, curry, kabob, salad, sauce, soup, stew, and stir fry. Of course, preparation and cooking time will vary with each type. Their preparation time will range anywhere from 15 to 60 minutes. They include setting up kitchen utensils and ingredients, such as taking out pot, knife, cutting board, oil, spices, meat, vegetables, etc. and cutting, dicing, marinating, peeling, slicing, trimming, and washing of the ingredients. Next part is the cooking time. This time is dependent only on the cooking technique and type of the ingredients used. Their time also vary, anywhere from 8 minutes (frying omelets) to 120 minutes (making soups by steaming).

But, most recipes, on the average, require only 90 minutes for preparing and cooking. The one-step-dish recipes in this book will take a lesser time, about 60 minutes for preparing and cooking. Furthermore, a simple precooking technique, simmer-saute, is used in most of the recipes. Thus, the traditional prebrowning step is avoided and reduces the most strenuous part of the cooking, over-the-stove, time from 5-20 minutes to only 2 minutes. The time consuming recipes (casseroles, kabob, battered fried foods, and steamed soups) are also included when you have time and motivation to enjoy the cooking.

Smelling and Tasting

Recognizing the aromas and flavors of freshly cooked foods is a useful skill to have. These are the same as the aromas and flavors that you get during their cooking. Once you have memorized these, you have developed the skills to judge the conditions of the ingredients during cooking, such as doneness, freshness, and burning or scorching. As you gain experience you may even be able to judge the imbalances of the proportions of the ingredients used in the cooking. You may also be able to notice when the cooked foods start to deteriorate. Because these foods develop distinct flavors and smells that are different from the aromas and flavors that you get during their cooking. Similarly, you can also identify the freshness of the fried foods (potato chips, toasted nuts, etc.). These foods give off the rancid odors and flavors of the oil. Old pretzels, crackers, breads, cookies, and so forth also produce distinct flavors and tastes that are different from the fresh ones. The chemical substances that are responsible for the aromas are volatile substances. One way of smelling them is by placing your nose at the perimeter of the food and fanning the vapors above the foods towards your nose with your palm.

CAUTION: Use your kitchen exhaust hood during cooking with one of your windoors at least slightly ajar, even in cold weather. If you don't have a hood or your hood is a recirculating type run a portable fan at one of the windoors and vent out the odors to the outdoor. Some food vapors (curry, herbs, oils, spices, etc.) given off during cooking could condense and adsorb on the kitchen wall, curtains, personal clothing, and so forth. Some of the odors, especially from the curry, could linger in the house the next day. Don't use air freshening spray to rid off the odors. The spray smells good but it contributes additional volatile chemicals to the food vapors. Prolong inhaling of the fragrance from the spray in a closed room is unhealthful and should be avoided. There is no substitute for the fresh clean air for breathing.

Recipes

Beef, 10

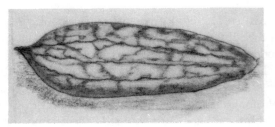

Bitter Gourd, *Momordica charantia*

1   Beef with Pickled Tofu

Group 1
32 oz beef, cut into 1/4-in slices
1 cup water
1 large garlic, diced
1 teaspoon ginger, diced
4 Tablespoons oil
Group 2
1 teaspoon soy sauce

1 teaspoon fish sauce
1/4 teaspoon MSG
3 cubes pickled tofu/red pepper/
    in rice wine
Group 3
4 stalks scallion, diced
1/4 teaspoon sesame oil
1/4 teaspoon pepper

Prepare beef per section 6a. Combine with the remaining Group 1 in pot. Mix well. Bring to boil at "Medium High" heat setting. Boil 1-2 minutes. Reset heat to "Medium Low", cover, and simmer 45 minutes. Mix occasionally. Remove cover and evaporate to sizzling. Cover and let self-saute 2-3 minutes. Mix occasionally. Add Group 2, mix, cover, and let self-saute 5 more minutes. Garnish with Group 3, and serve. Add 1/4 cup hot water for more sauce, if needed. Mix, salt to taste, and serve.

---

2   Cumin Beef*

Group 1
32 oz beef, cut into 1-in cubes
1 teaspoon ginger, diced
1/8 teaspoon red pepper
3 Tablespoons oil
1 medium onion, diced
3 medium garlic, diced
1/8 teaspoon turmeric

1 large fresh cayenne pepper,
    whole
1 teaspoon paprika
1 cup water
Group 2
2 teaspoons cumin powder
1/4 cup hot water

Prepare beef per section 6a. Combine with the remaining Group 1 in pot. Mix well. Bring to boil at "Medium High" heat setting. Boil 1-2 minutes. Reset heat to "Medium Low", cover, and simmer 45 minutes. Mix occasionally. Remove cover and evaporate to sizzling. Cover and let self-saute 2 minutes. Mix occasionally. Add Group 2, mix well, cover, simmer 3 minutes, and serve. Add 1/4 to 1 cup hot water for more sauce if needed. Mix, salt to taste, and serve.

3   Beef Minestrone

Group 1
24 oz beef, cut into 1/4-in slices
1/4 teaspoon pepper
3 Tablespoons olive oil
1/2 cup water
Group 2
1 cup hot beef broth

2 (10-oz) cans, Minestrone soup
Group 3
1 Tablespoon Parmesan cheese
  grated
1/2 cup onion/garlic flavored
  croutons, crushed

Prepare beef per section 6a. Combine with the remaining Group 1 in pot. Mix well. Bring to boil at "Medium High" heat setting. Boil 1-2 minutes. Reset heat to "Medium Low", cover, and simmer 25 minutes. Mix occasionally. Remove cover and evaporate to sizzling. Cover and let self-saute 2 minutes. Mix occasionally. Reset heat to "Medium", add Group 2, mix well, cover and let simmer 3 minutes. Garnish with Group 3, and serve. Add 1/4 cup hot water for more sauce, if needed. Mix, salt to taste, and serve.

4   Beef in Hoisin Sauce

Group 1
32 oz beef, cut into 1/4-in slices
1 large garlic, diced
5 Tablespoons oil
1 cup water
Group 2
2 Tablespoon Hoisin sauce

2 teaspoons soy sauce
1 Tablespoon rice wine
1/4 teaspoon MSG
1/2 teaspoon sugar
Group 3
4 stalks scallion, diced
1/4 teaspoon peeper

Prepare beef per section 6a. Combine with the remaining Group 1 in pot. Mix well. Bring to boil at "Medium High" heat setting. Boil 1-2 minutes. Reset heat to "Medium Low", cover, and simmer 45 minutes. Mix occasionally. Meanwhile, prepare Group 2 mixture and set aside. Remove cover and evaporate Group 1 to sizzling. Cover and let self-saute 2 minutes. Mix occasionally. Add Group 2, mix well, cover, and let self-saute 3 more minutes. Garnish with Group 3, and serve.

5   Tripe and Star Anise

Group 1
32 oz tripe, cut into 2-in pieces
1 large garlic, diced
1 Tablespoon ginger, diced
5-7 star anise
1/4 teaspoon MSG

3 Tablespoons oil
1 Tablespoon rice wine
2 cups water
3/4 teaspoon salt
Group 2
1/4 teaspoon pepper

Prepare beef per section 6a. Combine with the remaining Group 1 in pot. Mix well. Bring to boil at "Medium High" heat setting. Boil 1-2 minutes. Reset heat to "Medium Low", cover, and simmer 90-120 minutes. Mix occasionally. Remove cover and evaporate to sizzling. Mix occasionally. Reset heat to "Low", and let self-saute 5 minutes. Remove star anise from pot. Garnish with Group 2 and serve. Add 1/4 to 1 cup hot water to pot for more sauce, if needed. serve.

6   Kansas City Chili Classic

Group 1
32 oz lean ground beef
1/4 cup water
Group 2
2 cups hot beef broth
2 large garlic, diced
1 large onion, diced
1 cup bell pepper, diced
1 (16-oz) can, tomatoes and liquids

1 (18-oz) can, kidney beans and
   liquid
2 Tablespoons paprika
2 teaspoons cumin powder
1/4 teaspoon crushed red pepper
1/2 teaspoon pepper
1/2 teaspoon oregano flakes
3 Tablespoons oil
1 teaspoon salt

Combine Group 1 in pot. Mix well. Bring to boil at "Medium High" heat setting. Boil 1-2 minutes. Reset heat to "Medium Low", cover, and simmer 5 minutes. Mix occasionally. Reset heat to "Medium", remove cover, and evaporate to sizzling. Reset heat to "Low", cover, and let self-saute 5 minutes. Mix occasionally. Discard beef fat. Add Group 2, mix well. and bring to boil. Reset heat to "Medium Low", cover, and simmer 90 minutes. Add 1/4 to 1 cup hot water if more sauce is needed. Salt to taste and serve.

7   Karachi Kabob*

Group 1
1 small onion, diced
2 large garlic, diced
1 Tablespoon ginger, diced
1/2 teaspoon turmeric
1 teaspoon paprika
1/4 teaspoon red pepper, powder
1/2 teaspoon pepper
1/2 teaspoon pepper
2 Tablespoons Madras curry
    powder
1 medium lemon, juiced, seeded
1 cup plain yogurt

1 teaspoon salt
1 Tablespoon oil
Group 2
32 oz beef, cut in 2-in strips
Group 3
1/4 teaspoon pepper
1/4 teaspoon MSG
2 Tablespoons oil
1 medium lemon, quartered
1 medium onion, quartered
1 medium tomato, quartered
1 small bell pepper, quartered

Prepare beef per section 6a and set aside.. Combine Group 1 and marinate meat per section 5a or 5b. Cook marinated meat per section 21a, 21b or 21c. Garnish with Group 3 and serve.

8   Beef Chili Macaroni

Group 1
2 cups elbow macaroni
Group 2
24 oz lean ground beef
1/2 cup water
Group 3
3 Tablespoons oil
1 teaspoon salt
1 large onion, diced
1 medium bell pepper, diced
1/2 teaspoon pepper
1 large garlic, diced
1 teaspoon parsley flakes

2 (16-oz) cans, crushed tomatoes
    and liquid
2 Tablespoons chili powder
1/2 teaspoon Tabasco sauce
1 cup beef broth
Group 5
1 Tablespoon Romano cheese,
    grated
1 Tablespoon Parmesan cheese,
    grated
Group 6
1/4 cup onion/garlic flavored
    croutons, crushed

Prepare Group 1 per package instruction. Set aside. Combine Group 2. Mix and bring to boil at "Medium High" heat setting. Boil 1-2 minutes. Reset heat to "Medium Low", cover, and simmer 10 minutes. Mix occasionally. Reset heat to "Medium High", remove cover, and evaporate to dryness. Discard any beef fat. Add Group 3 to pot, mix well, and bring to boil. Reset heat to "Medium Low", cover. and simmer 30 minutes. Mix occasionally. Meanwhile, preheat oven at 325F. Remove cover and evaporate the sauce to sizzling. Add to 5-quart casserole bowl Group 1 and chili sauce. Mix and spread into a layer. Sprinkle Group 5 on top. Cover and bake 45-50 minutes. Garnish with Group 6 and serve.

---

9   Saffron Rice Casserole, Biryani*

This casserole is a popular festive meal commonly used in India, Pakistan, Burma, and many other Middle Eastern and Asian countries. I have made this complex recipe into a simple and quick version without sacrificing much of its AFTT and authenticity. Saffron is an expensive ingredient. Many of my friends who cannot afford to use the saffron would prepare a similar dish by substituting 1/4 to 1/2 teaspoon turmeric. It is called the poor people's Biryani. To substitute turmeric omit saffron and increase turmeric from 1/8 to 1/2 teaspoon in Group 2. Follow all other preparation steps.

Group 1
24 oz beef, cut into 2-in cubes
1 medium onion, diced
3 medium garlic, diced
1 Tablespoon ginger, diced
1 medium tomato, diced
1/4 teaspoon crushed red pepper
1 teaspoon paprika
1/4 teaspoon turmeric
2 Tablespoons Madras curry
    powder
2 teaspoons meat masala
2 teaspoons garam masala
2 Tablespoons oil
1 teaspoon salt
1 cup water

Group 2
1 Tablespoon saffron strands
1/4 cup whole milk
1 Tablespoon instant beef bouillon
2 (3-in) cinnamon sticks
6 cloves
8 cardamon, podded, seeds ground
1 large bay leaf
1/8 teaspoon turmeric
3 Tablespoons margarine
Group 3
1/2 cup plain yogurt, unsweetened
1/2 cup sour cream
Group 4
5 cups cooked rice

Prepare beef per section 6a. Combine with the remaining Group 1 in pot. Mix well. Heat to boiling at "Medium High" heat setting. Boil 1-2 minutes. Reset heat to "Medium Low", cover, and simmer 45 minutes. Mix occasionally. Meanwhile, add to 2-cup pot Group 2, bring to boil, turn heat off, cover, and set aside. Cook 3 cups extra long grain rice per section 23b and set aside. Reset heat to "Medium". Remove cover, and evaporate Group 1 to sizzling. Add Group 3, mix well, and turn heat off. Transfer Group 1 into a serving bowl. Set aside. Save the emptied pot. Preheat oven to 325F. Add Groups 2 and 4 in the emptied pot. Mix well. Remove half of the mixture into a bowl and prepare a rice bed with the remaining rice in the pot. Add Group 1 in the middle and make a bed. Cover it with the other half of the rice mixture. Seal and bake 45 minutes (see section 16a), and serve.

---

10   Beef and Turmeric

One of the simplest of all recipes given in this cookbook. Although turmeric is not one of the spices commonly used in American cooking, it is the spice which gives flavor and the yellow color to the mustard sauce which we use on hot-dog, ham, hamburger, sandwiches, etc. Don't let the turmeric discourage you to try this dish. You will be pleasantly surprised by its subtle flavor and aroma. We have not yet encountered a friend who disliked this dish. It is a very versatile recipe. You can use with pork, spare rib, lamb, chicken, and shrimp. If you are not concerned about fat and cholesterol you can also use this recipe with beef liver or chicken parts (wing, gizzard, heart, and liver). You can create many delicious and inexpensive dishes with this recipe.

Group 1
32 oz beef, cut into 1/4-in slices
1/4 teaspoon turmeric

4 Tablespoons oil
3/4 teaspoon salt
1 cup water

Prepare beef per section 6a. Combine with the remaining Group 1 in pot. Mix well. Bring to boil at "Medium High" heat setting. Boil 1-2 minutes. Reset heat to "Medium Low", cover, and simmer 45 minutes. Mix occasionally. Remove cover and evaporate to sizzling. Cover, let self-saute 2 minutes with occasional mixing, and serve.

11   Linguine with Meat Sauce

Group 1
24 oz lean ground beef
2 Tablespoons olive oil
1/4 teaspoon cracked pepper
1/2 cup water
1/2 teaspoon salt
Group 2
2 (10-oz) cans, minestrone soup
1/2 cup hot beef broth

Group 3
8 oz. linguine pasta
Group 4
2 Tablespoons margarine
Group 5
6 sprigs fresh parsley
2 Tablespoons Parmesan cheese,
   grated

Add to 3-quart pot, Group 1, mix, and bring to boil at "Medium High" heat. Boil 1-2 minutes. Reset heat to "Medium Low", cover, and simmer 15 minutes. Mix well. Remove cover, evaporate to sizzling and let self-saute 3 minutes. Mix occasionally. Stir in Group 2, mix well, cover and let simmer 10 minutes at "Low" setting. Meanwhile, prepare Group 3 per instruction on its package, and transfer into a 3-quart serving bowl. Add Group 4 to pasta and toss well. Pour Group 1 on pasta, garnish with Group 5, and serve.

12   Curried Beef Vegetable**

Group 1
24 oz beef, cut into 1/4-in slices
4 Tablespoons oil
1 cup water
1 large onion, diced
4 medium garlic, diced
1 teaspoon ginger, diced
1/4 teaspoon turmeric
1 teaspoons paprika
1/4 teaspoon crushed red pepper
1 Tablespoon Madras curry
   powder
6-8 fresh curry leaves
1 (3-in) cinnamon stick

1 teaspoon salt
Group 2
2 cups hot water
1 medium eggplant, cut into
   6 pieces
1 medium tomato, quartered
1 large fresh cayenne pepper,
   whole
1 large potato, cut into 8 pieces
Group 3
10 green beans, cut each into
   3 sections
6 whole okra, frozen
8 sprigs cilantro, diced

Prepare beef per section 6a. Combine with the remaining Group 1 in pot. Mix well. Bring to boil at "Medium High" heat setting. Boil 1-2 minutes. Reset heat to "Medium Low", cover, and simmer 45 minutes. Mix occasionally. Remove cover and evaporate to sizzling. Cover and let self-saute 3-5 minutes. Mix occasionally. Reset heat to "Medium", add Group 2, mix, bring to boil, reset heat to "Medium Low", cover, and simmer 15 more minutes. Mix occasionally. Add Group 3, simmer 5 more minutes, and serve. Add 1/4 to 1 cup hot water for more sauce if needed.

---

13 Chinese Curried Beef**

Group 1
24 oz beef, cut into 1/4-in slices
3 Tablespoons oil
2 large garlic, diced
1/4 teaspoon crushed red pepper
1/4 teaspoon salt
1/2 cup water
Group 2
1/4 cup water
2 Tablespoons soy sauce
1 teaspoon soybean paste
/2 Tablespoons Madras curry
    powder
1/4 teaspoon MSG

1 teaspoon sugar
1 Tablespoon rice wine
2 Tablespoons corn starch
Group 3
1/2 cup frozen pearl onions
1 medium fresh cayenne pepper
    diced
1 large potato, cut into 16 sections
2 cups hot broth
Group 4
1/2 cup frozen sweet peas
Group 5
3 stalks scallion, diced

Prepare beef per section 6a. Combine with the remaining Group 1 in pot. Mix well. Bring to boil at "Medium High" heat setting. Boil 1-2 minutes. Reset heat to "Medium Low", cover, and simmer 45 minutes. Mix occasionally. Meanwhile, prepare Group 2 (see section 2) and Group 3 vegetables. Set them aside. Remove cover and evaporate Group 1 to sizzling. Cover and let self-saute 3-5 minutes. Reset heat to "Medium High", add Group 3, mix well, and bring to a boil. Reset heat to "Medium Low", cover, and simmer 15 minutes. Add Group 4, mix, cover, and simmer 3 more minutes. Remix Group 2 and stir into pot. Stir continuously until the gravy thickens to smooth texture (see section 20a). Garnish with Group 5 and serve. Add 1/4 to 1/2 cup hot water if more sauce is needed. Mix, salt to taste, and serve.

18

14   Beef Noodle Soup

This dish is a popular one among Asians. The people, poor and rich alike, enjoy this meal at any time of the day. It is served as a main course, side dish or snack. There are many variations to it. They are served either as soups, stir-fries or salads prepared with variety of vegetables, meat, poultry, and seafood. The salads are usually prepared with hot peppers. They are inexpensive and simple to prepare. Practically every town in Asia has these roadside noodle stands throughout the town. Of course, there are many elaborate, complex, and expensive versions to these dishes as well. I have included a simple and inexpensive version. The usual methods used in their preparations are simplified for use with the simmer-saute method.

Group 1
16 oz beef, cut into 1/4-in slices
1 Tablespoon oil
1 medium garlic, diced
1/2 cup water
Group 2
5 cups hot water
Group 3
1/2 teaspoon sugar
4 seasoning bags came with
    noodle packages

2 teaspoons soy sauce
1 Tablespoon rice wine
1/4 teaspoon MSG
Group 4
4 (3-oz) packages, Oriental
    instant noodle
Group 5
4 stalks scallion, diced
1/4 teaspoon pepper
1/4 teaspoon sesame oil

Prepare beef per section 6a. Combine with the remaining Group 1 in pot. Mix well. Bring to boil at "Medium High" heat setting. Boil 2 minutes. Reset heat to "Medium Low", cover, and simmer 45 minutes. Mix occasionally. Remove cover and evaporate to sizzling. Cover and self-saute 3 minutes. Mix occasionally. Reset heat to "Medium", add Group 2, mix, and bring to boil. Add Group 3, mix, add Group 4, mix, and cook 5-7 minutes. Garnish with Group 5 and serve. Add 1/4 to 1 cup hot water for more sauce if needed. Mix, salt to taste, and serve.

15   Beef in Red Pepper Sauce*

Group 1
32 oz beef, cut into
   1/4-in slices
1 cup water
3 Tablespoons oil
Group 2
1/4 cup water
2 Tablespoons soy sauce
1 Tablespoon rice wine
1/4 teaspoon MSG
1 teaspoon sugar

2 Tablespoons corn starch
no salt
Group 3
2 Tablespoons garlic/black bean/
   red pepper sauce
1 teaspoon ginger, diced
Group 4
1 1/2 cups hot beef broth
Group 5
4 stalks scallion, diced
1/8 teaspoon pepper

Prepare beef per section 6a. Combine with the remaining Group 1 in pot. Mix well. Heat to boil at "Medium High" setting. Boil 1-2 minutes. Reset heat to "Medium Low", cover, and simmer 45 minutes. Mix occasionally. Meanwhile, combine Group 2, and mix well (see section 2). Set aside. Reset heat to "Medium", remove cover, and evaporate to sizzling. Add Group 3 in sizzling oil. Reset heat to "Medium Low", cover, and let self-saute 2-3 minutes. Remove cover, add Group 4, and mix well. Remix Group 2 mixture, add to pot, and mix continuously to smooth consistency (see section 20a). Garnish with Group 5 and serve.

16   Fried Rice with Beef*

Group 1
3 cups extra long grain rice
Group 2
16 oz lean ground beef
3 Tablespoons oil
1/4 teaspoon MSG
1/2 small onion, diced
1/4 teaspoon pepper
1 small garlic, diced
Group 3
1/8 teaspoon turmeric

1/4 teaspoon salt
2 Tablespoons soy sauce,
   Japanese or Chinese
2 medium fresh jalapeno pepper,
   diced
2 teaspoons Madras curry
   powder
Group 4
3 stalks scallion, diced
1/4 teaspoon white pepper

Cook Group 1 per section 23b and set aside. Add to 12-inch skillet, Group 2, saute 5-7 minutes at "Medium" heat setting, mix frequently, cover, reset heat to "Medium Low", and cook 5 minutes. Reset heat to "Medium", add Group 3, mix, add Group 1, mix, cover, reset heat to "Medium Low", and cook 3-5 minutes with occasional mixing. Garnish with Group 4 and serve

---

17   Burgundy Beef Stew

Group 1
24 oz beef, cut into
   1-in cubes
1 cup water
1/8 teaspoon pepper
1/2 teaspoon sugar
2 teaspoons instant
   beef bouillon
1/8 teaspoon MSG
1/4 teaspoon salt
3 Tablespoons oil
1/8 teaspoon white
   pepper

Group 2
1 Tablespoon corn starch
1/4 cup water
1 Tablespoon burgundy wine
Group 3
2 cups hot beef broth
Group 4
1 large carrot, cut into 16 pieces
2 large potatoes, cut into
   16 pieces
1/3 cup pearl onions, frozen
Group 6
1 Tablespoon burgundy wine

Prepare beef per section 6a. Combine with the remaining Group 1 in pot. Mix well. Bring to boil at "Medium High" heat setting. Boil 1-2 minutes. Reset heat to "Medium Low", cover, and simmer 60 minutes. Mix occasionally. Meanwhile, prepare Group 2 (see section 2) and Group 4. Set them aside. Remove cover and evaporate Group 1 to sizzling. Cover and let self-saute 3 minutes. Add Group 3 and mix. Remix Group 2 and stir into pot. Stir continuously until the gravy thickens to smooth consistency (see section 20a). Add Group 4. Mix well. Cover, and simmer 20 minutes. Add Group 5, mix well, and serve. Add 1/4 to 1/2 cup hot water if more sauce is needed. Salt to taste and serve.

18 Congo Combo

Group 1
4 oz lean ground beef
4 oz lean Italian sausage meat
1/4 cup water

Group 2
1 Tablespoon olive oil
12 oz pizza sauce

Group 3
2 (7-oz) flour packages, premixed
   for pizza

Group 4
2 Tablespoons corn oil

Group 5
1/2 teaspoon cracked pepper
1/2 teaspoon garlic powder
1/2 small onion, diced
1/4 small bell pepper, diced
1/4 teaspoon Italian seasoning

5 medium mushrooms, cut into
   15 slices

Group 6
1/4 cup Parmesan cheese, grated
1/2 cup mozzarella cheese, grated
1/4 cup Romano cheese, grated

Group 7
6 large shrimp, cut into 18 pieces
1 oz. pepperoni, slices
1 oz. Canadian bacon, diced

Group 8
1/4 cup sharp Cheddar cheese,
   grated

Group 9
1/4 cup croutons, onion/garlic
   flavored, crumbled
1/4 teaspoon crushed red pepper
1/8 teaspoon Italian seasoning

Combine Group 1 in pot, mix, and heat to boiling at "Medium High" heat setting. Reset heat to "Medium" and evaporate to sizzling. Reset heat to "Medium Low", remove fat, add Group 2, mix, cover, and let self-saute 3-5 minutes. Set aside. Prepare Group 3 crust mix per instructions on box. Set aside. Paint Group 4 evenly on 14-in. pizza pan floor. Place Group 3 at the center of the painted pan. Flatten Group 3 dough by pressing it outward into circular shape. Rotate the pan slightly in one direction after each pressing. Patch any holes formed during spreading. Remix Groups 1 and 2. Spread evenly. Sprinkle Groups 5 and 6 evenly. Place Group 7 evenly spaced. Sprinkle Group 8 and bake (see section 16b). Garnish with Group 9, section pizza, and serve.

19   Beef Noodle Salad*

Group 1
16 oz beef, cut into 1/4-in slices
1 cup water
2 Tablespoons oil
Group 2
1 medium fresh cayenne pepper,
   diced
1 medium onion, diced
10 sprigs cilantro, chopped
Group 3
5 cups water
3 (3-oz) packages, Oriental
   instant noodle

Group 4
1 Tablespoon oil
1 large garlic, diced
Group 5
1 Tablespoon soy sauce
1/4 teaspoon MSG
1 medium lemon, juiced, seeded
3 seasoning packages, from
   noodle packages
Group 6
1/4 teaspoon sesame oil
1/4 teaspoon pepper
1/8 teaspoon white pepper

Prepare beef per section 6a. Combine with the remaining Group 1 in pot. Mix well. Bring to boil at "Medium High" heat setting. Boil 1-2 minutes. Reset heat to "Medium Low", cover, and simmer 45 minutes. Mix occasionally. Meanwhile, prepare Group 2 and set aside in 4-quart serving bowl. Add to a 4-quart pot Group 3 and heat to boiling at "Medium High" setting. Mix and cook for 3-5 minutes. Drain noodles in colander immediately, combine with Group 2, and set aside. Fry Group 4 (see section 19f) and set aside. Add Groups 3 and 4 to Group 2. Set aside. Remove cover and evaporate Group 1 to sizzling. Cover and let self-saute 1-2 minutes. Add Group 1 to Groups 2, 3, and 4. Add Group 5 to Groups 1, 2, 3, and 4. Toss thoroughly. Garnish with Group 6, and serve.

20   Missouri Meat Loaf

Group 1

16 oz lean ground beef
16 oz ground turkey
1/4 cup onion, diced
1/4 cup celery, diced
3 slices bread, cut each into
     12 pieces
1 1/2 Tablespoons
     Worcestershire sauce
1 egg, beaten

1 cup whole milk
1/4 teaspoon sage
1/4 teaspoon pepper
1/4 teaspoon white pepper
1/4 teaspoon MSG
1 package onion soup mix
1 Tablespoon margarine, melted
1 teaspoon instant beef bouillon
     no salt

Preheat the oven at 350F. Combine Group 1. Mix well. Shape the mixture into a loaf. Place an aluminum foil in an oven tray (about 10 X 15 inch). Put meat loaf on the foil, bake 60-75 minutes, and serve.

21   Combo Curried Beef**

Group 1

32 oz beef, cut into 2-in cubes
5 Tablespoons oil
2 cups water
1 large onion, diced
4 medium garlic, diced
1 Tablespoon ginger, diced
1 medium fresh cayenne peppers,
     whole
1 medium tomato, diced

1/4 teaspoon turmeric
1 teaspoon paprika
1/4 teaspoon crushed red pepper
1 Tablespoon Madras curry
     powder
2 teaspoons meat masala
2 teaspoons garam masala
1 (3-in) cinnamon stick
1 1/4 teaspoons salt
1 small bay leaf

Prepare beef per section 6a. Combine with the remaining Group 1 in pot. Mix. Bring to a boil at "Medium High" heat setting. Boil 1-2 minutes. Reset heat to "Medium Low", cover, and simmer 90 minutes. Mix occasionally. Remove cover and evaporate to sizzling. Cover, self-saute 3-5 minutes with occasional mixing, and serve.

22   Beef in Curry Sauce

This is one of the simplest curry dishes you can make. Its aroma, flavor, and taste are as authentic as they can be. The secret here is a preblended curry sauce mix which comes loaded with most of the authentic Indian curry herbs and spices.

Group 1
32 oz lean beef, cut into
    1/4-in slices
1 Tablespoon oil
1 large onion, diced
1/2 cup water
no salt

Group 2
1 cup hot water
1 (4-oz) S&B Golden mild curry
    sauce mix
1 teaspoon fish sauce
1 teaspoon soy sauce, Chinese

Prepare beef per section 6a. Combine with the remaining Group 1 in pot. Bring to boil at "Medium High" heat setting. Boil 1-2 minutes, mix, reset heat to "Medium Low", cover, and simmer 45 minutes with occasional mixing. Remove cover, evaporate to sizzling with frequent mixing. Add Group 2, mix well to smooth consistency, reset heat to "Low", cover, simmer 5 minutes, and serve. Add 1/4 cup hot water to pot for more sauce, if needed. Mix, salt to taste, and serve.

23   Beef Stroganoff

Group 1
24 oz beef, cut into
    1-in cubes
3 Tablespoons oil
1 cup water
1 large onion, diced
1 medium garlic, diced
1/4 teaspoon pepper
1 Tablespoon beef
    bouillon
1/4 teaspoon salt

Group 2
1 cup hot water
1 (10-oz) can, cream of
    mushroom soup
1/4 cup whole milk
4 oz fresh mushroom, cut
    each into 4 pieces
Group 3
1/2 cup plain yogurt,
    unsweetened
1 cup sour cream

Prepare beef per section 6a. Combine with the remaining Group 1 in pot. Mix well. Bring to a boil at "Medium High" heat setting. Boil 1-2 minutes. Reset heat to "Medium Low", cover, and simmer 60 minutes. Mix occasionally. Remove cover and evaporate to sizzling. Cover and let self-saute 2-3 minutes. Reset heat to "Medium", add Group 2, mix well, and bring to boil. Add Group 3, mix, reset heat to "Medium Low", cover, simmer 3 minutes, and serve. Add 1/4 to 1 cup hot water if more sauce is needed. Mix. Salt to taste and serve.

---

24   Beef Salad

One of our favorite variations to the turmeric beef, Recipe 10, is making salads with it. We use this salad often for entertaining our guests. Every guest who has had the opportunity to try the salad enjoyed it very much.

Group 1
32 oz beef, cut into 1/4-in slices
4 Tablespoons oil
1/4 teaspoon turmeric
1 cup water
Group 2
15 sprigs cilantro, diced
1/4 head lettuce, shredded
1 large tomato, diced
1 medium onion, diced
1/2 medium cucumber, diced

1 large fresh cayenne pepper,
  diced
Group 3
1 Tablespoon oil
1 large garlic, diced
Group 4
1/4 teaspoon MSG
1 medium lemon, juiced, seeded
1/4 teaspoon sugar
3 Tablespoons fish sauce

Prepare beef per section 6a. Combine with the remaining Group 1 in pot. Mix well. Bring to boil at "Medium High" heat setting. Boil 1-2 minutes. Reset heat to "Medium Low", cover, and simmer 45 minutes. Mix occasionally. Meanwhile, prepare Group 2 and save in 4-quart salad serving bowl. Set aside. Remove cover and evaporate Group 1 to sizzling. Cover and let self-saute 2 minutes. Mix occasionally. Combine with Group 2 and set aside. Fry Group 3 (see section 19f) and combine with Groups 1 and 2 and, set aside. Add Group 4 to Groups 1, 2, and 3. Toss well and serve.

Chicken, 27

25   Curried Chicken Casserole*

Group 1

24 oz chicken, legs/thighs,
    disjointed
1 Tablespoon oil
1 medium onion, diced
2 teaspoons ginger, diced
2 medium garlic, diced
1/4 teaspoon cracked pepper
1 Tablespoon garam masala
1 teaspoon paprika
1/4 teaspoon turmeric
1 Tablespoon Madras curry
    powder
1 teaspoon salt
1 1/2 cups water

Group 2

1/3 cup hot water
1/3 cup hot whole milk
1 Tablespoon saffron strands
1 (3-in) cinnamon stick
4 cloves
8 cardamon pods, shelled,
    seeds cracked
1 medium bay leaf
4 Tablespoons margarine

Group 3

5 cups cooked rice
2 medium fresh cayenne peppers,
    whole

Disjoint chicken parts (see section 6c). Combine with the remaining Group 1. Mix well. Bring to boil at "Medium High" heat setting. Boil 1-2 minutes. Reset heat to "Medium Low", cover, and simmer 15 minutes. Mix occasionally. Meanwhile, add to 2-cup pot Group 2, bring to boil, turn heat off, cover, and set aside. Cook 3 cups extra long grain rice per section 23b and set aside. Remove cover and evaporate Group 1 to sizzling. Cover and let self-saute 2 minutes. Turn heat off. Transfer the entire contents into a serving bowl. Save the pot uncleaned. Set aside. Preheat oven at 325F. Add Groups 2 and 3 in the emptied pot. Mix well. Remove half of the mixture into a bowl and prepare a rice bed with the remaining rice in the pot. Add Group 1 in middle of the bed and cover it with the other half of the rice mixture. Seal, bake for 60 minutes (see 16a), and serve.

26   Chicken Vegetable Curry*

This is a chicken curry variation. This recipe is not limited to the use of vegetables listed in this recipe. You can substitute practically any vegetable of your choice. Chicken curry cooked with vegetables has its own subtle flavor. Nutritionally this dish is rich in natural fiber, minerals, and vitamins. This dish will give you an enjoyable and healthful meal.

Group 1
4 Tablespoons oil
1 medium onion, diced
1 large garlic, diced
2 teaspoons ginger, diced
1 medium tomato, quartered
1/4 teaspoon crushed red pepper
1 teaspoon paprika
1/8 teaspoon turmeric
1 Tablespoon cumin powder
2 teaspoons coriander powder
1/2 cup water
1 1/4 teaspoon salt

Group 2
3 cups hot water
24 oz chicken, legs/thighs
   disjointed
1 large potato, cut into 8 pieces
2 large white radishes, each
   quartered
1/4 cup green split peas

Group 3
1/4 cup okra, frozen
8 green beans, cut into halves
1 Tablespoon garam masala

Combine Group 1 in pot. Mix well. Bring to boil at "Medium High" heat setting. Boil 1-2 minutes. Reset heat to "Medium Low", cover, and simmer 15 minutes. Mix occasionally. Meanwhile, disjoint chicken per section 6c and set aside. Remove cover and evaporate Group 1 to sizzling. Add Group 2, mix well, and bring to boil at "Medium High" setting. Boil 1-2 minutes. Reset heat to "Medium Low", cover, and simmer 25 minutes. Mix occasionally. Reset heat to "Medium", stir in Group 3, mix well, cover, simmer 5 minutes, and serve. Add 1/4 to 1 cup hot water for more sauce if needed. Mix, salt to taste, and serve.

27   Chicken and Cucumber*

This dish is a typical provincial Burmese dish. In Burma, "bu-thee" (bottle gourd) is used in place of cucumber. Bottle gourd was not available when I was in Buffalo in 1960s. Hence, cucumber was substituted. Our family enjoys it so much that we still use cucumber in the dish. This is a simple, tasty, healthful, and inexpensive dish. I introduced this dish to my very close friend and colleague, Dr. Dennis Mulvey, who was then, my fellow graduate student. Ever since, he has been cooking this and other Burmese dishes often because, he said, the Burmese dishes taste great and are very inexpensive.

Group 1
1 medium onion, diced
2 medium garlic, diced
1 teaspoon ginger, diced
1 medium tomato, quartered
1/8 teaspoon crushed red pepper
1 teaspoon paprika
1/8 teaspoon turmeric
1 medium fresh cayenne pepper, whole
3 Tablespoons oil

1 teaspoon salt
1/2 cup water
Group 2
24 oz chicken, legs/thighs disjointed
1 medium cucumber, seeded, cut into 1/4-in slices
2 cups hot water
Group 3
10 sprigs cilantro, chopped

Combine Group 1 in pot. Mix well. Bring to boil at "Medium High" heat setting. Boil 1-2 minutes. Reset heat to "Medium Low", cover, and simmer 20 minutes. Mix occasionally. Meanwhile, prepare Group 2. Disjoint chicken parts per section 6c. Remove cover and evaporate Group 1 to sizzling. Cover and let self-saute 2 minutes. Add Group 2, mix well, and bring to boil at "Medium High" heat setting. Boil 1-2 minutes. Reset heat to "Medium Low", cover, and simmer 20 minutes. Garnish with Group 3 and serve. Add 1/4 to 1 cup hot water if more sauce is needed. Mix, salt to taste, and serve.

28   Sweet and Sour Chicken

This is for sharpening your skill and to have fun when you have time to spare. Part A is for making the nuggets and Part B is for the stir frying.

Part A
Group 1
24 oz chicken white meat, cut
    into 2-in cubes

2 Tablespoons baking powder
1 1/2 teaspoons pepper

Group 2
1 1/2 cups flour
2 teaspoons sugar
1 1/2 teaspoons MSG
1 1/2 teaspoons salt
1 1/2 Tablespoons garlic powder

Group 3
1 cup water
1/2 cup flour
2 teaspoons baking powder

Group 4
4 cups oil

Prepare Group 1 per section 6b. Set aside. Add to 2-quart bowl, Group 2, mix, and set aside. Add to 1-quart bowl, Group 3, mix well to disperse the flour globules (see section 4), and set aside. Add to 4-quart pot, Group 4 and heat 3 minutes at "Medium High" heat setting. Reset heat to between "Medium" and "Medium Low". Mop dry the nuggets with paper towel. Roll in Group 2, then, in Group 3, then, in Group 2 again, and deep fry in Group 4 (see section 19a). Turn over pieces every 2 minutes if needed. Fry the nuggets to light tan color. Remove, drip drain oil on paper, and set aside.

Part B
Group 5
4 Tablespoons corn starch
1/4 teaspoon MSG
1 Tablespoon soy sauce
1 Tablespoon rice wine
1/4 teaspoon salt
2 Tablespoons vinegar
2 Tablespoons sugar
1 Tablespoon oyster
    sauce

Group 6
2 cups chicken broth
1 small onion, quartered
1 medium carrot,cut into
    8 sections
1 small bell pepper, cut into
    8 sections
1 small tomato, quartered

Group 7
4 stalks scallion, diced
1/4 teaspoon pepper

Combine corn starch mixture Group 5 (see section 2) and set aside. Prepare Group 6 vegetables and set aside. Combine Group 6 and bring to boil at "Medium High" heat setting. Boil 2 minutes. Reset heat to "Medium Low". Remix Group 5 and add to pot. Mix continuously until gravy thickens to smooth consistency (see section 20a). Add fried nuggets from Part I to pot, mix well, garnish with Group 7 and serve. Add 1/4 to 1/2 cup hot water for more sauce if needed. Mix, salt to taste, and serve.

---

29   Chicken Asparagus

Group 1
24 oz chicken white meat, cut
  into 1/4-in slices
2 Tablespoons oil
1 medium garlic, diced
1/2 cup water

Group 2
25-30 stalks asparagus, washed,
  use tender parts only

Group 3
1/4 cup water
2 Tablespoons corn starch

1/4 teaspoon MSG
1 Tablespoon beef bouillon
1 teaspoon sugar
no salt

Group 4
1 cup hot chicken broth
2 Tablespoons white wine

Group 5
1/4 teaspoon pepper
1 Tablespoon Parmesan cheese,
  grated

Prepare chicken per section 6b. Combine with the remaining Group 1 in pot. Mix well. Bring to boil at "Medium High" heat setting. Boil 1-2 minutes. Reset heat to "Medium Low", cover, and simmer 20 minutes. Mix occasionally. Meanwhile, prepare Group 2 and Set aside. Prepare Group 3 mixture and set aside (see section 2). Remove cover and evaporate Group 1 to sizzling. Cover and let self-saute 3-5 minutes. Add Groups 2 and 4, mix, and simmer 2 minutes. Reset heat to "Medium". Remix Group 3 and stir into pot with continuous mixing until gravy thickens to smooth consistency (see section 20a). Garnish with Group 5 and serve. Add 1/4 to 1 cup hot water for more sauce if needed. Mix, salt to taste, and serve.

30   Chicken with Potato

Burmese provincial chicken stew. It tastes as good as it is simple to make. Flavor of turmeric is distinctive, mild, and very subtle.

Group 1

24 oz chicken, legs/thighs, disjointed
1/4 teaspoon MSG
1 medium onion, diced
1 large garlic, diced
1/8 teaspoon turmeric

3/4 teaspoon salt
4 Tablespoons oil
1/2 cup water

Group 2

1 1/2 cups hot water
2 large potatoes, each quartered

Disjoint chicken parts per section 6c. Combine with the remaining Group 1 in pot. Mix well. Bring to boil at "Medium High" heat setting. Boil 1-2 minutes. Reset heat to "Medium Low", cover, and simmer 10 minutes. Mix occasionally. Remove cover and evaporate to sizzling. Mix occasionally. Reset heat to "Medium", add Group 2, mix well, and bring to boil. Reset heat to "Medium Low", cover, simmer 30 minutes, and serve. Add 1/4 to 1 cup hot water for more sauce if needed.

31   Steamed Chicken Soup

Group 1

16 oz chicken, legs/thighs, disjointed
2 medium garlic, whole
1 teaspoon ginger, diced
2 teaspoons oil
1/4 teaspoon MSG
2 cups water

Group 2

1 cup pickled mustard green, cut into 1-in slices

Group 3

4 stalks scallion, diced
1/8 teaspoon white pepper
1/4 teaspoon pepper
1/4 teaspoon sesame oil

Disjoint chicken parts per section 6c. Set up steamer. Combine Group 1 and steam 60 minutes at "Medium Low" setting (see section 26c). Add Group 2, cover, and steam 90 minutes. Garnish with Group 3 and serve. Add 1/4 to 1 cup hot water for more sauce if needed.

32   Almond Chicken

This recipe has two parts to it. Part A is to make battered fried chicken nuggets. Part B is to make stir fried almond chicken.

Part A
Group 1
24 oz chicken white meat, cut
   into 2-in cubes
Group 2
1 1/2 cups flour
2 teaspoons sugar
1 1/2 teaspoons MSG
1 1/2 teaspoons salt
1 1/2 Tablespoons garlic powder

2 Tablespoons baking
   powder
1 1/2 teaspoons pepper
Group 3
1 cup water
1/2 cup flour
2 teaspoons baking powder
Group 4
4 cups oil

Prepare Group 1 per section 6b. Set aside. Add to 2-quart bowl, Group 2, mix, and set aside. Add to 1-quart bowl, Group 3, mix well to disperse the flour globules, and set aside (see section 20b). Add to 4-quart pot, Group 4 and heat 5 minutes at "Medium High" heat setting. Reset heat between "Medium" and "Medium Low". Mop dry the nuggets with paper. Roll in Group 2, then, in Group 3, then, in Group 2 again, and deep fry in Group 4, see section 19a. Turn the pieces over every 2 minutes if needed. Fry the nuggets to light tan or tan color. Remove drip drain oil on paper, and set aside.

Part B
Group 5
4 Tablespoons corn
   starch
1/4 teaspoon MSG
1 Tablespoon soy sauce
1 Tablespoon rice wine
1 teaspoon sugar
1 Tablespoon oyster
   sauce

Group 6
1/2 cup toasted almond
Group 7
2 cups chicken broth
Group 8
1/8 teaspoon white pepper
1/4 teaspoon sesame oil
4 stalks scallion, diced
1/4 teaspoon pepper

Combine corn starch mixture Group 5 (see section 2) and set aside. Prepare Group 6 and set aside (see section 24a). Add to 5-quart pot, Group 7, and heat at "Medium" setting for 3 minutes. Reset heat to "Medium Low", stir in Group 5,and mix continuously until gravy thickens to smooth texture (see section 20a). Add fried nuggets from Part I to pot, mix well, garnish with Groups 6 and 8, and serve. Add 1/4 to 1/2 cup hot water for more sauce if needed.

---

33   Chicken Cashews

Group 1

16 oz chicken white meat, cut into 1/4-in slices

4 Tablespoons oil

1 medium garlic, diced

1/2 cup water

Group 2

1/4 cup water

3 Tablespoons corn starch

1 Tablespoon soy sauce

1 Tablespoon rice wine

1/4 teaspoon MSG

2 teaspoons chicken bouillon

1 teaspoon sugar

Group 3

1/2 cup toasted cashews, unsalted

Group 4

1 1/2 cups hot chicken broth

Group 5

1/4 teaspoon sesame oil

1/4 teaspoon pepper

Prepare chicken per section 6b. Combine with the remaining Group 1 in pot. Mix well. Bring to boil at "Medium High" heat setting. Boil 1-2 minutes. Reset heat to "Medium Low", cover, and simmer 20 minutes. Mix occasionally. Meanwhile, mix Group 2 and set aside (see section 2). Toast Group 3 and set aside (see section 24a). Reset heat at "Medium". Remove cover and evaporate Group 1 to sizzling. Mix often. Reset heat to "Medium Low", cover, and let self-saute 1-2 minutes. Mix occasionally. Stir in Group 4, remix group 2 and add to pot. Mix continuously until gravy thickens to smooth texture (see section 20a). Garnish with Groups 3 and 5, and serve. Add 1/4 cup hot water for more sauce if needed. Mix, salt to taste, and serve.

34   Chicken Kabob I

Group 1
2 medium garlic, whole
2 teaspoons coriander powder
2 teaspoons caraway seeds
2 Tablespoons brown sugar
1/2 teaspoon pepper
4 Tablespoons dark soy sauce
1/4 teaspoon white pepper
1 large lemon, juiced, seeded

Group 2
32 oz chicken, legs/thighs disjointed
Group 3
2 Tablespoons oil
1/4 teaspoon MSG
1/4 teaspoon pepper
1 medium tomato, quartered
1 small bell pepper, quartered
1 small lemon, quartered

Combine Group 1 and puree in electric blender. Transfer puree in double layered 1-gallon plastic bag (see section 5a). Set aside. Disjoint chicken per section 6c. Add Group 2 to marinade, mix, and set aside at room temperature for 3 or more hours. Turn over the marinade bag occasionally to mix the content. Cook marinated chicken pieces using one of the techniques described in section 21. Garnish with Group 3 and serve.

35   Summit Chicken and Mushroom

This recipe is a modified version of a stir fried chicken dish to please chicken and mushroom lovers. It is very simple, easy, and quick to prepare. The overall flavor of this dish is subtle and no doubt it will become one of your favorites.

Group 1
24 oz chicken white meat, cut
    into 1/4-in slices
1 small garlic, diced
1 oz onion soup mix
1/2 teaspoon sugar
1/4 teaspoon MSG
1/4 teaspoon pepper
2 Tablespoons oil
1/2 cup water

no salt
Group 2
8 oz fresh mushroom cut each
    into 4 slices
Group 3
2 Tablespoons flour
Group 4
1 cup hot water
Group 5
2 Tablespoons white wine

36

Prepare chicken per section 6b. Combine with the remaining Group 1 in pot. Mix well. Bring to boil at "Medium High" heat setting. Boil 1-2 minutes. Reset heat to "Medium Low", cover, and simmer 15 minutes. Mix occasionally. Meanwhile, prepare Group 2. Remove cover and evaporate Group 1 to sizzling. Add Group 3 in sizzling oil, and let self-saute until it begins to turn tan color. Reset heat to "Medium High", stir in Group 4, and bring to boil while mixing continuously. Reset heat to "Low". Add Group 5, mix, cover, simmer 1 minute, and serve.

---

36   Nicky's Pizza

This recipe is for the chicken cacciatore buffs. The pizza is crowned with simmer-sauteed chicken.

Group A
6 oz chicken, white meat, cut
   into 1/4-in slices
1 Tablespoon olive oil
1/4 cup water
Group 1
2 (7-oz) flour packages,
   premixed for pizza
Group 2
2 Tablespoons corn oil
Group 3
12 oz pizza sauce
Group 4
1/4 teaspoon Italian seasoning

1 teaspoon diced garlic
1/4 teaspoon cracked pepper
Group 5
3/4 cup mozzarella/provolone/
   /Parmesan, premixed, grated
Group 6
2 Tablespoons Parmesan cheese,
   grated
Group 7
Group A chicken pieces
Group 8
1/2 teaspoon cracked pepper
1/4 cup croutons, onion/garlic
   flavored, crumbled

Prepare chicken per section 6b. Combine with the remaining Group A in pot, mix, and heat to boiling at "Medium High" heat setting. Reset heat to "Medium" and evaporate to sizzling. Reset heat to "Medium Low", mix, cover, and let self-saute 10 minutes. Set aside. Mix and raise crust mix (Group 1) per instruction on the package. Make pie crust and dress the pie as described in section 8 using the ingredient groups from this recipe. Use Group A as Group 7 ingredient. Bake per section 16b. Garnish with Group 8, section pizza, and serve.

37   Chicken in Black Bean Sauce**

Group 1

32 oz chicken white meat, cut
   into 1-in cubes
1 large garlic, diced
1/4 teaspoon pepper
2 Tablespoons oil
1/2 cup water
no salt

Group 2

1 teaspoon soy sauce

1 Tablespoon garlic/red pepper/
   /black bean sauce
1 Tablespoon rice wine
1 teaspoon fish sauce
1/4 teaspoon coarse shrimp paste

Group 3

4 stalks scallion, diced
   1/4 teaspoon sesame oil
1/8 teaspoon white pepper

Prepare chicken per section 6b. Combine with the remaining Group 1 in pot. Mix well. Bring to boil at "Medium High" heat setting. Boil 1-2 minutes. Reset heat to "Medium Low", cover, and simmer 15-20 minutes. Mix occasionally. Remove cover and evaporate Group 1 to sizzling. Cover and let self-saute 2 minutes. Add Group 2. Mix well. Cover and let self-saute 3 more minutes. Garnish with Group 3 and serve. Add 1/4 cup hot water if more sauce is needed.

38   Chicken and Snow Peas

Group 1

24 oz chicken white meat, cut
   into 1/4-in slices
1/2 cup water
3 Tablespoons oil
1 medium garlic, diced
1/4 teaspoon pepper

Group 2

1 teaspoon sugar
3 Tablespoons corn starch
1/4 cup water
1 Tablespoon rice wine
2 Tablespoons soy sauce

1/4 teaspoon MSG

Group 3

1/4 cup bamboo shoots in water,
   cut into 1/4-in slivers
8 water chestnuts, 1/4-in slivers
8 oz snow peas, frozen

Group 4

1 1/2 cups hot chicken broth

Group 5

3 stalks scallion, diced
1/4 teaspoon sesame oil
1/4 teaspoon white pepper

Prepare chicken per section 6b. Combine with the remaining Group 1 in pot. Mix well. Heat to boiling at "Medium High" heat setting. Boil 1-2 minutes. Reset heat to "Medium Low," cover, and simmer 20 minutes. Mix occasionally. Meanwhile, mix Group 2 and set aside (see section 2). Prepare Group 3 and set aside. Reset heat to "Medium". Remove cover and evaporate Group 1 to sizzling. Mix often. Stir in Groups 4 and 3. Reset heat to "Medium Low". Remix group 2 and add to pot. Mix continuously until gravy thickens to smooth consistency (see section 20a). Garnish with Group 5 and serve. Add 1/4 to 1/2 cup hot water for more sauce if needed. Mix, salt to taste, and serve.

39　　Chicken Corn Casserole

Group 1

24 oz chicken, legs/thighs,
　disjointed
1/4 teaspoon MSG
1 medium onion, diced
1 large garlic, diced
2 Tablespoons oil
1/2 teaspoon salt
1/4 teaspoon paprika
1/2 teaspoon thyme
1/4 teaspoon parsley
1/4 teaspoon pepper
1/2 cup water

Group 2

1/4 cup water
2 (10-oz) cans, cream of chicken
　soup

Group 3

4 cups cooked rice
10 pearl onions, frozen
1/4 cup corn, frozen
2 Tablespoons Parmesan cheese,
　grated
2 Tablespoons cheddar cheese,
　grated

Disjoint chicken parts per section 6c. Combine with the remaining Group 1 in pot. Mix well. Bring to boil at "Medium High" heat setting. Boil 1-2 minutes. Reset heat to "Medium Low", cover, and simmer 10 minutes. Mix occasionally. Meanwhile, mix Group 2 well and set aside. Remove cover and evaporate Group 1 to sizzling. Cover, let self-saute 2 minutes, and set aside. Preheat oven at 325F. Add Groups 2 and 3. Mix well. Turn heat off. Remove pot from stove. Seal pot, bake 45-50 minutes (see section 16a), and serve.

40 Chicken in Spicy Sauce*

Group 1
32 oz chicken white meat, cut
   into 1/4-in slices
1 small onion, diced
1 large garlic, diced
1 teaspoon paprika
1 teaspoon ginger, diced
4 Tablespoons oil
1 cup water

Group 2
1 Tablespoon black bean in
   soybean oil
2 teaspoons fish sauce
1 large fresh cayenne pepper,
   diced
no salt
Group 3
6 sprigs cilantro, diced

Prepare chicken per section 6b. Combine with the remaining Group 1 in pot. Mix well. Bring to boil at "Medium High" heat setting. Boil 1-2 minutes. Reset heat to "Medium Low", cover, and simmer 20 minutes. Mix occasionally. Reset heat to "Medium", remove cover, and evaporate to sizzling. Reset heat to "Medium Low", cover, and let self-saute 2 minutes. Mix occasionally. Add Group 2, mix well, cover, and let self-saute 3 minutes. Garnish with Group 3, and serve. Add 1/4 cup hot water for more sauce, if needed. Mix, salt to taste, and serve.

41 Chicken Gumbo*

Group 1
4 Tablespoons oil
3 sprigs fresh parsley
3/4 cup water
1 medium onion, diced
2 medium garlic, diced
1 stalk celery, diced
2 large tomatoes, diced
1 medium bell pepper, diced
1 Tablespoon gumbo file`
1 medium fresh jalapeno pepper,
   diced
1 medium bay leaf

1/8 teaspoon white pepper
1/8 teaspoon cayenne pepper
   powder
1 Tablespoons chicken bouillon
1/2 teaspoon salt
1/4 teaspoon pepper
Group 2
3 cups hot broth
24 oz chicken, legs/thighs,
   disjointed
Group 3
1 Tablespoon gumbo file`
6 oz okra, sliced, frozen

Combine Group 1 in pot. Mix well. Bring to boil at "Medium High" heat setting. Boil 1-2 minutes. Reset heat to "Medium Low", cover, and simmer 30 minutes. Mix occasionally. Meanwhile, disjoint chicken parts per section 6c. Set aside. Remove cover and evaporate Group 1 to sizzling. Cover and let self-saute 2 minutes. Reset heat to "Medium", add Group 2, bring to boil, reset heat to "Medium Low", cover, and simmer 30 minutes. Add Group 3, simmer 5 minutes, and serve. Add 1/4 to 1/2 cup hot water for more sauce if needed. Mix, salt to taste, and serve.

---

42   Chicken Kabob II

Group 1
1 small onion, diced
2 large garlic, diced
1 Tablespoon ginger, diced
1/2 teaspoon pepper
1/2 teaspoon turmeric
1 teaspoon paprika
1/4 teaspoon red pepper powder
1 Tablespoon garam masala
1 Tablespoon Madras curry
    powder
1 cup plain yogurt
1 medium lemon, juiced, seeded

2 Tablespoons oil
1 teaspoon salt
Group 2
32 oz chicken, legs/thighs,
    disjointed
Group 3
2 Tablespoons oil
1/4 teaspoon pepper
1/4 teaspoon MSG
1 small onion, quartered
1 small bell pepper, quartered
1 small lemon, quartered
1 medium tomato, quartered

Combine Group 1 and puree in electric blender. Transfer puree in double layered 1-gallon plastic bag. Set aside. Disjoint chicken per section 6c. Add Group 2 to marinade, mix, and set aside at room temperature for 3 or more hours (see section 5a). Turn over the marinade bag occasionally to mix the contents. Cook marinated chicken pieces using one of the techniques described in section 21. Garnish with Group 3 and serve.

43   Chicken Kabob III

Group 1
1 medium onion, diced
1 Tablespoon oregano
1 Tablespoon olive oil
1/2 teaspoon pepper
1/2 cup vinegar
1 teaspoon salt
1/4 teaspoon thyme
  flakes

Group 2
32 oz chicken, legs/thighs,
  disjointed
Group 3
1/4 teaspoon pepper
1/4 teaspoon MSG
2 Tablespoons olive oil
1 small onion, quartered
1 medium tomato, quartered

Combine Group 1 and puree in electric blender. Transfer puree in double layered 1-gallon plastic bag. Set aside. Disjoint chicken per section 6c. Add Group 2 to marinade, mix, and set aside at room temperature for 3 or more hours (see section 5a). Turn over the marinade bag occasionally to mix the contents. Cook marinated chicken pieces per section 21c. Garnish with Group 3 and serve.

44   Darjeeling Chicken Curry

Our (my brother and I) first experiences with the Chinese curry were in Darjeeling, India, in 1949. We were freshmen then at the St. Joseph College, North Point, Darjeeling.

Group 1
24 oz chicken, white meat, cut
  into 1/4-in slices
1 large garlic, diced
3 Tablespoons oil
1/2 cup water
Group 2
1/4 cup water
1/2 teaspoon sugar
2 teaspoons oyster sauce
1/4 teaspoon MSG

2 Tablespoons Madras curry
  powder
3 Tablespoons corn starch
1 Tablespoon rice wine
2 Tablespoons soy sauce
Group 3
2 cups hot chicken broth
Group 4
1/3 cup diced carrots, frozen
1/3 cup sweet peas, frozen
1/3 cup pearl onions, frozen

Prepare chicken per section 6b. Combine with the remaining Group 1 in pot. Mix well. Bring to boil at "Medium High" heat setting. Boil 1-2 minutes. Reset heat to "Medium Low", cover, and simmer 15 minutes. Mix occasionally. Meanwhile, mix Group 2 and set aside (see section 2). Reset heat at "Medium". Remove cover and evaporate Group 1 to sizzling. Mix often. Reset heat to "Medium Low", cover, and let self-saute 1-2 minutes. Mix occasionally. Stir in Group 3, remix Group 2, add to pot, and mix continuously until gravy thickens (see section 20a). Stir in Group 4, cover, simmer 5 minutes, and serve. Add 1/4 to 1/2 cup hot water for more sauce if needed. Mix, salt to taste, and serve.

---

45   Pecan Chicken

Group 1
32 oz chicken white meat, cut
   into 1/4-in slices
1/2 cup water
3 Tablespoons oil
1 large garlic, diced
Group 2
3 Tablespoons corn starch
1/4 cup water
2 Tablespoons soy sauce
1/4 teaspoon MSG
1 Tablespoon rice wine

1 teaspoon sugar
Group 3
1/2 cup toasted pecans
1/8 cup water chestnut, cut
   into 1/4-in slices
Group 4
2 cups hot chicken broth
Group 5
1/8 teaspoon pepper
1/8 teaspoon white pepper
1/4 teaspoon sesame oil
3 stalks scallion, diced

Prepare chicken per section 6b. Combine with the remaining Group 1 in pot. Mix well. Heat to boiling at "Medium High" setting. Boil 1-2 minutes. Reset heat to "Medium Low," cover, and simmer 15 minutes. Mix occasionally. Meanwhile, mix Group 2 and set aside (see section 2). Toast Group 3 and set aside (see section 24a). Slice each water chestnut into 3 slices and set aside. Reset heat at "Medium". Remove cover and evaporate Group 1 to sizzling. Mix often. Reset heat to "Medium Low", cover, and let self-saute 1-2 minutes. Mix occasionally. Stir in Group 4, remix group 2 and add to pot. Mix continuously until gravy thickens to smooth consistency (see section 20a). Add Group 3, mix, garnish with Group 5, and serve. Add 1/4 to 1/2 cup hot water for more sauce if needed. Mix, salt to taste, and serve.

46   Spicy Chicken*

This is a variation of beef and turmeric. This is a simple one-step dish. You will enjoy it's spicy flavor.

Group 1
32 oz chicken white meat, cut
   into 1/4-in slices
1/4 teaspoon MSG
1 medium garlic, diced
4 Tablespoons oil
1/2 cup water
1/2 teaspoon paprika

1/4 teaspoon turmeric
2 teaspoons S&B Oriental
   curry powder
1/4 teaspoon pepper
1/4 teaspoon white pepper
1/2 teaspoon salt
1 medium fresh cayenne pepper,
   diced

Prepare chicken per section 6b. Combine with the remaining Group 1 in pot. Mix well. Bring to boil at "Medium High" heat setting. Boil 1-2 minutes. Reset heat to "Medium Low", cover, and simmer 20 minutes. Mix occasionally. Remove cover and evaporate to sizzling. Mix often. Reset heat to "Low", cover, let self-saute 3-5 minutes, and serve. Add 1/4 to 1/2 cup hot water for more sauce if needed. Mix, salt to taste, and serve.

---

47   Chicken Green Salad

This chicken salad is a simple contemporary healthful dish and is easy and quick to prepare.

Group 1
24 oz chicken white meat, cut
   into 1/4-in slices
2 Tablespoons olive oil
1 small garlic, diced
1/4 teaspoon salt
1/4 teaspoon cracked pepper
1/2 cup water

Group 2
8 leaves endive, sliced
1 small cucumber, diced
1 small onion, diced
Group 3
6 Tablespoons Italian dressing,
   any brand

Prepare chicken per section 6b. Combine with the remaining Group 1 in pot. Mix well. Bring to boil at "Medium High" heat setting. Boil 1-2 minutes. Reset heat to "Medium Low", cover, and simmer 20 minutes. Mix occasionally. Meanwhile, prepare Group 2 and set aside in 3-quart salad bowl. Remove cover and evaporate Group 1 to sizzling. Cover and let self-saute 2 minutes. Empty entire contents into salad bowl. Add Group 3, toss well, and serve.

---

48   Chicken in Split Pea Sauce

This dish is flavored with thyme and a hint of fresh ginger. Split pea is a good source for fiber and protein. There are more ways to use the split pea than just ham and split pea soup. Omit bouillon if desired.

Group 1
1/2 cup green or yellow split pea
1 cup water
Group 2
24 oz chicken, legs/thighs,
    disjointed
3 Tablespoons oil
1 medium onion, diced
1 medium garlic, diced
1 teaspoon ginger, diced
1/2 teaspoon thyme flakes

1/8 teaspoon pepper
1/4 teaspoon parsley flakes
1 teaspoon chicken bouillon
1/2 cup water
1/2 teaspoon sugar
1/4 teaspoon salt
Group 3
2 cups hot chicken broth
1 medium carrot, cut into 8 pieces
2 medium potatoes, cut each into
    8 pieces

Add to 2-cup bowl, Group 1, and soak 1 hour in 1 cup water (see section 13g). Meanwhile, disjoint chicken parts per section 6c. Combine Group 2. Mix well. Bring to boil at "Medium High" heat setting. Boil 1-2 minutes. Reset heat to "Medium Low", cover, and simmer 20 minutes. Mix occasionally. Reset heat to "Medium", remove cover, and evaporate to sizzling. Cover and let self-saute 3 minutes. Add Group 1 (split pea only) and Group 3, mix well, and bring to boil. Reset heat to "Medium Low", cover, simmer 25-30 minutes, and serve. Add 1/4 to 1 cup hot water for more sauce if needed. Mix, salt to taste, and serve.

49   Chicken with Fried Red Pepper*

Group 1
32 oz chicken white meat, cut
   into 1-in cubes
1/4 teaspoon salt
1 large garlic, diced
3 Tablespoons oil
1/2 cup water
Group 2
2 Tablespoons soy sauce
3 Tablespoon corn starch

2 Tablespoons sugar
1/4 cup water
1 Tablespoon rice wine
1/4 teaspoon MSG
Group 3
2 cups hot chicken broth
Group 4
1 Tablespoon oil
3 large dried red pepper, each
   quartered

Prepare chicken per section 6b. Combine with the remaining Group 1 in pot. Mix well. Bring to boil at "Medium High" heat setting. Reset heat to "Medium Low", cover, and simmer 20 minutes with occasional mixing. Meanwhile, prepare Group 2 and set aside (see section 2). Reset heat to "Medium". Remove cover and evaporate Group 1 to sizzling. Reset heat to "Medium Low", cover and self-saute 2 minutes. Mix often. Stir in Group 3. Remix Group 2 and stir into pot. Mix continuously to smooth consistency (see section 20a). Fry Group 4 until red pepper turn to dark brown color (see section 19k, substitute red peppers in place of herbs/spices). Pour entire content (Group 4) over chicken and serve.

50   Chicken Kabob IV

Group 1
2 large garlic, diced
1 Tablespoon oil
1 Tablespoon ginger, diced
1/4 teaspoon MSG
2 teaspoons sugar
2 Tablespoons soy sauce
1 Tablespoon Hoisin sauce
1 teaspoon Chinese five-spice
2 Tablespoons rice wine

Group 2
32 oz chicken legs/thighs,
   disjointed
Group 3
2 Tablespoons oil
1/4 teaspoon pepper
1/8 teaspoon MSG
1 small onion, quartered
1 medium tomato, quartered
1 bell pepper, quartered

Combine Group 1 in double layered 1-gallon plastic bag. Set aside. Disjoint chicken per section 6c. Add Group 2 to marinade, mix, and set aside at room temperature for 3 or more hours (see section 5a). Turn over the marinade bag occasionally to mix the content. Cook marinated chicken pieces per section 21c. Garnish with Group 3 and serve.

51   Chicken Sauce on Fettuccine

Group 1
24 oz chicken white meat, cut
   into 1/4-in slices
1/4 teaspoon cracked pepper
2 Tablespoons olive oil
1 medium garlic, diced
1/2 cup water
no salt
Group 2
6 oz Fettuccine pasta

Group 3
3/4 cup 2% milk
2 (10-oz) cans, cream of chicken
   soup
2 Tablespoons margarine
Group 4
4 stalks scallion, diced
2 Tablespoons Parmesan cheese,
   grated

Prepare chicken per section 6b. Combine with the remaining Group 1, add to 4-quart pot, mix, and bring to boil at "Medium High" heat setting. Reset heat to "Medium Low", cover, and simmer 15 minutes. Prepare Group 2 per instruction on package and set aside in 3-quart serving bowl. Remove cover and evaporate Group 1 to sizzling. Rest heat to "Low", cover, and let self-saute 5 minutes. Stir in Group 3, mix well, and simmer 5 minutes. Pour Group 1 on Group 2, garnish with Group 4, and serve.

52   Chicken Vegetable

Group 1
16 oz chicken white meat, cut
   into 1/4-in slices
3 Tablespoons olive oil
1/4 teaspoon pepper
1/4 teaspoon MSG
1/2 cup water

1/4 teaspoon thyme flakes
Group 2
1 cup hot water
3 (10-oz) cans, vegetable soup
Group 3
2 Tablespoons Parmesan cheese,
   grated

Prepare chicken per section 6b. Combine with the remaining Group 1 in pot. Mix well. Bring to a boil at "Medium High" heat setting. Boil 1-2 minutes. Reset heat to "Medium Low", cover, and simmer 20 minutes. Mix occasionally. Reset heat to "Medium", remove cover, and evaporate to sizzling. Cover and let self-saute 2 minutes. Mix occasionally. Add Group 2, mix well, cover, reset heat to "Medium Low", and let simmer 5 minutes. Garnish with Group 3, and serve. Add 1/4 cup hot water for more sauce, if needed. Mix, salt to taste, and serve.

---

53   Curried Chicken and Potato*

Group 1
24 oz chicken, legs/thighs,
   disjointed
1 teaspoon ginger, diced
1 medium onion, diced
1 large garlic, diced
1 teaspoons salt
1/4 teaspoon crushed red pepper
2 Tablespoons S&B Oriental
   curry powder

1 teaspoon paprika
1/8 teaspoon turmeric
3/4 cup water
1 (3-in) cinnamon stick
4 Tablespoons oil
1 large tomato, diced
Group 2
2 cups hot water
   2 large potatoes, cut each
   into 8 pieces

Disjoint chicken parts (see section 6c). Combine with the remaining Group 1. Mix well. Bring to boil at "Medium High" setting. Boil 1-2 minutes. Reset heat to "Medium Low", cover and simmer 15 minutes. Remove cover and evaporate to sizzling at "Medium" setting. Mix occasionally. Let Group 1 sizzle 1-2 minutes. Mix often. Stir in Group 2. Bring to boil, reset heat to "Medium Low", cover, and simmer 15-20 minutes. Mix occasionally. Add 1/4 to 1/2 cup hot water to pot for more sauce, if needed. Mix, salt to taste, and serve.

54   Chicken Fingers

Group 1
32 oz chicken white meat, cut
   into 2-in strips
Group 2
1 1/2 cups flour
2 Tablespoons sugar
1 1/2 teaspoons MSG
1 1/2 teaspoons salt
1 teaspoon Italian seasoning

2 Tablespoons baking powder
2 teaspoons pepper
Group 3
1 1/2 cups water
3/4 cup flour
1 Tablespoon baking powder
Group 4
4 cups oil

Prepare Group 1 per section 6b. Set aside. Add to 2-quart bowl, Group 2, mix well, and set aside. Add to 1-quart bowl, Group 3, mix well to disperse the flour globules, and set aside. Add to 4-quart pot, Group 4 and heat 5 minutes at "Medium High" heat setting. Reset heat to between "Medium" and "Medium Low". Mop dry the strips with paper towel. Roll in Group 2, then, in Group 3, then, in Group 2 again, and deep fry in Group 4, see section 19a. Turn over pieces every 2 minutes if needed. Fry the strips to light tan color. Remove, drain oil on paper, and serve.

55   Budapest Chicken Paprikash

Group 1
1 small bell pepper, diced
3 Tablespoons oil
1 large garlic, diced
3 medium onions, diced
2 medium tomatoes,
   each quartered
1 cup celery diced
2 Tablespoons paprika
1/2 teaspoon thyme flakes
1/8 teaspoon oregano
1 small bay leaf

1/8 teaspoon white pepper
3/4 cup water
1 teaspoon salt
1/4 teaspoon pepper
Group 2
24 oz chicken legs/thighs,
   disjointed
1 cup hot water
Group 3
1/2 cup plain yogurt
1/2 cup hot whole milk

Combine Group 1 in pot. Mix well. Bring to boil at "Medium High" heat setting. Boil 1-2 minutes. Reset heat to "Medium Low", cover, and simmer 30 minutes. Mix occasionally. Meanwhile, disjoint chicken parts (see section 6c). Remove cover and evaporate to sizzling. Add Group 2, mix, add Group 3, mix, and reset heat to "Medium", and bring to boil. Reset heat to "Medium Low", mix, cover, and simmer 25 minutes. Add Group 4, mix, cover, simmer 2 minutes and serve.

---

56 Chicken in Sweet Sour Hot Sauce*

Group 1
24 oz chicken white meat, cut
   into 1-inch cubes
1 teaspoon salt
1 large garlic, diced
1/2 cup water
2 Tablespoons oil
Group 2
2 Tablespoons sugar
1 Tablespoon rice wine
1/4 cup water
3 Tablespoons corn starch
1/8 teaspoon MSG

2 Tablespoons vinegar
Group 3
1 small onion, quartered
1 medium carrot, cut into
   8 sections
1 small bell pepper, cut into
   8 sections
Group 4
1 1/2 cups hot chicken broth
Group 5
1 Tablespoon oil
4 dried red peppers, cut into
   halves

Prepare chicken per section 6b. Combine with the remaining Group 1 in pot. Mix well. Bring to a boil at "Medium High" heat setting. Reset heat to "Medium Low" cover, and simmer 15-20 minutes. Mix occasionally. Meanwhile, prepare Group 2 mixture and set aside (see section 2). Prepare Group 3 and set aside. Reset heat to "Medium", remove cover, and evaporate Group 1 to dryness. Reset heat to "Medium Low", cover, and let self-saute 2 minutes. Stir in Groups 4 and 3, cover, and simmer 10 minutes. Remix Group 2 and add to pot. Mix continuously until gravy thickens to smooth consistency (see section 20a). Set aside. Fry Group 5 until red peppers turn dark brown (see section 19k, substitute red peppers in place of herbs/spices). Pour Group 5 over chicken and serve. Add 1/4 cup hot water if more sauce is needed. Mix, salt to taste and serve.

57   Chicken Macaroni Casserole

Group 1
2 cups uncooked elbow macaroni
Group 2
24 oz chicken white meat, cut
    into 1-in cubes
1 small onion, diced
3 Tablespoons oil
1 medium garlic, diced
1/4 teaspoon parsley flakes

1 teaspoon basil flakes
1/4 teaspoon pepper
1/2 cup chicken broth
1 teaspoon salt
Group 3
1 cup American cheese, grated
Group 4
1/4 cup croutons, onion/garlic
    flavors

Prepare chicken per section 6b. Set aside. Prepare Group 1 per package instruction and set aside. Combine Group 2. Mix well. Bring to boil at "Medium High" heat setting. Boil 1-2 minutes. Reset heat to "Medium Low", cover, and simmer 15 minutes. Mix occasionally. Remove cover and evaporate to sizzling. Cover and let self-saute 2 minutes. Preheat oven at 325F. Combine Groups 1 and 2 in 4-quart casserole bowl. Sprinkle macaroni with Group 3, cover, and bake 45 minutes. Garnish with Group 4 and serve.

Egg, 52

Eggplant (Brinjal), *Solanum melongena*

58   Baked Eggs

Group 1
8 large eggs
Group 2
1/4 teaspoon thyme flakes
1/4 teaspoon pepper
1/4 teaspoon salt

2 Tablespoons Parmesan cheese,
grated
Group 3
2 Tablespoons Margarine
1 small garlic, diced

Boil Group 1 (see section 17f), shell, and cut each into halves, lengthwise. Set aside. Combine Group 2 in a bowl, mix well, and set aside. Add Group 3 to a casserole bowl. Spread them well. Lay the egg sections, with the yolk side faces down, on Group 3. Set aside. Preheat oven at 325F. Meanwhile, sprinkle Group 2 evenly over the eggs, bake in the oven 15 minutes uncovered, and serve.

---

59   Scrambled Egg Soup

Group 1
4 large eggs
Group 2
2 teaspoons soy sauce
1 teaspoon sugar
1/4 teaspoon MSG
1/2 teaspoon salt
Group 3
2 Tablespoons oil

Group 4
3 cups hot broth
Group 5
1/4 teaspoon sesame oil
1/4 teaspoon pepper
3 stalks scallion, diced
1/8 teaspoon white
pepper

Shell 2 eggs (Group 1) and separate their whites into a bowl. Discard the yolks. Shell remaining 2 eggs and add their whites and yolks to the bowl. Beat the mixture until the whites and the yolks are blended to yolk color (see section 19e). Set aside. Add to 1-cup bowl Group 2, mix, and set aside. Heat 10-inch skillet at "Medium High" heat setting for 60-90 seconds. Add Group 3 to the skillet and heat for 15-20 seconds. Reset heat to "Medium". Add eggs to skillet and scramble well. Fry 60-90 seconds. Add Group 4, mix well, and bring to boil. Add Group 2, mix, garnish with Group 5, and serve.

60   Pecan Omelet

Group 1
8 large eggs
Group 2
1/3 cup pecan nuts, unsalted

1/4 teaspoon pepper
1/4 teaspoon salt
Group 3
4 Tablespoons oil

Break 4 eggs (Group 1) and separate their whites into a bowl. Discard the yolks. Break the remaining 4 eggs and add their whites and yolks to the bowl. Beat the mixture until the whites and the yolks are blended to yolk color. Set aside. Prepare Group 2 and set aside. Heat a 10-inch skillet at "Medium High" heat setting for 60-90 seconds. Add Group 3 to the skillet and heat for 15-20 seconds. Reset heat to "Medium". Add Group 2, fry for 8 seconds, mix well, and add the egg mixture to the skillet immediately (see section 19d). When bottom of the omelet has set lift an edge of the omelet with spatula, tilt the skillet towards the lifted edge, and let uncooked eggs flow to the edge. Fry 10-20 seconds. Flip the omelet quickly. Turn heat off. Fry the omelet on the flipped side for additional 30-40 seconds and serve.

61   Egg Stew

Group 1
12 large eggs
Group 2
1 medium onion, diced
1 medium garlic, diced
1/4 teaspoon pepper
1/4 teaspoon thyme flakes
1 small bay leaf
1/2 teaspoon sugar
1 teaspoon salt
1 Tablespoon oil
1/4 cup water

Group 3
1 cup hot water
1/4 cup carrots, diced
1/4 cup pearl onions, frozen
Group 4
2 Tablespoons margarine
1/2 cup sour cream
1/2 cup yogurt, plain
Group 5
2 stalks scallion, diced
1 Tablespoon Parmesan cheese,
    grated

Boil Group 1 (see section 17f), shell, and cut each into halves, lengthwise. Remove yolks from 12 egg sections and discard. Save the remaining and set aside. Add to 4-quart pot, Group 2, mix well, and bring to boil at "Medium High" heat setting. Reset heat to "Medium Low", cover, and simmer 20 minutes. Prepare Group 3 and set aside. Reset heat to "Medium", remove cover, and evaporate Group 2 to sizzling. Cover and let self-saute 2 minutes. Add Group 3, mix well, cover, reset heat to "Medium Low", and simmer 15 minutes. Add Group 4, mix well, add Group 1 sections, don't mix, cover, and simmer 5-10 minutes. Garnish with Group 5 and serve. Add 1/4 to 1 cup hot water to pot for more sauce, if needed.

---

62   Cheese Omelet

Group 1
8 large eggs
Group 2
1/3 cup sharp Cheddar cheese, grated
1/4 teaspoon pepper

2 Tablespoons Parmesan cheese, grated
1/8 teaspoon salt
3 stalks scallion, diced
Group 3
4 Tablespoons oil

Break 4 eggs (Group 1) and separate their whites into a bowl. Discard the yolks. Break the remaining 4 eggs and add their whites and yolks to the bowl. Beat the mixture until the whites and the yolks are blended to yolk color (see section 19d). Set aside. Prepare Group 2 and set aside. Heat a 10-inch skillet at "Medium High" heat setting for 60-90 seconds. Add Group 3 to the skillet and heat for 15-20 seconds. Add egg mixture to the skillet and sprinkle Group 2 evenly over the omelet. Reset heat to "Medium". When bottom of the omelet has set lift an edge of the omelet with spatula, tilt the skillet towards the lifted edge, and let eggs flow to the edge. Fry 10-20 seconds. Flip the omelet. Turn heat off. Fry the omelet on the flipped side for additional 40 seconds and serve.

63   Egg and Rice Casserole

Group 1
6 large eggs

Group 2
1 medium garlic, diced
1 teaspoon Italian seasoning
2 Tablespoons olive oil
1/4 teaspoon pepper
1 medium fresh jalapeno
   pepper, diced
2 Tablespoons beef bouillon
1/4 cup water

Group 3
1/2 cup hot 2% milk

Group 4
1 cup lima beans, frozen
4 cups cooked rice
2 Tablespoons sharp Cheddar
   cheese, grated
2 Tablespoons margarine
1 Tablespoon Parmesan cheese,
   grated

Boil Group 1 (see section 17f), shell, and cut each into halves, lengthwise. Remove yolks from 6 egg sections and discard. Save the remaining and set aside. Cook 3 cups extra long grain rice per section 23b and set aside. Combine Group 2 in pot, mix well, and bring to boil at "Medium High" heat setting. Boil 1-2 minutes. Reset heat to "Medium Low", cover, and simmer 15 minutes. Mix occasionally. Remove cover and evaporate to sizzling. Preheat oven at 325F. Add Group 3, mix well, add Group 4, add Group 1 sections, and mix well. Seal the pot with aluminum foil (see section 16a), bake 30-45 minutes, and serve.

64   Bombay Scrambled Eggs*

Group 1
8 large eggs

Group 2
2 Tablespoons onion, diced
4 sprigs cilantro, diced
1 medium fresh jalapeno
   pepper, diced

1/4 teaspoon cumin powder
1/8 teaspoon turmeric
1/2 teaspoon coriander powder
1/4 teaspoon salt
1/4 teaspoon pepper

Group 3
4 Tablespoons oil

Break 4 eggs (Group 1) and separate their whites into a bowl. Discard the yolks. Break the remaining 4 eggs and add their whites and yolks to the bowl. Beat the mixture until the whites and the yolks are blended to yolk color (see section 19e). Set aside. Combine Group 2 and mix. Set aside. Heat 10-inch skillet at "Medium High" heat setting for 60-90 seconds. Add Group 3 and heat 30-40 seconds. Reset heat to "Medium", add Group 2, mix, and fry 10-20 seconds. Add eggs immediately and scramble well. Fry 60-90 seconds and serve.

---

65   Egg Curry*

Group 1

12 large eggs

Group 2

1 medium onion, diced

1 large garlic, diced

2 teaspoons ginger, diced

1/8 teaspoon turmeric

1 medium tomato, diced

1 Tablespoon Madras curry powder

1/8 teaspoon red pepper powder

1 teaspoon paprika

1/2 cup water

1 (2-in) cinnamon stick

1 teaspoon salt

3 Tablespoons oil

Group 3

1 large potato, cut into 8 sections

1 cup hot water

Group 4

8 sprigs cilantro, diced

2 medium fresh cayenne peppers, whole

Boil Group 1 (see section 17f), shell, and set aside. Add to 4-quart pot, Group 2, mix well, and bring to boil at "Medium High" heat setting. Reset heat to "Medium Low", cover, and simmer for 20 minutes. Reset heat to "Medium", remove cover, and evaporate Group 2 to sizzling. Cover and let self-saute 1-2 minutes. Add Group 3, mix, bring to boil, reset heat to "Medium Low", cover, and simmer 15 minutes. Add the eggs (whole), mix, cover, and simmer 10-15 minutes. Garnish with Group 4 and serve. Add 1/4 to 1 cup hot water to pot for more sauce, if needed. Mix, salt to taste, and serve.

66   Egg Rice Mushroom Casserole

Group 1
6 large eggs
Group 2
1 medium garlic, diced
2 Tablespoons oil
1/4 teaspoon pepper
1 1/2 teaspoons salt
1/4 cup water
Group 3
1/2 cup hot 2% milk

2 (10-oz) cans, cream of
    mushroom soup
3 Tablespoons margarine
Group 4
5 cups cooked rice
8 oz fresh mushroom, cut into
    1/4-in slices
1/4 cup pearl onions, frozen
2 Tablespoons Parmesan cheese,
    grated

Boil Group 1 (see section 17f), shell, and cut each into halves, lengthwise. Remove yolks from 6 egg sections and discard. Save the remaining and set aside. Cook 3 cups extra long grain rice per section 23b and set aside. Combine Group 2 in a 5-quat pot, mix well, and bring to boil at "Medium High" heat setting. Boil 1-2 minutes. Reset heat to "Medium Low", cover, and simmer 15 minutes. Mix occasionally. Remove cover and evaporate to sizzling. Preheat oven at 325F. Add Group 3, mix well, add Groups 4 and 1, and mix well. Seal pot with an aluminum foil (see section 16a), bake 30-45 minutes, and serve.

67   Provincial Egg Tomato Sauce*

The salted red snapper is similar to the taste and aroma of anchovy.

Group 1
5 large eggs
Group 2
1 small onion, diced
2 large garlic, diced
1 teaspoon paprika
1/8 teaspoon crushed red pepper
2 large tomatoes, diced
2 sections, salted red snapper
    in oil

2 medium fresh cayenne peppers,
    whole
1/8 teaspoon turmeric
1 teaspoon fish sauce
3 oz tomato paste
4 Tablespoons oil
3/4 cup water
Group 3
8 sprigs cilantro, cut each into
    4 sections

Boil Group 1 (see section 17f), shell, cut each into halves, lengthwise, and set aside. Add to 4-quart pot, Group 2, mix, bring to boil at "Medium" heat setting. Reset heat to "Low", cover, and simmer 15-20 minutes. Mix occasionally. Add Groups 1 and 3, mix, cover, simmer 5-10 minutes, and serve. Add 1/4 to 1/2 cup hot water for more sauce, if needed.

---

68   Egg and Salted Black Beans*

Group 1
12 large eggs
Group 2
1 large garlic, diced
1 teaspoon ginger, diced
3 Tablespoons oil
1/2 cup water
Group 3
2 Tablespoons corn starch
1 teaspoon black bean/red pepper
    sauce

1 Tablespoon black bean in oil
1/4 teaspoon MSG
1 Tablespoon soy sauce
1 Tablespoon rice wine
3/4 teaspoon sugar
1/4 cup water
no salt
Group 4
1 cup hot water
Group 5
3 stalks scallion, diced

Boil Group 1 (see section 17f), shell, and cut each into halves, lengthwise. Remove yolks from 12 egg sections and discard. Save the remaining and set aside. Add to 4-quart pot, Group 2, mix well, and bring to boil at "Medium High" heat setting. Reset heat to "Medium Low", cover, and simmer for 15 minutes. Set aside. Prepare Group 3 mixture and set aside (see section 2). Reset heat to "Medium", remove cover, and evaporate Group 2 to sizzling. Cover and self-saute 1-2 minutes. Add Group 4, mix, remix Group 3, and add to pot with mixing. Mix until the sauce thickens to a smooth texture (see section 20a). Add Group 1 sections, don't mix, cover, and simmer 5 minutes. Add 1/4 to 1 cup hot water to pot for more sauce, if needed. Mix, salt to taste. Garnish with Group 5 and serve.

69   Spicy Egg Stew*

Group 1
12 large eggs
Group 2
1 medium onion, diced
1 large garlic, diced
2 large tomatoes, diced
1/4 teaspoon pepper
1/2 teaspoon basil flakes
1/4 teaspoon thyme flakes
1/4 teaspoon parsley flakes
1 small bell pepper, diced

2 Tablespoons olive oil
1/8 teaspoon red pepper, powder
1/2 cup water
1/2 teaspoon sugar
1 teaspoon salt
Group 3
1/2 cup hot water
Group 4
1/3 cup oyster crackers, crumbled
1 Tablespoon Parmesan cheese,
    grated

Boil Group 1 (see section 17f), shell, and cut each into halves, lengthwise. Remove yolks from 12 egg sections and discard. Save the remaining and set aside. Add to 4-quart pot, Group 2, mix well, and bring to boil at "Medium High" heat setting. Reset heat to "Medium Low", cover, and simmer for 20 minutes. Reset heat to "Medium", remove cover, and evaporate Group 2 to sizzling. Cover and let self-saute 1-2 minutes. Add Group 3, mix, add Group 1 sections, don't mix, reset heat to "Medium Low", cover, and simmer 10 minutes. Garnish with Group 4 and serve. Add 1/4 to 1 cup hot water to pot for more sauce, if needed. Mix, salt to taste, and serve.

70   Egg Fried Rice*

Group 1
1 small onion, diced
1 small garlic, diced
1/8 teaspoon turmeric
2 teaspoons coriander powder
1 teaspoon cumin powder
2 medium fresh cayenne
    pepper, diced
1/2 teaspoon salt

2 Tablespoons
    margarine
2 Tablespoons oil
6 sprigs cilantro, diced
1/4 teaspoon pepper
Group 2
6 large eggs
Group 3
5 cups cooked rice

Cook 3 cups extra long grain rice per section 23b and set aside. Add to 12-inch skillet, Group 1, and saute at "Medium" heat setting with frequent mixing for 1 to 2 minutes, cover, reset heating to "Low", and let cook for 5 minutes. Meanwhile, shell half of the eggs (Group 2) and separate their whites into a bowl. Discard the yolks. Shell the remaining eggs and add their whites and yolks to the bowl. Beat the mixture until the whites and the yolks are blended well. Set aside. Reset heating to "Medium High", remove cover, wait 60 seconds, and add the beaten eggs to the skillet. Scramble ingredients immediately. Fry with mixing for 60 to 90 seconds. Add Group 3, mix well, reset heat to "Medium Low", cover and let cook for 2 to 3 minutes with occasional mixing, and serve.

---

71   Scrambled Egg with Eggplant*

Group 1
1 medium eggplant, peeled,
    chopped
4 Tablespoons oil
1/4 teaspoon pepper
1/2 teaspoon salt

1/4 cup water
Group 2
5 large eggs
Group 3
1 medium fresh jalapeno pepper,
    diced

Combine Group 1 in a 4-quart pot, mix well, and bring to boil at "Medium High" heat setting. Boil 1-2 minutes. Reset heat to "Medium Low", cover, and simmer, mixing occasionally, for 15-20 minutes. Meanwhile, break 2 eggs (Group 2) and separate their whites into a bowl. Discard their yolks. Shell 3 more eggs and add their whites and yolks to the bowl. Beat the mixture until the whites and the yolks are blended well to a yellow yolk color (see section 19e). Set aside. Reset heat to "Medium". Remove cover and evaporate Group 1 to sizzling while mashing eggplant in the pot. Add Groups 2 and 3 to pot. scramble well, saute 3-5 minutes, and serve.

72   Bill McEnroe Omelet

Group 1
8 large eggs
Group 2
4 Tablespoons oil

Group 3
1/4 teaspoon salt
1/4 teaspoon pepper

Break 4 eggs (Group 1) and separate their whites into a bowl. Discard the yolks. Break the remaining 4 eggs and add their whites and yolks to the bowl. Beat the mixture until the whites and the yolks are blended to yolk color (see section 19d). Set aside. Heat a 10-inch skillet at "Medium High" heat setting for 60-90 seconds. Add Group 2 to the skillet and heat for 15-20 seconds. Add the egg mixture to the skillet and sprinkle Group 3 evenly over the omelet. Reset heat to "Medium". When bottom of the omelet has set lift an edge of the omelet with spatula, tilt the skillet towards the lifted edge, and let uncooked eggs flow to the edge. Fry 10-20 seconds. Flip the omelet quickly. Turn off heat. Fry the omelet on the flipped side for additional 30-40 seconds and serve.

73   Cashew Scrambled Eggs

Group 1
8 large eggs
Group 2
1/3 cup cashew nuts, unsalted
Group 3
1/4 teaspoon pepper

3 stalks scallion,
    diced
1/4 teaspoon salt
Group 4
4 Tablespoons oil

Break 4 eggs (Group 1) and separate their whites into a bowl. Discard the yolks. Break the remaining 4 eggs and add their whites and yolks to the bowl. Beat the mixture until the whites and the yolks are blended to yolk color. Set aside (see section 19e). Prepare Group 2 and set aside. Heat a 10-inch skillet at "Medium High" heat setting for 60-90 seconds. Add Group 4 to the skillet and heat for 15-20 seconds. Reset heat to "Medium". Add Group 2, fry for 8 seconds with mixing, and add the egg mixture to the skillet immediately. Sprinkle Group 3 evenly over egg and scramble the egg well. Fry 60-90 seconds and serve.

74   Egg Rangoon

Group 1
12 large eggs
Group 2
1/4 teaspoon turmeric

1/4 teaspoon salt
Group 3
1 large garlic, diced
3 Tablespoons oil

Boil Group 1 (see section 17f), shell, and cut each into halves, lengthwise. Lay each section with its yolk side up in a 10-inch skillet (see section 19c). Sprinkle turmeric and salt on each section. Add Group 3 to the skillet. Heat at "Medium" for 2-3 minutes. Cover loosely, and fry undisturbed for 60-90 seconds. Flip each section over, cover, fry undisturbed for 60-90 seconds, and serve.

SAFETY CAUTION: The egg sections have tendency to pop and spit hot oil in the air during frying. Hence, the egg sections must be covered loosely during the frying.

Fish, 64

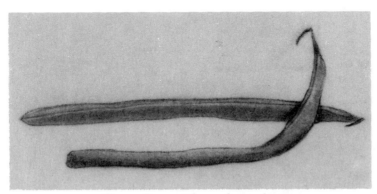

Green Bean, *Phaseolus vulgaris*

75   Flounder Parmesan

Group 1
32 oz flounder fillets
4 Tablespoons margarine
1 large garlic, diced
1/4 teaspoon cracked pepper
1/4 teaspoon salt
1/2 cup water

Group 2
2 Tablespoons Parmesan cheese,
   grated

Group 3
1/3 cup croutons, onion/garlic
   flavors, crumbled
1/8 teaspoon pepper

Combine Group 1 in pot. Mix well. Bring to boil at "Medium High" heat setting. Boil 1-2 minutes. Reset heat to "Medium Low", cover, and simmer 15 minutes. Mix occasionally. Remove cover and evaporate to sizzling. Sprinkle Group 2 on Group 1. Don't mix, cover, and let self-saute 1-2 minutes. Garnish with Group 3 and serve.

76   Ginger Tuna Loaf

Group 1
3 Tablespoons oil
1 small onion, diced
1/4 teaspoon salt
1/4 teaspoon pepper
1/4 cup water

Group 2
3 Tablespoons flour

Group 3
3/4 cup milk and tuna fish liquid

Group 4
1 egg, beaten

Group 5
3 (6-oz) cans, tuna fish
4 slices white bread, cubed
1 small sweet banana pepper,
   diced
1/2 teaspoon diced ginger, juiced
   with garlic press

Combine Group 1 in pot and evaporate to sizzling at "Medium" heat setting. Mix occasionally. Add Group 2 in sizzling oil and let self-saute until flour turns light tan color. Mix often. Remove pot from stove. Preheat oven at 325F. Add Group 3 and mix well. Stir in Group 4. Mix well. Add Group 5. Mix well and shape into a loaf. Place loaf on baking tray lined with aluminum foil. Bake 30-35 minutes and serve.

77   Salted Red Snapper Catsup*

Group 1
1 small onion, diced
1 large garlic, diced
1 teaspoon paprika
1/8 teaspoon crushed red pepper
2 large tomatoes, diced
2 sections, salted red snapper
    in oil

4 Tablespoons oil
2 medium fresh cayenne
    peppers, whole
1/8 teaspoon turmeric
2 teaspoons fish sauce
3/4 cup water
Group 2
8 sprigs cilantro, each quartered

Add to 3-quart pot, Group 1, mix, bring to boil at "Medium" heat setting. Reset heat to "Medium Low", cover, and simmer 15-20 minutes with occasional mixing. Add Group 2, mix, cover, simmer 2 minutes, and serve. Add 1/4 to 1 cup hot water to pot for more sauce, if needed. Mix, salt to taste, and serve.

78   Catfish Curry**

Group 1
1 large onion, diced
1 medium garlic, diced
1 teaspoon ginger, diced
1/4 teaspoon turmeric
1 teaspoon paprika
1/4 teaspoon crushed red pepper
1 medium fresh cayenne or
    jalapeno pepper, diced
1 Tablespoon Madras curry mix

1 medium tomato, diced
1 Tablespoon garam masala
1/4 cup water
3 Tablespoons oil
1 teaspoon salt
Group 2
1 cup hot water
24 oz catfish nuggets
Group 3
10 sprigs cilantro, cut into halves

Combine Group 1 in pot, mix, and bring to boil at "Medium High" heat setting. Boil 1-2 minutes, reset heat to "Medium Low", cover, and simmer 30 minutes. Meanwhile, prepare Group 2 catfish per section 3a and set aside. Remove cover and evaporate Group 1 to sizzling in oil. Cover and let self-saute 3 minutes mixing occasionally. Reset heat to "Medium", add Group 2, mix, and bring to boil. Reset heat to "Medium Low", add Group 3, cover, simmer 15 minutes, and serve.

79   Cod Fish Tomato Catsup*

Group 1
4 oz dried cod fish, cut into
  1-in pieces
1 cup hot water
Group 2
1 Tablespoon tamarind
1/2 cup hot water
Group 3
1 small onion, diced
1 large garlic, diced
1 teaspoon paprika
2 large tomatoes, diced

1/8 teaspoon crushed red
  pepper
2 teaspoons fish sauce
2 medium fresh cayenne peppers,
  whole
1 teaspoon shrimp paste
3/4 cup water
4 Tablespoons oil
no salt
Group 4
8 sprigs cilantro, each quartered

Combine Group 1 in 2-cup bowl. Soak 45 minutes. Set aside. Combine
Group 2. Soak in water 5-8 minutes. Disperse tamarind well and set
aside. Add to 3-quart pot, Groups 3 and 1 (only fish), mix, bring to boil
at "Medium" heat setting. Reset heat to "Medium Low", cover, and
simmer 45 minutes. Mix occasionally. Remove cover and evaporate
Group 1 to sizzling. Mix well. Remove tamarind pulps in Group 2, add
Group 2 to pot, mix, and simmer 10 more minutes. Add Group 4, cover,
turn heat off, stand 3 minutes, and serve. Add 1/4 cup to 1/2 hot water
for more sauce, if needed. Mix, salt to taste, and serve.

80   Red Snapper Hunan Style**

Group 1
1 large garlic, diced
3 Tablespoons oil
32 oz red snapper fillets,
  2-inch pieces
3/4 cup water
no salt
Group 2
1/4 teaspoon coarse shrimp paste

1 teaspoon soy sauce
1 teaspoon fish sauce
2 Tablespoons garlic/red pepper
  /black bean sauce
1 Tablespoon rice wine
Group 3
8 sprigs cilantro, cut into halves
1/8 teaspoon pepper

Combine Group 1 in pot. Mix gently. Bring to boil at "Medium High" heat setting. Reset heat to "Medium Low" cover, and simmer 10 minutes. Mix gently occasionally. Remove cover and evaporate to sizzling. Add Group 2. Mix gently. Reset heat to "Low", cover, and let self-saute 5-8 minutes. Add Group 3, do not mix, cover, turn heat off, stand 3 minutes, and serve. Add 1/4 to 1/2 cup hot water if more sauce is needed. Salt to taste and serve.

---

81 Anchovy Pizza*

Group 1
2 (7- oz) flour packages, premixed for pizza
Group 2
2 Tablespoons corn oil
Group 3
12 oz pizza sauce
Group 4
1/2 teaspoon cracked pepper
1 large hot pickled banana pepper, diced
1/4 teaspoon garlic powder
Group 5
1/2 cup blended cheese from pizza packages

1 medium garlic, diced
1/2 cup mozzarella/provolone/. Parmesan cheeses, grated
Group 6
1 (2-oz) can anchovies, diced
Group 7
1/2 cup mozzarella/provolone/ Parmesan cheeses, grated
1/2 cup blended cheese from pizza packages
1/4 teaspoon Italian seasoning
Group 8
1 Tablespoon Parmesan cheese, grated
1/4 teaspoon crushed red pepper

Mix and raise crust mix (Group 1) per instruction on the package. Make pie crust and dress the pie per section 8 using the ingredient groups in this recipe. Bake per section 16b. Garnish with Group 8, section pizza, and serve.

82   Steamed Cod Fish Fillets

Group 1
24 oz cod fillets, cut into
   2-inch pieces
4 stalks scallion, each quartered
1 small tomato, cut into 4 slices
1 Tablespoon oil
Group 2
1/2 cup water
1 Tablespoon corn starch
1 Tablespoon soy sauce
1/4 teaspoon MSG

2 teaspoons black bean in oil
1/2 teaspoon sugar
1 Tablespoon rice wine
Group 3
1 Tablespoon oil
1 teaspoon ginger, diced
1 medium garlic, diced
Group 4
1/8 teaspoon sesame oil
1/8 teaspoon pepper
1/8 teaspoon white pepper

Arrange Group 1 in a bowl and steam in a steamer about 40 minutes (see sections 26a and 26b). Meanwhile, mix Group 2, and set aside. Heat Group 3 in 1-cup pot at "Medium" heat setting and saute ingredients to light tan color (see section 19h). Reset heat to "Medium Low", remix Group 2, and add to Group 3. Mix to a smooth sauce. Set aside. Remove fish from steamer, pour Group 2 sauce over fish, garnish with Group 4, and serve.

83   Salmon in Ginger Cream Sauce

Group 1
3 Tablespoons oil
1 small onion, diced
1 medium garlic, diced
1/4 teaspoon parsley flakes
1/4 teaspoon cracked pepper
1/4 cup water
no salt
Group 2
2 Tablespoons flour
Group 3
1/2 cup whole milk

1 (10-oz) can, cream of
   mushroom soup
1/2 teaspoon sugar
1/2 cup hot water
Group 4
1 (15-oz) can, pink salmon,
   meat only
2 Tablespoons sharp Cheddar
   cheese, grated
1/2 teaspoon ginger, juiced with
   garlic press

Combine Group 1 in pot, mix well, and evaporate to sizzling at "Medium" heat setting. Add Group 2 in sizzling oil and let self-saute until flour turns light tan color. Mix often. Stir in Group 3, disperse soup, mix well to smooth paste, add Group 4 and mix breaking salmon chucks. Reset heat to "Medium Low", heat 15 minutes, and serve.

---

84   Mackerel with Mushroom

Group 1
1 Tablespoon oil
1 small onion, diced
1 medium garlic, diced
1 Tablespoon chicken bouillon
1/4 teaspoon pepper
1/4 teaspoon Italian Seasoning
1/2 cup water
no salt
Group 2
2 Tablespoons corn starch
1/2 teaspoon sugar

1 Tablespoon white wine
Group 3
4 (4-oz) cans, mackerel fillets in
   cotton seed oil
Group 4
6 oz fresh mushroom, cut each
   into 4 slices
Group 5
1 cup hot water
Group 6
1 Tablespoon Parmesan cheese,
   grated

Combine Group 1 in pot. Mix well. Bring to boil at "Medium High" heat setting. Boil 1-2 minutes. Reset heat to "Low", cover, and simmer 25 minutes. Mix occasionally. Meanwhile, prepare Group 2 and set aside (see section 2). Heat Group 3 (cans unopened) in boiling water 15 minutes, and set aside. Prepare Group 4 and set aside. Reset heating to "Medium", remove cover, and evaporate Group 1 to sizzling. Mix occasionally. Open mackerel cans, empty into 3-quart serving bowl, and set aside. Add to Group 1, Groups 4 and 5 and mix well. Remix Group 2, add to Group 1 (see section 20a), and mix until gravy thickens to smooth consistency. Pour Group 1 mixture over Group 3, garnish with Group 6, and serve.

85   Sardine Curry

This was a popular dish served at our dormitory dinning hall when I was an undergraduate student at the Rangoon University in the 1950s.

Group 1
1 small onion, diced
1 large garlic, diced
1/8 teaspoon turmeric
1 Tablespoon Madras curry
   powder
2 medium fresh cayenne peppers,
   diced
3 Tablespoons oil

1/2 cup water
1 teaspoon paprika
Group 2
1 teaspoon garam masala
2 (5-oz) cans sardines in tomato
   sauce
Group 3
5-8 sprigs cilantro, diced

Combine Group 1 in pot. Mix well. Bring to boil at "Medium High" heat setting. Reset heat to "Medium Low", cover, and simmer 30 minutes. Remove cover and evaporate to sizzling. Reset heat to "Low", add Group 2. mix gently, cover, simmer 20 minutes, add Group 3, cover, simmer 2 more minutes, and serve. Add 1/4 to 1/2 cup hot water if more sauce is needed. Salt to taste, garnish with Group 3, and serve.

86   Red Snapper with Black Beans

Group 1
32 oz red snapper, dressed
1 small onion, quartered
1 small tomato, quartered
Group 2
1 teaspoon ginger, diced
2 small garlic, diced
1 Tablespoon oil
1 Tablespoon dried
   black bean

Group 3
1/2 teaspoon sugar
1/4 teaspoon MSG
1 Tablespoon rice wine
1 teaspoon fish sauce
1 Tablespoon soy sauce
no salt
Group 4
1/8 teaspoon white pepper
1/8 teaspoon pepper

Place fish in 3-quart bowl. Place tomato and onion evenly around fish. Steam Group 1 for 90 minutes undisturbed (see sections 26a and 26b). Meanwhile, add to 1-cup pot Group 2 and fry at "Medium Low" setting for 3 minutes, maximum (see section 19i). Set aside. Mix Group 3 in 1-cup bowl and set aside. After steaming Group 1 remove cover, pour Group 3 over Group 1 (Caution: Don't let steam burn you), pour Group 2, cover, and steam for 25 more minutes. Garnish with Group 4 and serve.

87　　Sole on Red Pepper Sauce*

Group 1
1 small onion, diced
1 medium bell pepper, diced
2 medium garlic, diced
2 Tablespoons oil
1 teaspoon cumin powder
1/2 teaspoon paprika
1/2 teaspoon oregano
1/8 teaspoon basil flakes
1/8 teaspoon parsley flakes
1 medium fresh jalapeno
　 pepper, diced

1/8 teaspoon white pepper
1 large tomato, diced
1/4 teaspoon pepper
3/4 teaspoon salt
1/2 cup water
Group 2
32 oz Sole fillets, fresh or frozen
　 cut into halves
2 Tablespoons margarine
Group 3
　2 Tablespoons Parmesan cheese,
　 grated

Combine Group 1 in 3-quart pot. Mix well. Bring to boil at "Medium High" heat setting. Boil 1-2 minutes. Reset heat to "Low", cover, and simmer 20 minutes. Mix occasionally. Remove cover and evaporate to sizzling at "Medium Low". Mix occasionally. Meanwhile, preheat oven at 325F. Spread Group 1 in the pot, place Group 2 fillets side by side on Group 1, spread margarine on fillets. and sprinkle Group 3 evenly over fillets, baked 20-30 minutes, and serve.

88   Flounder Fettuccine Pasta

Group 1
1 medium garlic, diced
1 small onion, diced
1/4 teaspoon salt
2 Tablespoons oil
1/4 cup water
Group 2
6 oz fettucine pasta
Group 3
16 oz flounder, fillets

Group 4
2 (10-oz) cans, cream of
    chicken soup
1/2 cup 2% milk
2 Tablespoons margarine
1 cup hot water
Group 5
4 stalks scallion, diced
1/8 teaspoon pepper

Add to 4-quart pot, Group 1, mix well, and bring to boil at "Medium High" heat setting. Reset heat to "Medium Low", cover, and simmer 10-15 minutes. Meanwhile, prepare Group 2 per instruction on package and set aside. Remove cover and evaporate Group 1 to sizzling. Rest heat to "Low", cover and let self-saute 5 minutes. Mix occasionally. Reset heat to "Medium", add Group 3, mix breaking fish fillets into smaller pieces, add Group 4, mix well, cover, and simmer 5 minutes. Add Group 2 and mix well. Add 1/4 to 1/2 cup hot water for more sauce, if needed. Mix, salt to taste, garnish with Group 5 and serve.

89   Flounder Country Style*

Group 1
1 medium onion, diced
1 large garlic, diced
1 teaspoon paprika
1 medium fresh cayenne pepper,
    whole

3 Tablespoons oil
1/2 cup water
1/2 teaspoon salt
Group 2
1/4 cup hot water
32 oz flounder fillets

Combine Group 1 in pot, mix well, and bring to boil at "Medium High" heat setting. Boil 1-2 minutes. Reset heat to "Low", cover, and simmer 20 minutes. Mix occasionally. Reset heat to "Medium", remove cover, and evaporate to sizzling. Add Group 2, mix, cover, and simmer 20 minutes. Mix occasionally crushing fish chunks while mixing, and serve. Add 1/4 to 1/2 cup hot water to pot for more sauce, if needed. Mix, salt to taste, and serve.

---

90   Mandalay Catsup*

Group 1
1 small onion, diced
1 large garlic, diced
1 teaspoon paprika
1/8 teaspoon crushed red pepper
4 Tablespoons oil
2 large tomatoes, diced
1 teaspoon shrimp paste
2 teaspoons fish sauce

2 medium fresh cayenne peppers,
   whole
3/4 cup water
no salt
Group 2
1/4 cup hot water
1 Tablespoon tamarind
Group 3
8 sprigs cilantro, cut into halves

Add to 3-quart pot, Group 1, mix, bring to boil at "Medium" heat setting. Reset heat to "Medium Low", cover, and simmer 15-20 minutes. Mix occasionally. Meanwhile, soak Group 2 in hot water and disperse tamarind well. Set aside. Remove cover and evaporate Group 1 to sizzling. Add Group 2 (liquid only) discard pulp, add Group 3, mix, cover, simmer 15 minutes, and serve. Add 1/4 to 1 cup hot water to pot for more sauce, if needed. Mix, salt to taste, and serve.

91   Super Combo Pizza*

Group 1
2 (7 oz) flour packages,
  premixed for pizza
Group 2
2 Tablespoons corn oil
Group 3
4 oz fresh Italian sausage meat
4 oz lean ground beef
1/4 cup water
12 oz pizza sauce
Group 4
1/2 teaspoon cracked pepper
1/2 teaspoon garlic powder
1 small mild pickled banana
  pepper, diced
1/4 cup onion, diced
1/4 cup bell pepper, diced
Group 5
1/2 cup mozzarella/provolone/
Parmesan cheeses, premixed

1/2 cup blended cheese from
  pizza packages
Group 6
1 oz Canadian bacon,
  diced
6 medium shrimps, dressed,
  cut into halves
1 oz pepperoni slices
Group 7
1/4 teaspoon Italian
  seasoning
1/2 cup blended cheese from
  pizza packages
1/2 cup mozzarella/provolone/
  Parmesan cheeses, premixed
Group 8
1 Tablespoon Parmesan cheese.
  cheese, grated
1/4 teaspoon crushed red
  pepper

Mix and raise crust mix (Group 1) per instruction on the package. Set aside. Paint Group 2 evenly on the floor of pizza pan (16-inch diameter). Set aside. Meanwhile, combine Group 3, mix, heat to boiling at "Medium" heat setting, and evaporate to sizzling. Reset heat to "Medium Low", remove fat, add pizza sauce (remaining Group 3), mix, cover, and let self-saute 3 minutes. Set aside. Continue with pizza dressing beginning from flattening dough in section 8. Bake per section 16b. Garnish with Group 8, section pizza, and serve.

92   Salmon Moat-Hinn-Ghar

This is a simplified version of a national Myanmar salmon fish stew. This dish requires fish sauce, and rice and chick pea flours, which are available only in Asian grocery stores. In Myanmar, this sauce is usually served on noodle or on leftover rice. The noodle is made from fermented rice. It is not available in the US. A close substitute is a dried white noodle processed in Taiwan. The noodle is cooked per instruction on the package using two bundles for 4 servings. Alternatively this dish may be served on cooked rice. Although it is a simplified version its AFTT are as authentic as the ones prepared in Burma. This is a healthful dish.

Group 1
1 medium onion, diced
3 Tablespoons oil
3 medium garlic, diced
2 teaspoons ginger, diced
1/8 teaspoon turmeric
1 teaspoon paprika
1/4 teaspoon crushed red pepper
1 teaspoon pepper
1/2 cup water
no salt
Group 2
1/4 cup water
1 Tablespoon rice flour

1 Tablespoon chick pea flour
Group 3
4 cups hot water
Group 4
1 (15-oz) can, pink salmon
3 Tablespoons fish sauce
Group 5
2 bundles dried Chinese noodle
Group 6
1 small onion, 1/4-in slices
1 large garlic, diced
1/8 teaspoon turmeric
2 Tablespoons oil

Combine Group 1 in pot, mix well, and evaporate to sizzling at "Medium" heat setting. Meanwhile, disperse Group 2 in 1-cup bowl (see section 2). Set aside. Reset heat to "Medium Low", cover, and let self-saute 3-5 minutes. Mix occasionally. Reset heat to "Medium High". Stir in Group 3. Remix Group 2 and add to pot. Mix well. Add Group 4. Break salmon chunks and bring to boil. Boil 1-2 minutes. Reset heat to "Medium Low", cover, and simmer 50-60 minutes. Mix occasionally. Meanwhile, prepare Group 5 per instructions on package and set aside. Prepare Group 6 and fry per section 19g and set aside. Pour sauce on Group 5, garnish with Group 6, and serve. Add 1/4 to 1 cup hot water for more sauce if needed. Mix, salt to taste, and serve.

93   Burmese Monks' Delight*

The Burmese Buddhist religion requires the monks to receive their meals from the people. In cities, towns, and villages the monks would make their daily round in the mornings. The people set up tables by the roadside in front of their houses. They display pots, pans, plates, bowls etc. on the tables to signal the monks to stop by and receive the family's offerings. The bowls are filled with steamed rice, main dishes (fish, chicken, beef, pork, vegetables, etc.), and at least one version of the catsup. When the monks returned to their monasteries, chief of staffs of the monasteries would pool all the collections, combining all the beef curries, all the pork curries, all the tomato catsup, etc. together, and set the tables for the monks to eat their meals before noon. The religion prohibits the monks from eating after 12 noon everyday. The chiefs would take charge over the leftovers and serve the guests, patrons, sponsors, and students of the monastery. I must admit that when I was a little boy I enjoyed going to our family's monastery to feast on these hodge-podge leftovers. A version of the catsup is described below.

Group 1

1 small onion, diced	2 medium fresh cayenne peppers,
1 large garlic, diced	whole
1 teaspoon paprika	4 Tablespoons oil
1/8 teaspoon crushed red pepper	3/4 cup water
2 Tablespoons fish sauce	**Group 2**
2 large tomatoes, diced	8 sprigs cilantro, cut each into
no salt	4 sections

Add to 3-quart pot, Group 1, mix, bring to gentle boil at "Medium" heat setting. Reset heat to "Medium Low", cover, and simmer 15-20 minutes. Mix occasionally. Remove cover and evaporate to sizzling. Add Group 2, cover, and let self-saute 1-2 minutes. Add 1/4 to 1/2 cup hot water to pot for more sauce, if needed. Mix, salt to taste, and serve.

94   Jane McEnroe's Baked Fish

This recipe may be used with any fresh or salt water fish fillet of your favorite. We would resort to this recipe when we are not quite motivated to cook. Because, it is easy to prepare and we can always count on this dish, using yellow pike fillets, to give us flavorful and satisfying meal, every time.

Group 1

2/3 cup crushed saltine
   crackers
1/4 teaspoon garlic powder
1/4 teaspoon basil flakes
1/4 teaspoon oregano flakes
3 Tablespoons Parmesan
   cheese, grated

1/4 teaspoon salt

Group 2

1 Tablespoon olive oil
2 Tablespoon margarine

Group 3

24 oz fish fillets, whole or
   cut into bite-sized pieces

Add to 1-quart bowl, Group 1, mix well, and set aside. Add to baking dish (about 13"x9"), Group 2, warm to melt margarine, and mix well. Add Group 3 to Group 2, roll each fillet well, and set aside. Meanwhile, preheat oven at 350F. Sprinkle Group 1 on Groups 2 and 3 and roll coat each fillet piece well. Bake 25-30 minutes, and serve.

Lamb, 79

Onion, *Allium cepa*

95   Lamb and Bamboo Shoots*

Group 1
32 oz lean lamb, cut into
   1/4-in slices
2 Tablespoons oil
1 large garlic, diced
1 cup water
no salt
Group 2
1 teaspoon fish sauce

1 Tablespoon rice wine
1/2 teaspoon sugar
1/4 teaspoon MSG
1 teaspoon soy sauce
Group 3
1/2 cup braised bamboo shoots with
   red pepper

Combine Group 1 in pot. Mix well. Bring to boil at "Medium High" heat setting. Boil 1-2 minutes. Reset heat to "Medium Low", cover, and simmer 45 minutes. Mix occasionally. Remove cover, evaporate to sizzling, and let self-saute 2 minutes. Add Group 2. Mix well. Cover and simmer 2-4 minutes. Add Group 3, mix well, cover, let simmer 2-4 minutes, and serve. Add 1/4 cup hot water if more sauce is needed. Salt to taste and serve.

96   Italian Lamb Stew

Group 1
24 oz lean lamb, cut into
   1-in cubes
1/2 teaspoon Italian seasoning
2 Tablespoons oil
1 medium onion, diced
2 medium garlic, diced
1/4 teaspoon pepper

1 teaspoon salt
1 large bell pepper, diced
1 teaspoon paprika
1 large tomato, diced
1 cup water
Group 2
1 Tablespoon Parmesan cheese,
   grated

Combine Group 1 in pot. Mix well. Bring to boil at "Medium High" heat setting. Boil 1-2 minutes. Reset heat to "Medium Low", cover, and simmer 75 minutes. Mix occasionally. Remove cover and evaporate to sizzling. Cover and self-saute 3 minutes. Mix occasionally. Garnish with Group 2 and serve. Add 1/4 to 1/2 cup hot water for more sauce.

97　　Broiled Lamb Chops

Group 1
2 teaspoons pepper
1 teaspoon MSG
2 teaspoons salt

Group 2
8 lean lamb chops
Group 3
1 Tablespoon oil

Combine Group 1 in an empty spice bottle for use as spice shaker. Prepare chops per section f. Sprinkle copious amount of Group 1 mix from shaker on each side of chops. Broil each side 3 minutes per section 18. Broil twice on each side. Garnish with Group 3 and serve.

98　·　Lamb and Chana Curry*

Group 1
24 oz lamb, cut into 2-in cubes
1/4 teaspoon turmeric
4 Tablespoons oil
1 cup water
1 large onion, diced
2 large garlic, diced
1 Tablespoon ginger, diced
1 medium bay leaf
2 medium fresh cayenne pepper,
　whole
1 (3-in) cinnamon stick

1/4 teaspoon crushed red pepper
1 teaspoon paprika
1 Tablespoon Madras curry
　powder
2 teaspoons meat masala
1 teaspoon salt
Group 2
1/2 cup chana dahl
2 cups hot water
Group 3
2 teaspoons garam masala

Combine Group 1 in pot. Mix well. Bring to boil at "Medium High" heat setting. Boil 1-2 minutes. Reset heat to "Medium Low", cover, and simmer 45 minutes. Mix occasionally. Reset heat to "Medium", remove cover, and evaporate to sizzling. Mix occasionally. Reset heat to "Low", cover, and self-saute 3-5 minutes. Add Group 2, mix, bring to boil, cover, and simmer additional 60 minutes. Add Group 3, cover, simmer 5 more minutes, and serve. Add 1/4 to 1 cup hot water for more sauce if needed. Mix, salt to taste, and serve.

99   Spicy Broiled Lamb Chops*

Group 1
1 teaspoon paprika
1 teaspoon curry powder,
   any brand
1 teaspoon turmeric
1 teaspoon garlic powder
1 teaspoon pepper

1/2 teaspoon red pepper powder
2 teaspoons salt
1/2 teaspoon MSG
Group 2
8 lean lamb chops
Group 3
1 Tablespoon oil

Combine Group 1 in an empty spice bottle for use as spice shaker.
Prepare chops per section f. Sprinkle copious amount of Group 1 mix
from shaker on each side of chops. Broil each side 3 minutes per section
18. Broil twice on each side. Garnish with Group 3 and serve.

---

100   Hot Lamb Curry**

Group 1
32 oz lamb, cut into 2-in cubes
4 Tablespoons oil
2 cups water
1 large onion, diced
2 large garlic, diced
1 Tablespoon ginger, diced
2 medium fresh cayenne peppers,
   whole
1/4 teaspoon turmeric

1/4 teaspoon crushed red pepper
1 Tablespoon Madras curry
   powder
2 teaspoons meat masala
1 medium bay leaf
2 teaspoons garam masala
1 (3-in) cinnamon stick
1 teaspoon paprika
1 teaspoon salt

Combine Group 1 in pot. Mix well. Bring to boil at "Medium High" heat
setting. Boil 1-2 minutes. Reset heat to "Medium Low", cover, and
simmer 90 minutes. Mix occasionally. Reset heat to "Medium", remove
cover, and evaporate to sizzling. Mix occasionally. Reset heat to "Low",
cover, let self-saute 3-5 minutes, and serve. Add 1/4 to 1 cup hot water
for more sauce if needed. Mix, salt to taste, and serve.

101   Rumanian Lamb Stew

Group 1

24 oz lean lamb, cut into
   1-in cubes
3 Tablespoons oil
1 large onion, cut into 8 sections
1 1/2 cups hot water
2 medium garlic, diced
1/4 teaspoon pepper
1 Tablespoon beef bouillon

1 large tomato, diced
1 large red bell pepper, diced
2 Tablespoons paprika
5 cloves
1 cup water
1/4 teaspoon salt
Group 2
1 small green bell pepper, diced

Combine Group 1 in pot. Mix well. Bring to boil at "Medium High" heat setting. Boil 1-2 minutes. Reset heat to "Medium Low", cover, and simmer 75 minutes. Mix occasionally. Remove cover and evaporate to sizzling. Cover and let self-saute 3-5 minutes. Mix occasionally. Garnish with Group 2 and serve. Add 1/4 to 1/2 cup hot water for more sauce if needed. Mix, salt to taste, and serve.

102   Homemade Lamb Stew

Group 1

24 oz lean lamb, cut into
   1-in cubes
2 cups water
1 medium bay leaf
1/8 teaspoon oregano
1/8 teaspoon thyme flakes
1/8 teaspoon pepper
1 medium garlic, diced
1/8 teaspoon white pepper
3 Tablespoons oil
1/2 teaspoon sugar
1/2 teaspoon salt
1 Tablespoon beef
   bouillon

Group 2
1 Tablespoon Worcestershire
   sauce
5 teaspoons corn starch
1/4 cup water
Group 3
1 1/2 cups hot water
Group 4
2 medium onions, each quartered
1 large potato, cut each into
   8 pieces
2 large carrots, cut into 16 pieces
Group 5
4 sprigs fresh parsley, cut in
   halves

Combine Group 1 in pot. Mix well. Bring to boil at "Medium High" heat setting. Boil 1-2 minutes. Reset heat to "Medium Low", cover, and simmer 75 minutes. Mix occasionally. Meanwhile, prepare Groups 2 (see section 2) and 4. Set them aside. Remove cover and evaporate Group 1 to sizzling. Cover and let self-saute 5 minutes. Add Group 3 and mix. Remix Group 2 and stir into pot (see section 20a). Stir continuously until gravy thickens to smooth consistency. Add Group 4, mix, cover, and simmer 20 minutes. Add Group 5, mix, and serve. Add 1/4 to 1 cup hot water if more sauce is needed. Salt to taste and serve.

---

103   Taiwanese Lamb Curry*

Group 1

32 oz lamb, cut into 1/4-in slices
1/2 cup water
3 Tablespoons oil
1 large garlic, diced
1/4 teaspoon pepper
1/4 teaspoon salt

Group 2

1/4 cup water
2 Tablespoons corn starch
2 Tablespoons soy sauce

1 Tablespoon Madras curry
  powder
1/2 teaspoon sugar
1 Tablespoon rice wine
1/4 teaspoon MSG

Group 3

1 1/2 cups hot water

Group 4

1 Tablespoon black bean in oil
1 large fresh cayenne pepper, diced

Combine Group 1 in pot. Mix well. Bring to boil at "Medium High" heat setting. Boil 1-2 minutes. Reset heat to "Medium Low", cover, and simmer 45 minutes. Mix occasionally. Meanwhile, prepare Group 2 (see section 2) and set aside. Remove cover and evaporate Group 1 to sizzling. Cover and let self-saute 5 minutes. Add Group 3, mix. add Group 4, mix, remix Group 2, and stir into pot (see section 20a). Stir continuously until the gravy thickens to smooth consistency and serve. Add 1/4 to 1/2 cup hot water if more sauce is needed. Salt to taste and serve.

104   Lamb Stroganoff

Group 1

24 oz lean lamb, cut into
   1-in cubes
2 Tablespoons burgundy wine
1 medium onion, diced
1/4 teaspoon pepper
2 Tablespoons margarine
1/8 teaspoon oregano
1/4 teaspoon thyme flakes
1 cup water
1/4 teaspoon salt

Group 2

1 cup hot 2% milk
2 (10-oz) cans, cream of
   mushroom soup

Group 3

1 cup hot water
2 large potatoes, each quartered

Group 4

1/2 cup sour cream
1/2 cup plain yogurt

Combine Group 1 in pot. Mix well. Bring to boil at "Medium High" heat setting. Boil 1-2 minutes. Reset heat to "Medium Low", cover, and simmer 45 minutes. Mix occasionally. Meanwhile, prepare Group 2 and set aside. Reset heat to "Medium", remove cover, and evaporate Group 1 to sizzling. Stir in Group 3, mix, cover, and simmer 30 minutes. Remix Group 2 and add to Groups 1 and 3, mix, cover, and simmer 5 minutes. Add Group 4, mix well, and serve. Add 1/4 to 1/2 cup hot water for more sauce if needed. Mix, salt to taste, and serve.

105 Lamb Chop Salad

Group 1
1 teaspoon pepper
1/2 teaspoon MSG
1 teaspoon salt
Group 2
1 small onion, diced
1 small tomato, diced

1 small bell pepper, diced
1 cup chopped lettuce
Group 3
6 lamb chops
Group 4
4 Tablespoons Italian salad
    dressing, any brand

Combine Group 1 in an empty spice bottle for use as spice shaker. Set aside. Prepare Group 2 and set aside in 3-quart serving bowl. Prepare chops per section f. Sprinkle copious amount of Group 1 mix from shaker on each side of chops. Broil each side 3 minutes per section 18. Broil twice on each side. Trim fat of each chop and discard fat. Carve meat from each chop, discard bones, and cut trimmed meat into bite-size pieces. Add meat pieces to Group 2, add Group 4, toss well, and serve.

106 Lamb and Vegetables Curry***

Group 1
24 oz lamb, cut into 1-in cubes
3 Tablespoons oil
1 cup water
2 medium garlic, diced
1 large onion, diced
1/4 teaspoon turmeric
1/4 teaspoon crushed red pepper
2 Tablespoons Madras curry
    powder
1 teaspoon salt
1 Tablespoon ginger, diced
Group 2
2 cups hot water

1 medium fresh cayenne pepper,
    whole
1 small eggplant, cut into 8 pieces
1 large potato, cut into 6 pieces
1 medium tomato, quartered
Group 3
1/2 cup sour cream
1/2 cup plain yogurt
4 oz okra, frozen, whole
Group 4
1 Tablespoon oil
2 teaspoons black mustard seeds
6-8 fresh curry leaves

Combine Group 1 in pot. Mix well. Bring to boil at "Medium High" heat setting. Boil 1-2 minutes. Reset heat to "Medium Low", cover, and simmer 45 minutes. Mix occasionally. Meanwhile, prepare Group 2 vegetables. Set aside. Remove cover and evaporate Group 1 to sizzling. Cover and let self-saute 3 minutes. Mix occasionally. Reset heat to "Medium", add Group 2, mix well, and bring to boil. Reset heat to "Medium Low", cover, and simmer 15 minutes. Mix occasionally. Reset heat to "Medium", add Group 3, mix, and simmer 3 minutes. Fry Group 4 (see section 19b), pour over Group 1, and serve. Add 1/4 to 1 cup hot water for more sauce if needed. Mix.

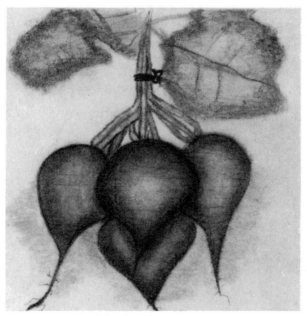

Radish, *Raphanus savitus*

Pork, 88

107 Broiled Pork Chop Salad**

Group 1
1 teaspoon turmeric
1 teaspoon paprika
1 teaspoon Madras curry
   powder
1 teaspoon garlic powder
1/2 teaspoon red pepper powder
1 teaspoon pepper
1/2 teaspoon MSG
2 teaspoons salt

Group 2
1 small onion, diced
1 small tomato, diced
1 cup chopped lettuce
2 medium fresh cayenne peppers
   diced

Group 3
2 Tablespoons fresh lemon juice

Group 4
8 lean pork chops

Combine Group 1 in an empty spice bottle for use as spice shaker. Set aside. Prepare Group 2 vegetables in 3-quart serving bowl. Add Group 3 to Group 2, toss well, and set aside. Sprinkle copious amount of Group 1 mix from shaker on one side of each chop (Group 4). Broil the sides 3-5 minutes per section 18. Turn over the chops to the other sides and sprinkle copious amount of Group 1 mix. Broil 3-5 minutes. Broil two more times on each side. Garnish with Groups 2 and 3, and serve.

108 Pork Chops in Oyster sauce

Group 1
8 pork chops, rib or loin
3 Tablespoons oil
1 medium garlic, diced
1 teaspoon ginger, diced
1 cup water

1 Tablespoon soy sauce
1/4 teaspoon sugar
1 teaspoon beef bouillon
1 Tablespoon rice wine
no salt

Group 2
1/4 cup water
2 Tablespoons corn starch
1/4 teaspoon MSG
1 Tablespoon oyster sauce

Group 3
2 cups hot broth

Group 4
4 stalks scallion, diced
1/4 teaspoon pepper

Combine Group 1 in pot. Mix well. Bring to boil at "Medium High" heat setting. Boil 1-2 minutes. Reset heat to "Medium Low", cover, and simmer 60 minutes. Mix occasionally. Meanwhile, prepare Group 2 mixture (see section 2). Remove cover and evaporate to sizzling. Cover and let self-saute 2 minutes. Mix occasionally. Remove chops and put in 3-quart serving bowl. Add Group 3 to pot, heat 2 minutes, remix Group 2, and add to pot. Mix continuously until gravy thickens to smooth texture (see section 20a). Pour Group 2 over chops, garnish with Group 4, and serve.

---

109   Pork Meat Ball Soup

Group 1
16 oz lean ground pork
1/4 teaspoon salt
1 medium garlic, diced
1 teaspoon ginger, diced
1 teaspoon corn starch
1 teaspoon soy sauce
1 teaspoon rice wine
1/4 teaspoon MSG
2 teaspoons sugar
1/4 teaspoon pepper
Group 2
2 cups broth or water

Group 3
1/4 cup water
2 teaspoons rice wine
1 teaspoon soy sauce
1 teaspoon corn starch
Group 4
1/2 cup sliced sour bamboo shoot
1/2 cup hot broth or water
Group 5
1/4 teaspoon sesame oil
1/8 teaspoon white pepper
4 stalks scallion, diced
1/4 teaspoon pepper

Combine Group 1 in 2-quart bowl, mix well, and make 15-20 meat balls. Set aside. Add to 3-quart pot, Group 2, and bring to boil at "Medium High" heat setting. Add Group 1 (meat balls), bring to boil, and let boil 2-3 minutes. Reset heat to "Medium Low" and simmer 30 minutes. Meanwhile, prepare Group 3 and set aside (see section 2). Reset heat to "Medium" and add Group 4, mix, and bring to boil. Boil 5 minutes. Remix Group 3, stir into pot, mix, sprinkle Group 5, and serve.

110   Sicilian Grilled Pork

Group 1
1 medium onion, diced
1 Tablespoon oregano
1/4 teaspoon thyme flakes
1/2 cup vinegar
1/2 teaspoon pepper
1 Tablespoon olive oil
1 teaspoon salt
1/4 teaspoon white pepper
Group 2
32 oz pork, fresh ham, cut into

2-in strips
Group 3
1/4 teaspoon pepper
1 small bell pepper, quartered
1/4 teaspoon MSG
2 Tablespoons olive oil
1 medium tomato, quartered
1 medium lemon, quartered
1 medium onion, quartered

Combine Group 1 and marinate Group 2 per section 5a. Cook marinated meat using one of the techniques described in section 21. Garnish with Group 3 and serve.

111   Broiled Pork Chops

Group 1
2 teaspoons pepper
1 teaspoon MSG
2 teaspoons salt
2 teaspoons garlic powder
Group 2
2 Tablespoons oil
1/4 teaspoon pepper

1/4 teaspoon MSG
1 medium tomato, quartered
1 medium onion, quartered
1 small bell pepper, quartered
1 medium lemon, quartered
Group 3
8 lean pork chops

Combine Group 1 in an empty spice bottle for use as spice shaker. Set aside. Prepare Group 2 vegetables and set aside. Sprinkle copious amount of Group 1 mix from shaker on one side of each chop (Group 3). Broil the sides 3-5 minutes per section 18. Turn over the chops to the other sides and sprinkle copious amount of Group 1 mix. Broil 3-5 minutes. Broil two more times on each side. Garnish with Group 2 and serve.

112   Pork in Mango Pickle Sauce**

Group 1

32 oz lean pork, cut into
   1-in cubes
1 medium onion, diced
1 large garlic, diced
1/8 teaspoon turmeric
1 medium fresh jàlapeno
   pepper, whole

1 teaspoon paprika
3 Tablespoons oil
1 cup water
no salt
Group 2
2 Tablespoons mild mango pickle
   in oil

Combine Group 1 in pot. Mix well. Bring to boil at "Medium High" heat setting.   Boil 1-2 minutes. Reset heat to "Medium Low", cover, and simmer 60 minutes. Mix occasionally. Remove cover and evaporate to sizzling. Cover and let self-saute 2 minutes. Add Group 2, mix well, cover, let self-saute 3 minutes, mix occasionally, and serve.

113   Punjabi Pork Kabob*

Group 1
1 small onion, diced
2 large garlic, diced
1 Tablespoon ginger, diced
2 Tablespoons fresh lemon juice
1/2 teaspoon turmeric
1 teaspoon paprika
1/4 teaspoon red pepper powder
1/2 teaspoon pepper
1 teaspoon salt
1 cup plain yogurt
2 Tablespoons oil

3 Tablespoons garam masala
Group 2
32 oz pork, fresh ham, cut into
   2-in strips
Group 3
2 Tablespoons oil
1/4 teaspoon pepper
1/4 teaspoon MSG
1 medium onion, quartered
1 medium tomato, quartered
1 medium lemon, quartered
1 small bell pepper, quartered

Combine Group 1 and marinate Group 2 per section 5a. Cook marinated meat using one of the techniques described in section 21. Garnish with Group 3 and serve.

114   Beijing Pork Barbecue

Chinese five-spice is a mixture of (star anise, black pepper, fennel, cloves, and cinnamon).

Group 1
3 large garlic, diced
1 teaspoon ginger, diced
1/4 teaspoon MSG
2 teaspoons sugar
2 Tablespoons soy sauce
2 Tablespoons Hoisin sauce
1 Tablespoon oil
1 Tablespoon rice wine
1 teaspoon Chinese
   five-spice

Group 2
32 oz pork, fresh ham, cut
   into 2-in strips
Group 3
1/4 teaspoon pepper
1/4 teaspoon MSG
2 Tablespoons oil
1 medium tomato, quartered
1 small bell pepper, quartered
1 medium onion, quartered
1 medium lemon, quartered

Combine Group 1 and marinate Group 2 per section 5a. Cook marinated meat using one of the techniques described in section 21. Garnish with Group 3 and serve.

115   Pasta Sauce

Group 1
24 oz lean pork, cut into
   1/4-in slices
1 large garlic, diced
1 small onion, diced
1/2 teaspoon Italian seasoning
1/2 teaspoon sugar
1 teaspoon paprika
1/4 teaspoon MSG
1/4 teaspoon cracked pepper
2 Tablespoons olive oil
1/4 teaspoon anise seeds,
   cracked

1/2 cup water
3/4 teaspoon salt
Group 2
8 oz linguine pasta
1 Tablespoon margarine
Group 3
1 cup hot broth
1 (6-oz) can, tomato paste
1 (16-oz) can, tomatoes
Group 4
1/2 small onion, diced
2 Tablespoons Parmesan
   cheese, grated

Combine Group 1 in pot. Mix well. Bring to boil at "Medium High" heat setting. Reset heat to "Medium Low", cover, and simmer 15 minutes with occasional mixing. Prepare Group 2 per instruction on package and mix with margarine in a 4-quart serving bowl. Set aside. Reset heat to "Medium", remove cover, and evaporate Group 1 to sizzling. Mix well. Reset heat to "Medium Low", cover, and simmer 4 minutes. Mix often. Add Group 3, mix well, bring to boil at "Medium High" setting. Reset heat to "Medium Low", cover, and simmer 60 minutes. Add 1/4 to 1/2 cup hot water if more sauce is desired. Salt to taste. Combine with Group 1, mix well, garnish with Group 4, and serve.

116　Sebastina Rice Casserole

Group 1

24 oz lean pork, cut into
　1-in cubes
1 medium bay leaf
2 Tablespoons oil
1 medium onion, diced
2 medium garlic, diced
1 Tablespoon ginger, diced
1 teaspoon garam masala
1 Tablespoon Madras curry
　powder
1/4 teaspoon turmeric
1 teaspoon paprika
1/4 teaspoon pepper

1 (3-in) cinnamon stick
1 cup water
1 1/2 teaspoon salt
Group 2
1/2 cup hot 2% milk
Group 3
1/4 cup hot water
1 cup yogurt, plain
2 Tablespoons fresh lemon juice
Group 4
5 cups cooked rice
Group 5
2 Tablespoons margarine

Combine Group 1 in pot. Mix well. Bring to boil at "Medium High" heat setting. Boil 1-2 minutes. Reset heat to "Medium Low", cover, and simmer 30 minutes. Mix occasionally. Meanwhile, cook 3 cups extra long grain rice per section 23b and set aside. Remove cover and evaporate Group 1 to sizzling. Cover and self-saute 2 minutes. Mix occasionally. Preheat oven to 325F. Combine Groups 1, 2, and 3. Mix well. Add Group 4 and mix well. Add Group 5 spreading evenly on top. Turn heat off. Seal pot, bake 50-60 minutes (see section 16a), and serve.

117 Pork Kabob

Group 1
2 medium garlic, diced
2 teaspoons coriander powder
2 Tablespoons Madras curry
   powder
2 teaspoons cumin powder
2 Tablespoons fresh lemon juice
1/2 teaspoon pepper
4 Tablespoons dark soy sauce
Group 2
32 oz pork, fresh ham, cut into

2-in strips
Group 3
2 Tablespoons oil
1/4 teaspoon MSG
1/4 teaspoon pepper
1 medium lemon, quartered
1 small bell pepper, quartered
1 small onion, quartered
1 medium tomato,
   quartered

Combine Group 1 and marinate Group 2 per section 5a. Cook marinated meat using the technique described in section 21a or 21c. Garnish with Group 3 and serve.

118 Alicia's Five-Spice Delight*

Group 1
32 oz lean pork, cut into
   1/4-in slices
1 medium fresh cayenne
   pepper, diced
4 Tablespoons oil
1 cup water
1 medium garlic, diced
1 teaspoon ginger, diced
Group 2
1/4 cup water
2 Tablespoons corn starch

1 teaspoon sugar
1 Tablespoon soy sauce
1/4 teaspoon MSG
1/4 teaspoon pepper
1/2 teaspoon Chinese five-spice
1 Tablespoon rice wine
Group 3
1 cup hot broth
Group 4
1/4 teaspoon sesame oil
4 stalks scallion diced

Combine Group 1 in pot. Mix well. Bring to boil at "Medium High" heat setting. Boil 1-2 minutes. Reset heat to "Medium Low", cover, and simmer 20 minutes. Mix occasionally. Meanwhile, prepare Group 2 mixture (see section 2). Remove cover and evaporate Group 1 to sizzling. Cover and let self-saute 2 minutes. Mix occasionally. Add Group 3 to pot, remix Group 2, and add to pot. Mix continuously until gravy thickens to smooth consistency (see section 20a). Garnish with Group 4, and serve.

---

119   Pork Chop Rice Casserole

Group 1

4 lean pork chops	1/4 teaspoon salt
1 Tablespoon oil	2 Tablespoons margarine
1 medium garlic, diced	1/4 teaspoon pepper
1 cup water	**Group 3**
Group 2	5 cups cooked rice
1/4 cup hot water	10 fresh or frozen pearl onions
1/4 cup 2% milk	**Group 4**
2 (10-oz) cans, cream of chicken soup	2 Tablespoons Parmesan cheese, grated

Combine Group 1 in pot. Mix well. Bring to boil at "Medium High" heat setting. Boil 1-2 minutes. Reset heat to "Medium Low", cover, and simmer 20 minutes. Mix occasionally. Meanwhile cook 3 cups extra long grain rice and set aside (see section 23b). Remove cover and evaporate to sizzling. Cover and let self-saute 2 minutes. Mix occasionally. Preheat oven to 325F. Add Group 2 to Group 1, mix well, stir in Group 3, mix well, and remove pot from burner. Seal pot and bake 50 minutes (see section 16a). Garnish with Group 4 and serve.

96

120 Spicy Broiled Pork Chops*

Group 1
1 teaspoon garlic powder
1 teaspoon turmeric
1 teaspoon paprika
1 teaspoon Madras curry
   powder
1/2 teaspoon red pepper powder
1 teaspoon pepper
1/2 teaspoon MSG
2 teaspoons salt

Group 2
1/4 teaspoon MSG
1/4 teaspoon pepper
1 Tablespoon oil
1 medium onion, quartered
1 medium tomato, quartered
1 medium lemon, quartered
1 small bell pepper, quartered

Group 3
8 lean pork chops

Combine Group 1 in an empty spice bottle for use as spice shaker. Set aside. Prepare Group 2 vegetables and set aside. Sprinkle copious amount of Group 1 mix from shaker on one side of each chop (Group 3). Broil the sides 3-5 minutes per section 18. Turn over the chops to the other sides and sprinkle copious amount of Group 1 mix. Broil 3-5 minutes. Broil two more times on each side. Garnish with Group 2 and serve.

121 Xinjiang Pork Curry

Group 1
24 oz lean pork, cut into
   1/4-in slices
2 Tablespoons oil
1/4 teaspoon salt
1 large garlic, diced
1/2 cup water

Group 2
2 Tablespoons soy sauce
1/4 cup water
1 1/2 Tablespoons S&B
   Oriental curry powder

2 Tablespoons corn starch
1/4 teaspoon MSG
2 Tablespoons rice wine
1/2 teaspoon sugar

Group 3
2 cups hot broth
1 large potato, cut into 16 pieces

Group 4
1/2 cup sweet peas, frozen

Group 5
4 stalks scallion, diced

Combine Group 1 in pot. Mix well. Bring to boil at "Medium High" heat setting. Boil 1-2 minutes. Reset heat to "Medium Low", cover, and simmer 30 minutes. Mix occasionally. Meanwhile, prepare Group 2 (see section 2) and Group 3. Set them aside. Remove cover and evaporate Group 1 to sizzling. Cover and let self-saute 5 minutes. Reset heat to "Medium", add Group 3, mix well, and bring to boil. Reset heat to "Medium Low", cover, and simmer 15 minutes. Remix Group 2 and stir into pot. Stir until gravy thickens to smooth consistency (see section 20a). Garnish with Group 5 and serve. Add 1/4 to 1/2 cup hot water if more sauce is needed. Salt to taste and serve.

---

122   Pork with Red Pepper Sauce**

Group 1
32 oz lean pork, cut into
   1-in cubes
3 Tablespoons oil
no salt
1 teaspoon garlic, diced
1 cup water
Group 2
1/4 cup water
2 Tablespoons corn starch

1 Tablespoon soy sauce
1 teaspoon fish sauce
1/4 teaspoon MSG
Group 3
1 Tablespoon rice wine
1 Tablespoon garlic/red pepper sauce
Group 4
1 cup hot broth
Group 5
8 sprigs cilantro, diced

Combine Group 1 in pot. Mix well. Bring to boil at "Medium High" heat setting. Reset heat to "Medium Low", cover, and simmer 60 minutes with occasional mixing. Meanwhile, mix Group 2 and set aside (see section 2). Remove cover and evaporate Group 1 to sizzling. Add Group 3, mix, and let self-saute 3 minutes. Add Group 4 and mix. Remix Group 2 and stir into pot. Mix continuously until the sauce thickens to smooth texture (see section 20a). Garnish with Group 5 and serve. Add 1/4 to 1/2 cup hot water if more sauce is needed.

123   Fried Rice with Pork

Group 1
16 oz lean ground pork
3 Tablespoons oil
1/4 teaspoon MSG
1 small onion, diced
1 small garlic, diced
1/4 teaspoon pepper
Group 2
1 teaspoon soybean paste
1 teaspoon oyster sauce

1 Tablespoon soy sauce,
    Japanese or Chinese
1 teaspoon dark soy sauce
1/2 teaspoon sugar
Group 3
4 cups cooked rice
Group 4
3 stalks scallion, diced
1/8 teaspoon white pepper

Cook 3 cups extra long grain rice per section 23b and set aside. Add to 12-inch skillet, Group 1, and saute at "Medium" heat setting with frequent mixing for 5 minutes, cover, reset heating to "Low", and cook 5 minutes. Meanwhile, combine Group 2 in 1-cup bowl and set aside. Reset heating to "Medium", add Group 2, mix, add Group 3, mix, cover, and cook 5 minutes with occasional mixing. Garnish with Group 4 and serve

124   Portuguese Pork Patty

Group 1
1/4 cup flour
1 teaspoon sugar
1/4 teaspoon MSG
1/4 teaspoon salt
1/4 teaspoon pepper
1 teaspoon garlic powder
2 teaspoons baking powder
1/8 teaspoon onion powder
Group 2
24 oz lean ground pork

Group 3
1 Tablespoon margarine
2 (10-oz) cans, cream of
    mushroom soup
1/2 cup hot 2% milk
Group 4
6 Tablespoons oil
Group 5
2 Tablespoons sharp Cheddar
    cheese, grated

99

Combine Groups 1 and 2 in 2-quart bowl, mix well, and make 8-10 thin patties. Set them aside. Combine Group 3 in 4-cup pot, disperse well, heat 10 minutes at "Medium Low" heat setting, and set aside. Meanwhile, heat 1 Tablespoon Group 4 in 8-in skillet at "Medium Low" heat setting. Fry each side of patty to tan color. Fry one patty at a time. Set fried patties on paper and drain oil. Remix Group 3 and pour on patties, garnish with Group 5, and serve.

---

125   New Orleans Pork Chop*

Group 1
8 pork chops, loin
3 Tablespoons oil
1 cup water
Group 2
1/8 teaspoon turmeric
1/2 teaspoon paprika
1/4 teaspoon garlic powder

1/2 teaspoon Madras curry
  powder
1/4 teaspoon red pepper powder
1/4 teaspoon pepper
1/4 teaspoon sugar
1/4 teaspoon MSG
Group 3
2 teaspoons soy sauce

Combine Group 1 in pot. Mix well. Bring to boil at "Medium High" heat setting. Boil 1-2 minutes. Reset heat to "Medium Low", cover, and simmer 45 minutes. Mix occasionally. Meanwhile, combine Group 2 in 1-cup bowl and set aside. Remove cover and evaporate Group 1 to sizzling. Cover and let self-saute 2 minutes. Mix occasionally. Add Group 2 in sizzling oil, and let self-saute 1 minute. Add Group 3, mix, cover, let self-saute 2 more minutes, and serve. Add 1/4 to 1/2 cup hot water for more sauce if needed. Mix, salt to taste, and serve.

126   Bulgarian Goulash

Group 1

24 oz lean pork, cut into
   1-in cubes
3 Tablespoons oil
1 large red bell pepper, diced
1 large onion, cut into 8 sections
2 medium garlic, diced
1/2 teaspoon pepper
1 Tablespoon beef bouillon
1 cup water

2 Tablespoons paprika
1 large tomato, diced
1 Tablespoon caraway seeds,
   cracked
1/4 teaspoon salt
Group 2
1/4 teaspoon white pepper
1 small onion, diced
1 small green bell pepper, diced

Combine Group 1 in pot. Mix well. Bring to boil at "Medium High" heat setting. Boil 1-2 minutes. Reset heat to "Medium Low", cover, and simmer 60 minutes. Mix occasionally. Remove cover and evaporate to sizzling. Cover and let self-saute 3 minutes. Mix occasionally. Garnish with Group 2 and serve. Add 1/4 to 1/2 cup hot water for more sauce if needed. Mix, salt to taste, and serve.

127   Pork Split Pea Soup

Group 1

16 oz lean pork, cut into
   1-in cubes
1 medium garlic, diced
2 Tablespoons oil
1/2 cup water
1 medium onion, diced
3 stalks celery, diced
1/2 teaspoon thyme flakes
1/4 teaspoon parsley flakes
1/4 teaspoon MSG

1 teaspoon salt
1/2 teaspoon pepper
1 teaspoon sugar
Group 2
2 large carrots, cut each into
   6 pieces
1 cup green split peas
4 cups hot water or broth
Group 3
1/3 cup oyster crackers, crumbled

Combine Group 1 in pot. Mix well. Bring to boil at "Medium High" heat setting. Boil 1-2 minutes. Reset heat to "Medium Low", cover, and simmer 15 minutes. Mix occasionally. Reset heat to "Medium", remove cover, and evaporate to sizzling. Add Group 2. Mix well. Reset heat to "Medium Low", cover, and simmer 60 minutes. Garnish with Group 3 and serve. Add 1/4 to 1 cup hot water for more sauce.

---

128   Pork and Pickled Bamboo Shoots

Group 1
24 oz lean pork, cut into
    1/4-in slices
3 Tablespoons oil
1 medium garlic, diced
1 teaspoon ginger, diced
3/4 cup water
1/4 teaspoon pepper
Group 2
15 medium Chinese dried
    mushroom
1 cup hot water

Group 3
no salt
1/4 cup water
2 Tablespoons corn starch
2 teaspoons soy sauce
1 Tablespoon rice wine
1/4 teaspoon MSG
Group 4
2 cups sliced sour bamboo shoots
1/2 cup hot water
Group 5
1 1/2 cups hot water

Combine Group 1 in pot. Mix well. Bring to boil at "Medium High" heat setting. Boil 2 minutes. Reset heat to "Medium Low", cover, and simmer 60 minutes. Mix occasionally. Meanwhile, combine Group 2 and set aside 5 minutes. Combine Group 3 mixture (see section 2) and set aside. Remove Group 2 and squeeze out water, cut each into 3 slices, and set aside. Remove cover and evaporate Group 1 to sizzling. Cover and let self-saute 2 minutes. Mix occasionally. Reset heat to "Medium". Add Group 4 to pot, mix well, add Group 2, mix well, cover, and simmer 5 minutes with occasional mixing. Reset heat to "Medium Low", add Group 5, mix well, wait 1 minute, remix Group 3, and stir into pot (see section 20a). Stir continuously until gravy thickens to smooth texture and serve.

129   Susan's Pizza

This recipe uses raw Italian pork sausage as a topping ingredient. The sausage is precooked to reduce fat and to cook the meat partially. Since commercial sausages contain substantial amount of fat, you may like to prepare your own, using lean meat. Of course, this will add one more hour to your plan if you have to make the sausage at the same time. Nevertheless, I would like to call your attention to Recipes #135, 136, and 138 for making Italian sausages.

Group A
4 oz Italian sausage meat, roll
    into small bite-sized meat balls
Group 1
2 (7-oz) flour packages,
    premixed for pizza
Group 2
2 Tablespoons Corn oil
Group 3
12 oz pizza sauce
Group 4
1 teaspoon cracked
    pepper
1 teaspoon garlic powder
Group 5
1/2 cup blended cheese from
    pizza packages

1/2 cup mozzarella/provolone/
    /Parmesan cheeses, grated
Group 6
16 slices, pepperoni
Italian sausage, Group A
Group 7
1/2 cup mozzarella/provolone/
    /Parmesan cheeses, grated
1/2 cup blended cheese from pizza
    packages
1/4 teaspoon Italian seasoning
Group 8
1 Tablespoon Parmesan Cheese.
    grated
1/8 teaspoon crushed red pepper
1/4 teaspoon cracked pepper

Prepare Group A into bite-size pieces. Heat in covered 4-in frying pan at "medium Low" heat setting. Let self-saute in its own juices 5-8 minutes. Discard fat and use the sausage along with Group 6. Prepare and dress pizza crust (see section 8). Bake per section 16b. Garnish with Group 8 and serve.

130   Pasta Sauce with Pork

Group 1
16 oz lean pork, cut into
   1/4-in slices
1 large garlic, diced
1 small onion, diced
1 cup chopped celery
1 small bell pepper, diced
1/4 teaspoon parsley flakes
1/8 teaspoon crushed red pepper
1/4 teaspoon cracked fennel seeds
1/2 teaspoon basil flakes
1/4 teaspoon cracked pepper
1/2 teaspoon sugar
1/2 teaspoon paprika
1/4 teaspoon oregano

1 teaspoon salt
1/2 cup water
2 Tablespoons olive oil
1/2 teaspoon cumin powder
Group 2
8 oz linguine pasta
1 Tablespoon margarine
Group 3
1 cup hot broth
1 (6-oz) can, tomato paste
1 (16-oz) can, tomatoes
Group 4
1/2 small onion, diced
1 Tablespoon sharp Cheddar
   cheese, grated

Combine Group 1 in pot. Mix well. Bring to boil at "Medium High". Reset heat to "Medium Low", cover, and simmer 15 minutes. Mix occasionally. Meanwhile, prepare Group 2 per manufacturer's instructions, mix with margarine in a 4-quart serving bowl, and set aside. Reset heat to "Medium", remove cover, and evaporate Group 1 to sizzling. Mix well. Reset heat to "Medium Low", cover, and let self-saute 3 minutes. Mix often. Add Group 3, mix well, cover, and simmer 60 minutes. Mix often. Add 1/4 to 1/2 cup hot water if more sauce is desired. Salt to taste. Combine with Group 1 in serving bowl, mix well, garnish with Group 4, and serve.

131   Pork Chops Romano

Group 1

8 pork chops, rib or loin
1 teaspoon Italian seasoning
2 Tablespoons olive oil
1 medium onion, diced
1 medium garlic, diced
1 large tomato, diced
1 small bell pepper, diced
2 teaspoons beef bouillon
1 cup water
1/4 teaspoon pepper
1/4 teaspoon salt

Group 2

1/4 cup hot beef broth

Group 3

2 Tablespoons Parmesan cheese
   grated

Combine Group 1 in pot. Mix well. Bring to boil at "Medium High" heat setting. Boil 1-2 minutes. Reset heat to "Medium Low", cover, and simmer 45 minutes. Mix occasionally. Remove cover and evaporate to sizzling. Cover, and, let self-saute 2 minutes. Mix occasionally. Add Group 2 and mix. Garnish with Group 3 and serve.

132   Alana's Casserole

Group 1

1/2 cup green split peas

Group 2

20 oz lean pork, cut into
   1-in cubes
1 Tablespoon oil
1 medium garlic, diced
2 Tablespoons beef bouillon
1/4 teaspoon pepper
1/4 teaspoon turmeric
1 cup water

no salt

Group 3

1/2 cup hot water
1 (3-in) cinnamon stick
3 Tablespoons margarine
5 cups cooked rice
8 pearl onions, frozen

Group 4

2 Tablespoons Parmesan cheese,
   grated

Prepare Group 1 (see section 13g). Combine Group 2 in pot. Mix well. Bring to boil at "Medium High" heat setting. Boil 1-2 minutes. Reset heat to "Medium Low", cover, and simmer 15 minutes. Mix occasionally. Meanwhile, cook 3 cups extra long grain rice per section 23b and set aside. Remove cover and evaporate Group 1 to sizzling. Cover and let self-saute 2 minutes. Mix occasionally. Preheat oven to 325F. Combine Groups 1, 2, and 3, mix well, sprinkle Group 4, and remove pot from burner. Turn heat off. Seal pot, bake 50-60 minutes (see section 16a), and serve.

---

133   Picadilly Pork Patty

Group 1
1 teaspoon sage flakes
1 teaspoon salt
1 teaspoon pepper
1 Tablespoon flour
Group 2
4 (8-oz) lean pork cutlets
Group 3
2 Tablespoons oil

Group 4
2 (10-oz) cans, cream of
    mushroom soup
1/2 cup hot 2% milk
2 Tablespoons margarine
Group 5
2 Tablespoons Parmesan cheese,
    grated
1/4 teaspoon pepper

Combine Group 1 in a cup and set aside. Pound each Group 2 cutlet with meat tenderizer and set them aside. Heat Group 3 in 12-inch skillet 1-2 minutes at "Medium High" heat setting. Reset heat to "Low". Roll Group 2 in Group 1 mix on both sides. Add Group 2 in skillet, cover and simmer 20 minutes. Remove cover and evaporate to sizzling. Fry each side to tan color. Set them aside on paper towel. Meanwhile, combine Group 4 in 3-cup pot. Mix to disperse soup mix to a smooth mixture and heat at "Medium Low" 5-10 minutes. Mix often. Pour Group 4 over patties, garnish with Group 5, and serve.

134   Pork and Sour Bamboo Shoots*

This is a typical Myanmar dish. The pork and pickled bamboo shoots combination has a unique flavor which is unfamiliar to most Westerner. The use of pickled vegetables in Western meat stews is almost unknown. I highly recommend you to try it. I might also add that the pickled bamboo shoots we get in the U.S. is pickled with vinegar and salt. The Burmese pickles the bamboo shoots with fermented cooked rice. I personally find the later to taste less acidic and smoother than the others.

Group 1
24 oz lean pork, cut into 1-in cubes
1/8 teaspoon turmeric
1 medium onion, diced
2 medium garlic, diced
1 teaspoon ginger, diced
1 medium tomato, quartered
1 teaspoon paprika

2 medium fresh cayenne peppers,
    whole
3 Tablespoons oil
1 cup water
no salt
Group 2
2 cups hot water
2 cups sliced sour bamboo shoots

Combine Group 1 in pot. Mix well. Bring to boil at "Medium High" heat setting. Boil 1-2 minutes. Reset heat to "Medium Low", cover, and simmer 45 minutes. Mix occasionally. Remove cover and evaporate to sizzling. Cover and let self-saute 2 minutes. Mix occasionally. Add Group 2, mix well, cover, simmer 15 minutes, and serve. Add 1/4 to 1/2 cup hot water for more sauce.

135   Italian Sausage Meat, Mild

Group 1

32 oz lean ground pork
1 teaspoon oregano
2 teaspoons anise seeds, whole
2 teaspoons sugar

1 teaspoon garlic powder
1/2 teaspoon cracked pepper
1/2 teaspoon MSG
1 1/2 teaspoon salt

Add to a 1-quart bowl Group 1. Mix well. Set aside 2 hours or overnight in refrigerator. Make 12 thin patties of Group 1. Set them aside. Meanwhile, heat 12-in skillet at "Medium" heat setting for 3 minutes. Reset heat to "Medium Low", add 2 Tablespoons oil, add patties, cover, and let simmer 30 minutes. Remove cover and fry each patties to tan color on each side. Remove patties, drain oil on paper towel, and serve.

136   Italian Sausage Meat, Spicy

Group 1

32 oz lean ground pork
1 teaspoon oregano
2 teaspoons anise seeds, whole
2 teaspoons sugar
1 teaspoon paprika

1 teaspoon garlic powder
1/2 teaspoon cracked pepper
1 teaspoon parsley flakes
1/2 teaspoon MSG
1 1/2 teaspoon salt

Sausage patties may be prepared and cooked as above (see Recipe #135).

137   Breakfast Sausage Meat

Group 1

32 oz lean ground pork
2 teaspoons sage
2 teaspoons sugar

1 teaspoon cracked pepper
1 1/2 teaspoons salt
1/2 teaspoon MSG

Sausage patties may be prepared and cooked as above (see Recipe #135).

138 Italian Sausage Meat, Hot*

Group 1
32 oz lean ground pork
1 teaspoon oregano
2 teaspoons anise seeds, whole
2 teaspoons sugar
2 teaspoons paprika

1 teaspoon garlic powder
1/2 teaspoon MSG
1 teaspoon cracked pepper
1 teaspoon parsley flakes
1/4 teaspoon crushed red pepper
1 1/2 teaspoon salt

Sausage patties may be prepared and cooked as above (see Recipe #135).

139 Polish Sausage Meat

Group 1
32 oz lean ground pork
2 teaspoons sugar
2 Tablespoons cracked white
     mustard seeds

1 teaspoon cracked pepper
1/2 teaspoon MSG
1 teaspoon garlic powder,
1 1/2 teaspoons salt

Sausage patties may be prepared and cooked as above (see Recipe #135).

140 Pork with Kim Chee**

Group 1
24 oz lean pork, cut into
     1/4-in slices
1/2 cup water

3 Tablespoons oil
Group 2
2 cups Kim Chee

Combine Group 1 in pot. Mix well. Bring to boil at "Medium High" heat setting. Boil 1-2 minutes. Reset heat to "Medium Low", cover, and simmer 45 minutes. Mix occasionally. Remove cover and evaporate to sizzling with occasional mixing. Cover and let self-saute 2 minutes. Add Group 2, mix well, cover, let self-saute 5 minutes, mix occasionally, and serve.

Seafood, 110

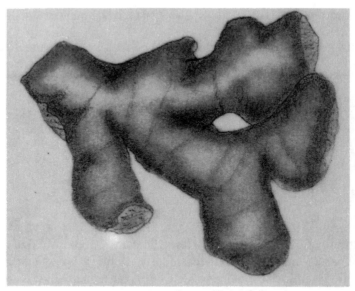

Ginger, *Zingiber officinale*

141   Seafood Delight

Group 1

4 oz medium shrimp, dressed	2 Tablespoons olive oil
4 oz Haddock, cut into 2-in pieces	1/4 cup water
4 oz oysters, diced	**Group 2**
4 oz scallops, diced	1 Tablespoon margarine
1 medium garlic, diced	4 stalks scallion, each cut into
1/2 teaspoon basil flakes	3 sections
1/4 teaspoon salt	2 Tablespoons Parmesan cheese,
1/4 teaspoon cracked pepper	grated

Dress seafood and shrimp (see section 10 and 11). Combine Group 1 in pot, mix, and bring to boil at "Medium High" heat setting. Boil 1-2 minutes. Reset heat to "Medium Low", cover, and simmer 15 minutes. Remove cover and let evaporate to sizzling. Reset heat to "Low" and let self-saute 5 minutes. Add Group 2, reset heat to "Medium Low", don't mix, cover, let self-saute 5 minutes, and serve. Add 1/4 cup hot water to pot for more sauce, if needed. Mix, salt to taste, and serve.

142   Seafood Spaghetti Sauce

Group 1

1 medium onion, diced	
2 stalks celery, diced	**Group 3**
1 large garlic, diced	1 cup hot seafood or chicken
1/4 teaspoon pepper	broth
1/8 teaspoon white pepper	**Group 4**
1/2 teaspoon salt	2 oz scallops, diced
1/4 teaspoon oregano	3 oz king crab meat, diced
1/2 teaspoon basil flakes	2 oz oysters, diced
1/4 teaspoon parsley flakes	4 oz shrimp, cut into
1/2 cup water	halves
3 Tablespoons olive oil	2 oz clams, diced
Group 2	**Group 5**
1 Tablespoon flour	2 Tablespoons Parmesan cheese,
	grated

Add to 4-quart pot, Group 1, mix, and bring to boil at "Medium High" heat setting. Reset heat to "Medium Low", mix, cover, and simmer 45 minutes. Mix occasionally. Remove cover and evaporate to sizzling. Cover and let self-saute 5 minutes. Reset heat to "Medium. Push some ingredients aside, add Group 2 into sizzling oil, and stir only the flour until it turns light tan color. Stir in Group 3 and mix well. Add Group 4, mix, reset heat to "Medium Low", cover, and let simmer 8-10 minutes. Garnish with Group 5 and serve. Add 1/4 to 1/2 cup hot water to pot for more sauce, if needed.

---

143   Seafood Pasta Sauce

Group 1
1 small onion, diced
3/4 cup celery, diced
1 medium garlic, diced
1/4 teaspoon pepper
1/8 teaspoon white pepper
1/2 teaspoon salt
1/2 teaspoon Italian seasoning
1/2 cup water
2 Tablespoons olive oil
Group 2
1/4 cup water

2 teaspoons corn starch
Group 3
1 cup hot seafood or chicken
  broth
4 oz shrimp, diced
2 oz clams, diced
2 oz oysters, diced
2 oz scallops, diced
2 oz king crab meat
Group 4
2 Tablespoons Parmesan cheese,
  grated

Dress seafood and shrimp per sections 10 and 11. Combine Group 1 in pot, mix, and bring to boil at "Medium High" heat setting. Reset heat to "Medium Low", mix, cover, and simmer 30-45 minutes. Mix occasionally. Meanwhile, prepare Group 2 (see section 2) and set aside. Remove cover and evaporate Group 1 to sizzling. Reset heat to "Low", cover, and let self-saute 5 minutes. Reset heat to "Medium Low", add Group 3, mix, cover, and let simmer 5 minutes. Remix Group 2 and stir into pot. Stir continuously until the gravy thickens to smooth consistency (see section 20a). Garnish with Group 4 and serve.

144   Seafood Gumbo*

Group 1

1 medium onion, diced
1 large garlic, diced
1 stalk celery, diced
1 large tomato, diced
1 medium jalapeno pepper, diced
1 medium bell pepper, diced
2 Tablespoons gumbo file`
1 Tablespoon chicken bouillon
1/2 teaspoon parsley flakes
1 teaspoon paprika
1/4 teaspoon pepper
1/4 teaspoon white pepper
1/4 teaspoon red pepper, powder

1 teaspoon Tabasco sauce
1 cup water
3 Tablespoons oil
1/2 teaspoon salt

Group 2

4 oz shrimp, diced
2 cups hot seafood broth or water
2 oz Haddock, 1-in cubes
2 oz oysters, diced
2 oz scallops, diced

Group 3

1 teaspoon gumbo file`
8 oz okra, whole, frozen

Dress seafood (see section 10). Combine Group 1 in pot, mix, and bring to boil at "Medium High" heat setting. Boil 1-2 minutes. Reset heat to "Medium Low", mix, cover, and simmer 45 minutes. Mix occasionally. Remove cover and evaporate to sizzling. Reset heat to "Medium", add Group 2, mix, and bring to boil. Reset heat to "Medium Low" cover, and simmer 10 minutes. Stir in Group 3, mix, simmer 5 minutes, and serve. Add 1/4 to 1 cup hot water for more sauce if needed.

145   Seafood Rice Casserole

Group 1
1 large garlic, diced
3/4 teaspoon basil flakes
1/8 teaspoon parsley flakes
1/8 teaspoon white pepper
1/4 teaspoon cracked pepper
4 Tablespoons margarine
1 cup seafood or chicken broth
no salt
Group 2
8 oz medium shrimps, dressed
1 teaspoon paprika
4 oz oysters
4 oz scallops

4 oz imitation crab meat.
Group 3
1/4 cup hot whole milk
4 oz sweet peas, frozen
4 cups cooked rice
Group 4
10 black olives, cut into halves
2 Tablespoons Parmesan cheese,
   grated
Group 5
4 stalks scallion, diced
1/4 cup croutons, onion/garlic
   flavored, crushed

Combine Group 1 in pot. Mix well. Bring to boil at "Medium". Boil 1-2 minutes. Reset heat to "Medium Low", cover, and simmer 15 minutes with occasional mixing. Meanwhile, prepare Group 2 (oysters, and shrimps per sections 10 and 11), and set aside. Cook 3 cups extra long grain rice per section 23b and set aside. Remove cover and evaporate Group 1 to sizzling. Meanwhile, preheat oven to 325F. Add Group 2, mix, add Group 3, and mix well. Sprinkle Group 4 on top. Seal and bake 50 minutes (see 16a). Garnish with Group 5 and serve.

146   Stir Fried Seafood

Group 1
4 stalks scallion, each quartered
1 teaspoon ginger, diced
1 large garlic, diced
1/4 teaspoon pepper
1 Tablespoon oil
1/4 cup water
Group 2
2 whole eggs
2 egg whites, yolks discarded
Group 3
1/2 teaspoon sugar
1/8 teaspoon MSG

1 Tablespoon rice wine
2 Tablespoons oyster sauce
8 oz shrimp, cut into halves
2 oz scallops, diced
4 oz imitation crab meat, diced
2 oz oysters, diced
1/2 teaspoon salt
Group 4
3 Tablespoons oil
Group 5
1/4 teaspoon sesame oil
1/8 teaspoon white pepper

Combine Group 1 in pot. Mix well. Bring to boil at "Medium High". Boil 1-2 minutes. Reset heat to "Medium Low", cover, and simmer 20 minutes. Mix occasionally. Meanwhile, prepare Groups 2 and 3. Set aside. Reset heat to "Medium". Remove cover and evaporate Group 1 to sizzling. Add Group 3, mix, cover and simmer 5 minutes with occasional mixing. Add Group 4, mix well, add Group 2, mix continuously until Group 2 is cooked. Garnish with Group 5 and serve.

147   Noodle with Oyster Sauce

Group 1
5 cups water
3 (3-oz) packages, instant
   Oriental noodle
Group 2
1 cube hot pickled tofu
1/4 cup water
2 Tablespoons corn starch
1/4 teaspoon MSG
2 teaspoons soy sauce
2 Tablespoons oyster sauce
2 teaspoons rice wine

3 seasoning bags, from
   noodle packages
Group 3
1 medium garlic, diced
3 Tablespoons oil
Group 4
2 cups hot seafood or chicken
   broth
Group 5
4 stalks scallion, diced
1/4 teaspoon pepper
1/8 teaspoon white pepper

Add to 4-quart pot 5 cups water and heat to boiling at "Medium High" heat setting. Add Group 1, mix well, and boil 3 minutes, maximum. Remove noodles immediately into a 4-quart serving bowl. Set aside. Discard the liquid. Prepare Group 2 mixture (see section 2). Set aside. Fry Group 3 per section 19f and set aside. Add to 2-cup pot Group 4 and heat at "Medium Low" setting. Remix Group 2, stir into Group 4, and mix continuously to smooth consistency (see section 20a). Pour Groups 2 and 3 over Group 1, toss well, garnish with Group 5 and serve.

Shrimp, 117

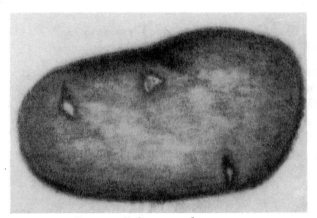

Potato, *Solanum tuberosum*

148   Shrimp and Rice Casserole

Group 1
1 small onion, diced
1 large garlic, diced
1/2 teaspoon paprika
4 Tablespoons margarine
2 Tablespoons chicken bouillon
1/2 teaspoon thyme flakes
1/4 cup seafood or chicken broth
1/2 teaspoon parsley flakes
1/4 teaspoon cracked pepper
no salt

Group 2
4 cups cooked rice
1/4 cup pearl onions, frozen
1/4 cup whole milk
16 oz shrimp, cut into halves

Group 3
2 Tablespoons sharp cheddar
    cheese, grated
10 black olives, diced
4 stalks scallion, diced

Combine Group 1 in pot. Mix well. Bring to boil at "Medium" heat setting. Boil 1-2 minutes. Reset heat to "Medium Low", cover, and simmer 20 minutes with occasional mixing. Meanwhile, dress shrimp per section 11 and set aside. Cook 3 cups extra long grain rice per section 23b and set aside. Remove cover and evaporate Group 1 to sizzling. Cover and let self-saute 2 minutes. Preheat oven to 325F. Add Group 2 to Group 1 and mix well. Sprinkle Group 3 on top, cover, bake 45 minutes (see section 16a), and serve.

149   Shrimp and Pumpkin*

Group 1
1 medium onion, diced
1 large garlic, diced
1 teaspoon ginger, diced
1 medium fresh cayenne pepper,
    whole
1 teaspoon paprika
1/8 teaspoon crushed red pepper
1/8 teaspoon turmeric
2 teaspoons fish sauce

4 Tablespoons oil
1/2 teaspoon salt
1/4 cup water

Group 2
1 cup hot water
6 oz pumpkin, peeled, seeded,
    cut into 8 sections

Group 3
16 oz shrimp, whole

Combine Group 1 in pot. Mix well. Bring to boil at "Medium High" heat setting. Reset heat to "Medium Low", cover, and simmer 25 minutes with occasional mixing. Meanwhile, section a small pumpkin (Group 2) into quarters along its vertical axis (top to bottom). Peel each section. Scrape the core and seeds with a metal spoon from each section and discard them. Cut each section into 3-4 pieces and set aside. Remove cover and evaporate Group 1 to sizzling. Reset heat to "Low", cover, and let self-saute 2-3 minutes. Reset heat to "Medium", add Group 2, mix, cover, and simmer 20 minutes. Mix occasionally. Add Group 3, mix, cover, and simmer 5 more minutes. Add 1/4 to 1/2 cup hot water if more sauce is needed. Salt to taste and serve.

---

150   Shrimp and Potato*

This is a typical provincial Burmese dish. A simple combination of shrimp, turmeric, and potato with a subtle aroma, flavor, and taste. It is an easy dish to prepare when you are too busy for the cooking.

Group 1
1 medium onion, diced
1 large garlic, diced
1/4 teaspoon salt
1/4 teaspoon turmeric
1 large fresh cayenne pepper,
    whole
1/4 cup water
3 Tablespoons oil

Group 2
3 medium potatoes, each
    quartered
1/4 teaspoon MSG
2 teaspoons fish sauce
1 1/2 cups hot water
Group 3
24 oz shrimp, whole

Combine Group 1 in pot. Mix well. Bring to boil at "Medium High" heat setting. Reset heat to "Medium Low", cover, and simmer 15 minutes with occasional mixing. Remove cover and evaporate to sizzling. Reset heat to "Low", cover and let self-saute 5 minutes. Reset heat to "Medium", add Group 2, mix, and bring to boil. Reset heat to "Medium Low", cover, and simmer 20-25 minutes. Mix occasionally. Meanwhile, clean shrimp (see section 11) and set aside. Add Group 3, mix, cover, and simmer 5 more minutes. Add 1/4 to 1/2 cup hot water if more sauce is needed. Salt to taste and serve.

119

151   Shrimp and Turmeric

This is just like the beef and turmeric dish (see Recipe #10), unusually simple and quick to prepare. It is very flavorful, tasty, and a versatile dish. It may be used as a main or snack dish. This dish may also be mixed with any fresh vegetables for making Asian or Western shrimp salads (see Recipe #24).

Group 1

32 oz shrimp, whole	4 Tablespoons oil
1 small garlic, diced	1/2 teaspoon salt
1/4 cup water	1/4 teaspoon turmeric

Add to 3-quart pot, Group 1, mix, and evaporate to sizzling in oil at "Medium" heat setting. Mix occasionally. Reset heat to "Medium Low", cover, let self-saute 3 minutes, and serve.

152   Shrimp Country Style*

Group 1

1 medium onion, diced	1/2 teaspoon salt
1 large garlic, diced	2 teaspoons fish sauce
1 teaspoon paprika	1/4 cup water
1/8 teaspoon crushed red pepper	**Group 2**
3 Tablespoons oil	1/2 cup hot water
1 medium fresh cayenne	32 oz shrimp, whole
pepper, whole	8 sprigs cilantro, whole

Combine Group 1 in pot. Mix well. Bring to boil at "Medium High" heat setting. Reset heat to "Medium Low", cover, and simmer 25 minutes with occasional mixing. Meanwhile, clean shrimp (see section 11) and set aside. Remove cover and evaporate Group 1 to sizzling. Reset heat to "Low", cover, and let self-saute 3 minutes. Reset heat to "Medium", add Group 2, and bring to boil. Reset heat to "Medium Low", cover, and simmer 5 minutes with occasional mixing. Add 1/4 to 1/2 cup hot water if more sauce is needed. Salt to taste and serve.

153   Shrimp Pasta Salad*

Group 1
16 oz shrimp, whole
1/8 teaspoon pepper
1 small garlic, diced
1 Tablespoon olive oil
Group 2
6 oz fettucine
4 cups water
Group 3
1/2 teaspoon salt

10 black olives, diced
1 small fresh jalapeno pepper,
  diced
5 sprigs fresh basil,
  diced
1 Tablespoon olive oil
Group 4
2 Tablespoons Parmesan cheese,
  grated

Clean shrimp (see section 11) and set aside. Add to 3-quart pot, Group 1, and heat at "Medium" heat setting until shrimp sizzle in oil. Reset heat to "Low", cover, and let self-saute 5 minutes. Remove Group 1 from stove and set aside. Prepare Group 2 per instruction on its package and set aside. Combine Groups 1 (includes its oil), 2, and 3 in 3-quart serving bowl. Toss well, garnish with Group 4 and serve.

154   Eggplant Shrimp Scampi

Eggplant and shrimp combination has a very subtle flavor. This will please both the eggplant and shrimp lovers.

Group 1
1 large eggplant, cut into
  4 sections, lengthwise
1/4 cup water
2 Tablespoons olive oil
1/2 teaspoon salt
Group 2
1 large garlic, diced
24 oz shrimp, whole
1/4 teaspoon cracked pepper

1 Tablespoon olive oil
1/2 teaspoon Italian seasoning
1/4 cup water
Group 3
2 Tablespoons Parmesan cheese,
  grated
Group 4
10 black olive, cut into halves
1 Tablespoon chives, diced

Clean shrimp (see section 11) and set aside. Add to 3-quart pot, Group 1, mix, and bring to boil at "Medium" heat setting. Reset heat to "Medium Low", cover, and simmer 30-40 minutes. Meanwhile, add to 4-quart pot Group 2, mix, and bring to boil at "Medium" heat setting. Reset heat to "Medium Low" and evaporate to sizzling, mixing occasionally. Set aside. Spread Group 2 on Group 1. Sprinkle Group 3 on top, cover, and let self-saute 2-3 minutes. Garnish with Group 4 and serve.

---

155   Shrimp and Snow Pea

Group 1

4 stalks scallion, each quartered	2 Tablespoons corn starch
1 medium garlic, diced	2 teaspoons rice wine
1/4 teaspoon pepper	1/4 teaspoon MSG
3 Tablespoons oil	1 teaspoon sugar
1/4 teaspoon salt	**Group 4**
1/4 cup water	1 1/2 cups hot shrimp or chicken
Group 2	broth
24 oz shrimp, whole	12 oz fresh snow peas, ends
Group 3	trimmed, whole, washed
1/4 cup water	**Group 5**
2 Tablespoons soy sauce,	1/4 teaspoon sesame oil
Japanese or Chinese	1/8 teaspoon white pepper

Add to 4-quart pot, Group 1, mix, and bring to boil at "Medium High" heat setting. Reset heat to "Medium Low", mix, cover, and simmer 20 minutes. Mix occasionally. Meanwhile, prepare Group 2 and set aside (see section 11). Prepare Group 3 mixture and set aside (see section 2). Prepare snow peas (Group 4) and set aside or use frozen snow peas (see section 14). Remove cover and evaporate Group 1 to sizzling. Add Group 2, mix, cover, and let simmer 5 minutes. Add Group 4 and mix. Remix Group 3 and add to Group 1. Reset heat to "Medium" and mix continuously until gravy thickens to a smooth consistency (see section 20a). Remove pot from stove. Garnish with Group 5 and serve.

156   Shrimp Macaroni Sauce

Group 1
1 small onion, diced
1 medium garlic, diced
1 stalk celery, diced
1 large tomato, diced
1 (6-oz) tomato paste
1 small bell pepper, diced
1/2 teaspoon salt
1/2 teaspoon Italian seasoning
1/4 teaspoon sugar
1/4 teaspoon pepper

2 Tablespoons olive oil
1/2 cup water
Group 2
6 oz elbow macaroni, uncooked
Group 3
1 Tablespoon margarine
Group 4
20 oz shrimp, cut into halves
Group 5
2 Tablespoons Parmesan cheese,
   grated

Combine Group 1 in pot. Mix and bring to boil at "Medium High" heat setting. Boil 1-2 minutes. Reset heat to "Medium Low', cover, and simmer 45 minutes. Meanwhile, prepare Group 2 per instruction on package. Spread Group 3 evenly on cooked Group 2 and set aside. Clean Group 4 (see section 11) and set aside. Remove cover and evaporate Group 1 to sizzling. Add Group 4 to Group 1, mix, cover, and let simmer 5 minutes. Add Group 2 to Group 1, mix well, garnish with Group 5 and serve.

157   Egg and Shrimp Stir Fried

Group 1
1/4 cup water
3 Tablespoons oil
1 teaspoon ginger, diced
1/8 teaspoon salt
1 medium garlic, diced
1/4 teaspoon pepper
4 stalks scallion, section
   into quarters
Group 2
24 oz shrimp. whole

Group 3
2 Tablespoons soy sauce,
   Japanese or Chinese
2 teaspoons rice wine
1/4 teaspoon MSG
1/2 teaspoon sugar
Group 4
3 eggs, whole
3 egg, whites, discard yolks
Group 5
1/4 teaspoon sesame oil

Add to 4-quart pot, Group 1, mix, and bring to boil at "Medium High" heat setting. Reset heat to "Medium Low", mix, cover, and simmer 20 minutes. Mix occasionally. Meanwhile, clean Group 2 and set aside (see section 11). Combine Group 3 and set aside. Combine Group 4, beat, and set aside. Remove cover and evaporate Group 1 to sizzling. Add Group 4, and scramble until eggs are cooked. Add Group 2, mix, add Group 3, mix, and cook 5 minutes while mixing. Garnish with Group 5 and serve.

---

158   Curried Shrimp**

Group 1
1 medium onion, diced
2 large garlic, diced
2 Tablespoons Madras curry
    powder
1/8 teaspoon turmeric
1 teaspoon paprika
1/4 teaspoon crushed red pepper
4 Tablespoons oil
1 teaspoon salt

1/2 cup water
Group 2
4 small potatoes, cut in halves
1 1/2 cups hot water
1 medium tomato, quartered
1 medium fresh cayenne pepper,
    whole
Group 3
24 oz shrimp, whole
8 sprigs cilantro, cut in halves

Combine Group'1 in pot. Mix well. Bring to boil at "Medium High" heat setting. Reset heat to "Medium Low", cover, and simmer 20 minutes with occasional mixing. Remove cover and evaporate Group 1 to sizzling. Reset heat to "Low", cover, and let self-saute 3 minutes. Reset heat to "Medium High", add Group 2, mix, and bring to boil. Reset heat to :Medium Low", cover, and simmer 20 minutes with occasional mixing. Meanwhile, clean shrimp per section 11 and set aside. Add Group 3, mix, cover, and simmer 5 minutes. Add 1/4 to 1/2 cup hot water if more sauce is needed. Salt to taste, garnish with Group 4, and serve.

159 Sally Shrimp Scampi

This dish is prepared on stove with simmer-saute method.

Group 1
32 oz shrimps, whole
1 medium garlic, diced
1/2 teaspoon thyme flakes
1/4 teaspoon cracked pepper
2 Tablespoons olive oil
1/2 teaspoon salt

Group 2
2 Tablespoons Parmesan cheese,
grated

Group 3
10 black olives, cut into halves
3 stalks scallion, diced

Clean shrimp (see section 11) and set aside. Add to 4-quart pot, Group 1, mix, and heat at "Medium" setting until shrimps sizzle in oil. Reset heat to "Low", sprinkle Group 2 on top, cover, and let self-saute 5 minutes. Garnish with Group 3 and serve.

160 Shrimp Green Bean Stir Fried

This dish is very tasty and flavorful. It is simple and quick to prepare.

Group 1
2 Tablespoons oil
1 large garlic, diced
1/4 cup water

Group 2
24 oz shrimp, cut into halves

16 oz green beans, ends trimmed,
cut into halves

Group 3
1/4 teaspoon MSG
1/2 teaspoon salt

Prepare green beans and set aside (see section 13h). Clean shrimp and set aside (see section 11). Combine Group 1, mix, and bring to boil at "Medium" heat setting. Reset heat to "Medium Low", cover and let simmer 10 minutes. Reset heat to "Medium", remove cover, and evaporate to sizzling. Add Group 2, mix, cover, and cook 5 minutes. Sprinkle Group 3, mix well, and serve.

161   Little Italy Shrimp Salad

Group 1
1 medium garlic, diced
1/2 teaspoon Italian seasoning
2 Tablespoons vinegar
1 Tablespoon water
2 Tablespoons olive oil
2 teaspoons sugar
1/4 teaspoon pepper
1/2 teaspoon salt

Group 2
1/4 medium cucumber, peeled,
   seeded, bite-sized cubes
1 small Bermuda onion, diced
1/4 head lettuce, diced
1 medium tomato, cut
   into 8 sections
10 black olives, diced
1 medium bell pepper, diced

1 small mild pickled banana
   pepper, diced
3 stalks scallion, diced
1 medium carrot, peeled,
   1/2-in slices

Group 3
1/4 teaspoon salt
20 oz shrimp, dressed,
   cut in halves
1/4 cup water
1/8 teaspoon thyme flakes
1 Tablespoon olive oil
1/8 teaspoon oregano

Group 4
1/4 teaspoon cracked
   pepper
2 Tablespoon Parmesan
   cheese, grated

Combine Group 1 in salad dressing bottle, shake well 3 times in 30 seconds installments, and set aside. Prepare Group 2 vegetables in 3-quart salad bowl and set aside. Meanwhile, clean shrimp per section 11. Combine Group 3 in 2-quart pot and evaporate to sizzling at "Medium" heat setting with occasional mixing. Add entire Group 3 to Group 2, remix Group 1, and add to Group 2. Toss well, garnish with Group 4, and serve.

Turkey, 127

Garlic, *Allium sativum*

162   Turkey Trot

It is topped with a combination of smoked turkey, turkey pastrami, and fresh garlic.

Group 1
2 (7-oz) flour packages,
   premixed for pizza

Group 2
2 Tablespoons corn oil

Group 3
12 oz pizza sauce

Group 4
1/4 teaspoon cracked pepper,
   cracked
1/4 teaspoon Italian seasoning

Group 5
1/2 cup mozzarella/provolone/
   Parmesan cheeses, premixed

1/4 cup blended cheeses
   from pizza packages

Group 6
4 oz turkey pastrami, diced
1 large garlic, diced
4 oz smoked turkey, diced

Group 7
1/2 cup mozzarella/provolone/
   Parmesan cheeses, premixed

Group 8
1/4 teaspoon Italian seasoning
1/4 teaspoon crushed
   red pepper

Mix and raise crust mix (Group 1) per instruction on the package. Make pie crust and dress pie as described in section 8 using ingredient groups in this recipe. Bake per section 16b. Garnish with Group 8, section pizza, and serve.

163   Fried Turkey Steak Salad*

Group 1
10 oz lean ground turkey

Group 2
1/4 head lettuce, diced
1 medium tomato, diced
1 small onion, diced
1/4 cucumber, seeded, diced
1 medium fresh jalapeno
   pepper, diced

1 Tablespoon olive oil

Group 3
1 Tablespoon oil per patty

Group 4
1/2 cup Italian dressing, commercial

Group 5
2 Tablespoons Parmesan cheese,
   grated
1/4 teaspoon pepper

Make 4 thin patties of Group 1. Set aside. Prepare Group 2 in 3-quart salad bowl. Set aside. Add to 8-inch skillet, 1 Tablespoon oil (Group 3), and fry one patty at a time on "Medium" heat setting. Fry each side twice and fry 3 minutes each time. Drain oil, cut each patty into 1/4 inch slices, and combine with Group 2. Add Group 4 to Groups 1 and 2. Toss well. Garnish with Group 5 and serve.

---

164   Turkey Egg Rice Casserole

Group 1
1 small onion, diced
1/4 teaspoon cracked pepper
1 large garlic, diced
1/8 teaspoon turmeric
no salt
3 Tablespoons margarine
1/2 teaspoon Italian seasoning
1 Tablespoon beef bouillon
1/4 cup water
Group 2
3 hard boiled eggs, 1/2-in slices
Group 3
2 cups turkey leftover, cut into

bite-sized pieces
Group 4
1/2 cup 2 % milk
2 (10-oz) cans, cream of
  mushroom soup
Group 5
2 cups broccoli florets, frozen
1/2 cup American cheese,
  diced
3 cups cooked rice
Group 6
2 Tablespoons sharp Cheddar
  cheese, grated

Combine Group 1 in pot. Mix well. Bring to boil at "Medium". Boil 1-2 minutes. Reset heat to "Medium Low", cover, and simmer 15 minutes with occasional mixing. Meanwhile, prepare Group 2 and set aside (see section 17f). Cook 3 cups extra long grain rice per section 23b and set aside. Remove cover, evaporate Group 1 to sizzling, add Group 3, mix, cover, and self-saute 2 minutes. Meanwhile, preheat oven to 325F. Trim turkey meat per section 6i and set aside. Reset heat to "Medium". Add Group 4 to Group 1 and mix well. Add Group 5 to Groups 1 and 4 and mix well. Place Group 2 on top, seal pot, and bake 45-50 minutes (see section 16a). Garnish with Group 6 and serve.

165   Fried Turkey Patty

This recipe consists of two parts. Part A makes fried patties and Part B makes sauce.

Part A
Group 1
1/4 cup flour
1/4 teaspoon garlic powder
1/2 teaspoon Italian seasoning
1/4 teaspoon MSG
1/2 teaspoon sugar
1/2 teaspoon pepper
1 teaspoon baking powder
1/2 teaspoon salt

Group 2
1/3 cup flour
1 teaspoon baking powder
Group 3
24 oz lean ground turkey
2 Tablespoons water
Group 4
3 cups oil

Add to 2-cup bowl Group 1, mix, and set aside. Add to 12-inch dining plate Group 2, mix, and set aside. Add to 2-quart bowl Group 3, mix well, then add Group 1 mixture, mix well, divide into 8 portions, and set aside. Heat Group 4 in 2-quart frying pan at "Medium" heat setting for 3 minutes. Make one thin patty with each of the 8 portions. Roll each patty on both sides in Group 2 and deep fry in oil. Fry each side 2-3 minutes and fry each side twice. Drain oil on paper. Repeat as above with remaining patties. Make and fry one patty at a time. Serve patties with gravy (see Part B below).

Part B
Group 5
1 cup hot whole milk
2 Tablespoon margarine
1 (10-oz) can, cream of chicken
  soup

1 cup sour cream
Group 6
2 Tablespoons Parmesan cheese,
  grated

Add to 5-cup pot, Group 5, mix well, heat at "Medium Low" setting 5 minutes with occasional mixing, and pour over fried turkey patties. Garnish with Group 6 and serve.

166   Turkey Rice Casserole

Group 1
1 medium garlic, diced
1 small onion, diced
1/2 teaspoon thyme flakes
1/4 teaspoon parsley flakes
1/4 teaspoon cracked pepper
1/3 cup water
3 Tablespoons margarine
1 Tablespoon beef bouillon
Group 2
2 (10-oz) cans, cream of
     mushroom soup

1/2 cup hot whole milk
Group 3
3 cups cooked rice
1/3 cup sweet peas, frozen
1/3 cup pearl onions, frozen
2 cups turkey leftover,
     bite-sized pieces
Group 4
1/2 cup sharp Cheddar
     cheese, grated
Group 5
1/3 cup croutons, garlic flavor

Combine Group 1 in pot, mix, and bring to boil at "Medium High" heat setting. Reset heat to "Medium Low", mix, cover, and simmer 15 minutes. Mix occasionally. Meanwhile, mix Group 2 well and set aside. Cook 3 cups extra long grain rice per section 23b and set aside. Remove cover and evaporate Group 1 to sizzling. Mean while, preheat oven at 325F. Trim turkey meat per section 6i and set aside. Add Group 2 to Group 1, mix, add Group 3, and mix. Spread Group 4 on top of Groups 1, 2, and 3, seal, and bake 45-55 minutes (see section 16a). Garnish with Group 5 and serve.

167   Turkey Salad*

Group 1
3 cups turkey leftover, bite-sized
Group 2
1/4 cucumber, seeded, diced
1/4 head lettuce, diced
1 small Bermuda onion, diced
1 medium tomato, diced
1 small bell pepper, diced
1 small fresh jalapeno pepper,
     diced

1 medium carrot, cut into
     1/4-in slices
10 black olives, diced
1/4 teaspoon pepper
1 Tablespoon olive oil
Group 3
1/2 cup Italian dressing, any brand
Group 4
3 Tablespoons Parmesan cheese,
     grated

Prepare Group 1 per section 6i and set aside. Prepare Group 2 in 3-quart salad bowl. Add Groups 1 and 3 to Group 2. Toss well, garnish with Group 4, and serve.

---

168   Turkey Macaroni Casserole

Group 1
2 cups uncooked elbow

Group 2
1/4 teaspoon cracked pepper
3 Tablespoons margarine
1/2 teaspoon thyme flakes
no salt
1/4 teaspoon parsley flakes
1/4 cup water

Group 3
1/2 cup 2% hot milk

2 (10-oz) cans, cream of
  mushroom soup

Group 4
4 cups turkey leftover,
  bite-sized pieces

Group 5
1 Tablespoon Parmesan
  cheese, grated
1 Tablespoon sharp Cheddar
  cheese, grated

Prepare Group 1 per package instruction and set aside. Combine Group 2 in pot, mix well, and bring to boil at "Medium High" heat setting. Reset heat to "Medium Low", cover, and simmer 10 minutes. Meanwhile, add to 3-cup bowl, Group 3, disperse well, and set aside. Trim turkey meat per section 6i and set aside. Turn off heat and add Groups 3, 4, and 1 to Group 2. Mix well. Meanwhile, preheat oven at 325F. Sprinkle Group 5 over macaroni mix, seal, and bake 45 minutes (see section 16a).

169   Turkey Pasta Casserole

Group 1
8 oz linguine pasta
1 Tablespoon margarine
Group 2
1 small onion, diced
1/4 cracked teaspoon pepper
1/4 cup water
1 Tablespoon beef bouillon
2 Tablespoons margarine
Group 3
2 (10-oz) cans, Minestrone soup

Group 4
4 cups leftover turkey, bite-sized
   pieces
1 medium garlic, diced
1/2 cup mixed vegetables, frozen
Group 5
2 Tablespoon Parmesan cheese,
   grated
Group 6
1/2 cup oyster cracker, crumbled
1/2 cup hot whole milk

Prepare Group 1 per instruction on the package. Mix pasta with margarine and set aside. Combine Group 2, mix, and bring to boil at "Medium High" heat setting. Reset heat to "Medium Low", mix, cover, and simmer 15 minutes. Mix occasionally. Meanwhile, mix Group 3 well and set aside. Trim turkey meat per section 6i and set aside. Remove cover and evaporate Group 2 to sizzling. Meanwhile, preheat oven at 325F. Add Group 3 to Group 2, mix, add Group 4, mix, add Group 1 and mix. Spread Group 5 on top, seal, and bake 45 minutes (see section 16a). Garnish with Group 6 and serve.

Vegetable, 134

170   Potato Yogurt Curry**

Group 1
3 large potatoes, with skin, cut
   each into 8 sections
Group 2
1 medium onion, diced
2 large garlic, diced
1 Tablespoon ginger, diced
1/3 teaspoon turmeric
2 medium fresh cayenne peppers,
   diced

1 teaspoon salt
2 teaspoons cumin seeds, cracked
1/2 cup water
5 Tablespoons oil
1/4 teaspoon crushed red pepper
Group 3
2 Tablespoons fresh lemon juice
1 cup plain yogurt
1/2 cup sour cream

Add to 3-quart pot, Group 1. Add water just enough to cover potatoes.
Bring to boil at "Medium High" heat setting. Boil 1-2 minutes, reset heat
to "Medium Low", and simmer 15-20 minutes. Meanwhile, prepare Group
2. Drain Group 1 potatoes in colander and set aside. Combine Group 2
in 4-quart pot, mix well, and bring to boil at "Medium High" heat setting.
Boil 1-2 minutes. Reset heat to "Medium Low", cover, and simmer 25
minutes. Mix occasionally. Remove cover and evaporate to sizzling. Stir
in Groups 3 and 1, cover, turn heat off, let stand 2 minutes, and serve.

171   Fried Green Tomatoes

Group 1
2 large green tomatoes, cut
   into 1/2-in slices
Group 2
1 1/2 cups flour
1 1/2 teaspoons sugar
1 1/2 teaspoons MSG
1 1/2 teaspoons cracked pepper
1 1/2 teaspoon salt
1 teaspoon Italian seasoning
2 Tablespoons baking powder

Group 3
1 cup water
1/2 cup flour
2 teaspoons baking powder
Group 4
4 cups oil
Group 5
2 10-oz.) cans, Minestrone soup
1/2 cup hot water
Group 6
1 Tablespoon Parmesan cheese,
   grated

Wash and slice Group 1 into 1/2-in. slices, and set aside. Add to 2-quart bowl, Group 2, mix, and set aside. Add to 1-quart bowl, Group 3, mix well to disperse the flour globules, and set aside. Add to 4-quart pot, Group 4 and heat at "Medium High" heat setting. Roll Group 1 slices in Group 2, then, in Group 3, then, in Group 2 again, and deep fry in Group 4 (see section 19a). Turn the pieces over every 2-3 minutes if needed. Fry to light tan or tan color. Remove drip drain excess oil on paper towel, and set aside. Meanwhile, combine Group 5 in 1-quart pot, mix well, and heat at "Medium" setting 5 minutes. Pour Group 5 over fried Group 1 slices, garnish with Group 6, and serve.

---

172   Fried Zucchini on Cream Sauce

Group 1
1 medium zucchini, cut into
   1/2-in slices

Group 2
1 1/2 cups flour
1 1/2 teaspoons sugar
1 1/2 teaspoons MSG
1 1/2 teaspoons salt
1 1/2 Tablespoons garlic powder
1 1/2 teaspoons pepper
2 Tablespoons baking powder

Group 3
1 cup water

1/2 cup flour
2 teaspoons baking powder

Group 4
4 cups oil

Group 5
2 (10-oz) cans, cream of
   mushroom soup
1/2 cup whole milk
1 Tablespoon margarine

Group 6
2 Tablespoons sharp Cheddar
   cheese, grated

Prepare Group 1 per section 13b and slice into 1/2-in slices, and set aside. Add to 2-quart bowl, Group 2, mix, and set aside. Add to 1-quart bowl, Group 3, mix well to disperse the flour globules, and set aside. Add to 4-quart pot, Group 4 and heat 3 minutes at "Medium High" heat setting. Reset heat to between "Medium" and "Medium Low". Roll Group 1 slices in Group 2, then, in Group 3, then, in Group 2 again, and deep fry in Group 4, see section 19a. Turn the pieces over every 2-3 minutes if needed. Fry to light tan or tan color. Remove drip drain excess oil on paper, and set aside. Meanwhile, combine Group 5 in 1-quart pot, mix well, and heat at "Medium" setting 5 minutes. Pour Group 5 over fried Group 1 slices, garnish with Group 6, and serve.

173   Sambar***

This is a fully vegetarian dish. It is extra hot, pungent, and sour all rolled up in one flavor. I like this dish extremely well. By popular requests from my South Indian friends I prepared this soup for them at two different dinner parties. This dish was the first one among several other dishes to be used up by their guests, at both the parties. The Indians guests at the parties frankly admitted to me that they never expected this dish to taste anywhere near the sambar they make in South India. They were genuinely flabbergasted. This is a big compliment to me. They asked for the recipe and I obliged their requests. Vegetables used are quite flexible. You can substitute any other vegetables of your liking. It tastes as good as it is easy to prepare, an anti-Murphy's Law.

Group 1
6 cups water
1 (7-oz) Instant Sambar Mix
Group 2
1 medium tomato, quartered
1 small eggplant, cut into 8 pieces
2 small potatoes, cut into 8 pieces
2 medium fresh cayenne peppers, whole
Group 3
1 small radish (diakon), cut into 8 pieces
1 small zucchini, cut into 8 pieces

1 small bitter melon or bitter gourd cut into 8 pieces, seeded
Group 4
4 oz okra, whole or sections, frozen
8 sprigs cilantro, cut into halves
Group 5
1 Tablespoon oil
Group 6
1 teaspoon black mustard seeds
Group 7
3 medium dried red peppers, whole
8 fresh curry leaves

Bring 6 cups water to boil at "Medium High" heat setting. Stir in Group 1, reset heat to "Medium Low", and cook for 30 minutes. Meanwhile, prepare Groups 2 and 3. Set aside. Add to Group 1, Group 2, and cook 15 minutes. Mix, every 5 minutes or so. Scrape side and bottom during mixing. Add Group 3, mix, and cook 15 more minutes. Add Group 4, mix well, and cook 2 more minutes. Fry Groups 6 and 7 in Group 5 per section 19b, pour over somber, and serve. Add 1/4 to 1 cup hot water for more sauce if needed. Mix, salt to taste, and serve.

174   Stir Fried Bok Choy

Group 1
1 large garlic, diced
3 Tablespoons oil
1/4 teaspoon MSG
3/4 teaspoon salt
1/4 cup water
Group 2
16 oz boa chop, cut into 1-in pieces

Combine Group 1 in pot, mix, and bring to boil at "Medium" heat setting. Reset heat to "Medium Low", cover and let simmer 20 minutes. Meanwhile, prepare Group 2 and set aside. Reset heat to "Medium", remove cover, and evaporate to sizzling. Add Group 2, mix, cover, cook 3 minutes, and serve.

175   Fried Tofu in Soybean Sauce

Group 1
1 medium garlic, diced
3 Tablespoons oil
1/4 cup water
Group 2
1/4 cup water
3 Tablespoons corn starch
1/4 teaspoon MSG
2 Tablespoons soy sauce
2 teaspoons sherry wine
1/2 teaspoon sugar
1 Tablespoon black bean in
    soybean oil
no salt
Group 3
12 oz fried tofu, frozen
1 1/2 cups hot water
Group 4
6 sprigs cilantro, diced
1/4 teaspoon sesame oil
1/8 teaspoon pepper

Combine Group 1 in pot. Mix well. Bring to boil at "Medium High" heat setting. Boil 1-2 minutes. Reset heat to "Medium Low", cover, and simmer 10-15 minutes. Mix occasionally. Meanwhile, prepare Group 2 mixture and set aside (see section 2). Remove cover and evaporate Group 1 to sizzling. Cover and let self saute 2 minutes. Add Group 3, mix well, and simmer 5 minutes. Reset heat to "Low", stir in Group 2, and mix continuously to smooth consistency (see section 20a). Garnish with Group 4 and serve.

176   Vegetarian Vegetable Soup**

This recipe is dedicated to one of the World's renown mathematicians, Siri Nivasa Ramanujan (1887-1920), who died of malnutrition at the age of 32. He was a vegetarian of the extreme. His untimely death was not due to his dietary discipline but due to his complete negligence to his general health and his poor eating habits. He was completely focussed in his work that he often forgot to eat his meals.

This soup is a vegetarian soup of almost an at the end of one side of the vegetarian spectrum. It is strictly vegetables. It is not only free of bouillon, meat broth, meat, poultry, and fish, it even excludes alcohol, wine, egg, and dairy products such as, milk, butter, yogurt, cheese, etc.

Group 1
1/2 cup water
1 medium onion, quartered
1/4 teaspoon turmeric
1 medium garlic, diced
2 teaspoons ginger, diced
1 teaspoon salt
1 Tablespoon Madras curry
    powder
1/4 teaspoon cayenne
    pepper, powder
1/4 teaspoon pepper
3 Tablespoons oil
1 medium tomatoes,
    quartered

Group 2
1/4 cup hot water
1 Tablespoon tamarind
Group 3
2 cups hot water
1 small eggplant, cut into 8 pieces
1 medium potato, cut into 8 pieces
1 medium fresh cayenne pepper,
    whole
1 teaspoon paprika
Group 4
4 oz okra, frozen, whole or slices
10 green beans, both ends trimmed,
    cut into halves
1 teaspoon garam masala

Combine Group 1 in pot. Mix well. Heat to boil at "Medium High heat setting. Boil 1-2 minutes. Reset heat to "Medium Low", cover, and simmer 20-30 minutes. Mix occasionally. Meanwhile, soak Group 2 in 1/4 cup hot water and set aside. Remove cover and evaporate Group 1 to sizzling. Mix well. Cover and let self saute 2-3 minutes. Reset heat to "Medium". Add Group 2 liquid, discard tamarind pulp, add Group 3, mix well, and bring to boil. Reset heat to "Medium Low", cover, and simmer 20-30 minutes. Mix occasionally. Add Group 4, mix well, cover, simmer 3 minutes, and serve. Add 1/4 to 1 cup hot water if needed.

177   Chana Paste*

Group 1
1 cup chana dahl
Group 2
3 cups water
Group 3
1 cup water
1 (3-in) cinnamon stick
5 cloves, whole
1 small bay leaf
1/4 teaspoon turmeric

3/4 teaspoon salt
1 medium fresh cayenne pepper,
  diced
Group 4
2 Tablespoons oil
1 Tablespoon ginger, diced
2 large garlic, diced
1 medium onion, diced
Group 5
2 Tablespoons margarine

Wash Group 1 per section 13g. Add Group 1 and Group 2 to 4-quart pot. Bring to boil at "Medium High" heat setting. Boil 1-2 minutes. Reset heat to "Medium Low" and simmer 60 minutes. Mix occasionally. Meanwhile, prepare Group 3 and set aside. Mash Group 1 (chana) with potato masher. Add Group 3 to Group 1, mix, and simmer 30 more minutes at "Medium Low" setting. Mix occasionally. Meanwhile, fry Group 4 (see section 19g). Add fried Group 4 to Groups 1 and 2 mixture. Mix well. Garnish with Groups 4 and 5, mix well, and serve. Add 1/4 cup hot water if more gravy is desired, mix well, salt to taste, and serve.

178   Baked Parmesan Potato

Group 1
4 large potatoes, cut into halves,
  with skin
Group 2
1 small garlic, diced
1/4 teaspoon cracked pepper

3 Tablespoons margarine
1/4 teaspoon Italian seasoning
2 Tablespoons Parmesan cheese,
  grated
1 Tablespoon chives, minced
1/2 teaspoon salt

Wash Group 1 well, cut into halves, and place in baking dish with their cut faces facing up, Set aside. Meanwhile, preheat oven at 325F. Combine Group 2 and spread on Group 1 evenly, bake 45-50 minutes, and serve.

179   Pink Lentil with Cilantro

Group 1
1 cup pink lentil
Group 2
3 cups water
1/8 teaspoon tumeric
1 teaspoon ginger, diced
2 medium fresh cayenne peppers, diced

1 teaspoon salt
Group 3
3 Tablespoons oil
2 large garlic, diced
1 medium onion, diced
Group 4
6 sprigs cilantro, diced

Wash Group 1 per section 13g. Add Group 1 and Group 2 to 4-quart pot. Bring to boil at "Medium High" heat setting. Boil 1-2 minutes. Reset heat to "Medium Low", and simmer 45 minutes. Mix occasionally. Meanwhile, prepare Group 3 and fry per section 19g. Add fried Group 3 and Group 4 to pot, mix, simmer 10 minutes, and serve. Add 1/4 to 1 cup hot water if more gravy is desired, mix well, salt to taste, and serve.

180   Jane McEnroe's Salad

Group 1
6 large eggs
Group 2
8 medium new red potatoes, with skin
Group 3
4 stalks scallion, diced

1 cup celery, diced
Group 4
2 1/2 Tablespoons French dressing
1 1/2 teaspoons mustard sauce
2 Tablespoons mayonnaise
1/4 teaspoon cracked pepper
1 teaspoon sugar

Boil Group 1 and cut into 1/4-in slices (see section 17f). Add to 5-quart pot Group 2, add water to cover potatoes, and boil at "Medium" heat setting for 15 minutes. Meanwhile, prepare Group 3 and set aside. Remove cooked Group 2 from pot and cut each into 8 sections. Combine Groups 1, 2, 3, and 4 immediately, toss well, and serve.

181   Vegetarian Spaghetti Sauce*

Group 1
1 large onion, diced
1 medium bell pepper, diced
1 medium garlic, diced
3 Tablespoons olive oil
2 Tablespoons Parmesan cheese,
     grated
1/4 teaspoon thyme flakes
1/2 teaspoon basil flakes

2 (6-oz) cans, tomato paste
1 teaspoon sugar
1/4 teaspoon parsley, flakes
1/4 teaspoon pepper
2 large tomatoes, diced
1/4 teaspoon cayenne pepper,
     powder
2 cups water
3/4 teaspoon salt

Combine Group 1 in pot. Mix well. Bring to boil at "Medium High" heat setting. Boil 1-2 minutes. Reset heat to "Medium Low", cover, and simmer 60 minutes. Mix occasionally. Add 1/4 to 1 cup hot water for more sauce if needed. Mix, salt to taste, and serve.

182   Corn and Rice Casserole

Group 1
3 Tablespoons oil
1 medium onion, diced
1 large garlic, diced
1 large tomato, diced
1 small bell pepper, diced
1/2 teaspoon basil flakes
1 1/2 teaspoon salt
1/4 teaspoon pepper

1/4 cup water
Group 2
1/2 cup hot whole milk
Group 3
5 cups cooked rice
1/2 cup sweet corn, frozen
Group 4
2 Tablespoons Parmesan cheese,
     grated

Combine Group 1 in pot. Mix well. Bring to boil at "Medium High" heat setting. Boil 1-2 minutes. Reset heat to "Medium Low", cover, and simmer 20 minutes. Mix occasionally. Meanwhile, cook 3 cups extra long grain rice per section 23b and set aside. Remove cover and evaporate Group 1 to sizzling. Preheat oven to 325F. Add Group 2, mix, add Group 3, mix, sprinkle Group 4 on top of rice, seal pot, and bake 30-45 minutes (see section 16a).

183   Fried Corn Nibblers

Group 1

3 Tablespoons oil
1 medium onion, diced
1 medium garlic, diced
1/8 teaspoon turmeric
1/8 teaspoon pepper

1/2 teaspoon salt
1/4 cup water
1/8 teaspoon MSG
Group 2
3 cups corn nibblers, frozen

Combine Group 1 in pot, mix, and bring to boil at "Medium" heat setting. Reset heat to "Medium Low", cover and let simmer 20 minutes. Meanwhile, prepare Group 2 and set aside (see section 14). Reset heat to "Medium", remove cover, and evaporate to sizzling. Add Group 2, mix, cover, let vegetable cook for 3 minutes, and serve.

184   Curried Cabbage*

Group 1
1 medium onion, diced
2 large garlic, diced
1 Tablespoon ginger, diced
1/4 teaspoon crushed red pepper
2 medium fresh cayenne
     pepper, diced
1 teaspoon cumin seeds, cracked
1/2 cup water

1/4 teaspoon turmeric
4 Tablespoons oil
3/4 teaspoon salt
Group 2
16 oz cabbage, 1/4-in slices
1/4 cup hot water
Group 3
2 teaspoons garam
     masala

Combine Group 1 in pot. Mix well. Bring to boil at "Medium High" heat setting. Boil 1-2 minutes. Reset heat to "Medium Low", cover, and simmer 25 minutes. Mix occasionally. Meanwhile, prepare Group 2 cabbage and set aside. Remove cover and evaporate Group 1 to sizzling. Add Group 3, mix, cover, and let self-saute 2 minutes. Add Group 2, mix well, cover, cook 5 minutes and serve.

185   Stir Fried Green Bean

Group 1
1/2 teaspoon salt
3 Tablespoons oil
1/4 teaspoon MSG
1 large garlic, diced

1/4 cup water
Group 2
16 oz green beans, ends trimmed, cut
  each into 3 sections

Combine Group 1 in pot, mix, and bring to boil at "Medium" heat setting. Reset heat to "Medium Low", cover and let simmer 20 minutes. Meanwhile, prepare Group 2 and set aside. Reset heat to "Medium", remove cover, and evaporate Group 1 to sizzling. Add Group 2, mix, cover, cook 3 minutes, and serve.

186   Baked Eggplant

Group 1
1 medium onion, diced
1 medium garlic, diced
1 small green bell pepper, diced
1 Tablespoon olive oil
1/2 teaspoon Italian seasoning
1/4 teaspoon pepper
1 large tomato, diced
1/2 teaspoon salt
1/2 cup water

Group 2
2 large eggplants, cut each into
  4 sections
3 Tablespoons margarine
Group 3
1 cup mozzarella cheese, grated
2 Tablespoons Parmesan cheese,
  grated
1/8 teaspoon cracked pepper

Combine Group 1 in 3-quart pot, mix well, and bring to boil at "Medium High" heat setting. Boil 1-2 minutes, cover, reset heat to "Medium Low", and simmer 30 minutes. Meanwhile, prepare eggplants and lay them side by side in a casserole dish. Spread margarine on eggplants. Set aside. Preheat oven at 325F. Remove cover and evaporate Group 1 to sizzling. Let self saute 2 minutes and pour evenly over eggplant sections. Sprinkle Group 3 evenly over the eggplants, bake in the oven for 45 minutes, and serve.

187   Eggplant in Yogurt Sauce**

Group 1
16 oz eggplant, cut into 16 pieces
1 medium fresh cayenne pepper
   diced
1/4 teaspoon cracked pepper
3/4 teaspoon salt
2 Tablespoons oil
1/4 teaspoon turmeric
1/2 cup water

Group 2
1/2 cup hot water
1 cup plain yogurt
1 cup sour cream
Group 3
1 Tablespoon oil
1 teaspoon black mustard seeds
4 medium dried cayenne pepper,
   cut each into halves

Combine Group 1 in pot. Mix well. Bring to a boil at "Medium High" heat setting. Reset heat to "Medium Low", cover, and simmer 30 minutes. Mix occasionally. Remove cover and evaporate to sizzling. Add Group 2, mix well, cover, and let simmer 5 minutes at "Low" heat setting. Meanwhile, fry Group 3 (see section 19b) until cayenne peppers turn dark brown color. Pour over eggplant and serve. Add 1/4 to 1/2 cup hot water to pot for more sauce, if needed. Mix, salt to taste, and serve.

---

188   Burmese Soybean Catsup**

Group 1
1 medium onion, diced
2 large garlic, diced
1 large tomato, diced
2 medium fresh cayenne
   peppers, whole
1 teaspoon paprika
1/4 teaspoon crushed
   red pepper

3 Tablespoons oil
1/2 cup water
no salt
Group 2
2 Tablespoons black bean in
   soybean oil
6 cilantro, cut each into
   4 sections

Combine Group 1 in 3-quart pot, mix well. Bring to boil at "Medium High" heat setting. Boil 1-2 minutes. Reset heat to "Medium Low", cover, and simmer 20 minutes. Mix occasionally. Remove cover and evaporate to sizzling. Add Group 2, cover, let self saute 2 minutes, and serve.

189   Fredrico Fettuccine

Group 1
1 medium garlic, diced
1/4 teaspoon pepper
1 Tablespoon olive oil
1/4 cup water
Group 2
2 (10-oz) cans, cream of
   mushroom soup
3/4 cup hot whole milk

Group 3
6 oz fettuccine
Group 4
2 Tablespoons margarine
Group 5
10 black olives, diced
2 Tablespoons sharp Cheddar
   cheese, grated
5 sprigs fresh basil, diced

Add to 3-quart pot, Group 1, mix, and bring to boil at "Medium" heat setting. Reset heat to medium Low", cover, and simmer 5 minutes. Mix well. Remove cover and evaporate to dryness with occasional mixing. Stir in Group 2, mix well, cover and let simmer 5 minutes at "Low" setting. Meanwhile, prepare Group 3 per instruction on its package, and transfer into a 3-quart serving bowl. Add Group 4 to Group 3 and toss well. Pour Group 1 on pasta, toss well, garnish with Group 5, and serve.

190   Vegetarian Chili Sauce*

Group 1
1 large onion, diced
2 large garlic, diced
2 large tomatoes, diced
1 medium bell pepper, diced
3 Tablespoons oil
1 teaspoon paprika
1 1/2 teaspoons cumin powder
1/2 teaspoon oregano

1 (16-oz) can, red kidney beans
   and liquid
1 teaspoon pepper
1/8 teaspoon red pepper powder
1 teaspoon Tabasco sauce
1 small fresh jalapeno pepper, diced
2 cups water
3/4 teaspoon salt

Combine Group 1 in pot. Mix well. Bring to boil at "Medium High" heat setting. Boil 1-2 minutes. Reset heat to "Medium Low", cover, and simmer 60-90 minutes. Mix occasionally. Add 1/4 to 1 cup hot water for more sauce if needed. Mix, salt to taste, and serve.

191 Spicy Tofu

Group 1
4 Tablespoons oil
1 (6-oz) cans, hot pickled
    mustard

1/4 cup water
Group 2
1 block fresh tofu,
    cut into 8 pieces

Combine Group 1 in pot, mix well, and evaporate to sizzling at "Medium High" heat setting. Reset heat to "Low", cover, and let self saute 5 minutes. Meanwhile, prepare Group 2 and set aside. Add Group 2, don't mix, cover, simmer 8 minutes, and serve.

192 Cajun Vegetable Stew*

Group 1
1 medium onion, diced
2 medium garlic, diced
1 teaspoon paprika
2 stalks celery, diced
3 sprigs parsley, fresh, chopped
1 large tomato, diced
1 medium fresh jalapeno pepper,
    diced
1/8 teaspoon cayenne pepper
    powder
1 Tablespoon gumbo file`

2 teaspoons Tabasco sauce
1 small green bell pepper, diced
1 cup water
1 teaspoon salt
4 Tablespoons oil
Group 2
1 small eggplant, cut into 8 pieces
2 cups hot water
Group 3
4 oz okra, whole or slices,
    frozen
1 Tablespoon gumbo file`

Combine Group 1 in pot. Mix well. Bring to boil at "Medium High" heat setting. Boil 1-2 minutes. Reset heat to "Medium Low", cover, and simmer 30 minutes. Mix occasionally. Remove cover and evaporate to sizzling. Reset heat to "Low", cover, and let self saute 5 minutes. Reset heat to "Medium", add Group 2, mix well, and bring to boil. Reset heat to "Medium Low" and simmer 20 minutes. Mix occasionally. Add Group 3, mix well, turn heat off, cover, let stand 2-3 minutes, and serve. Add 1/4 to 1 cup hot water for more sauce if needed. Mix, salt to taste, and serve.

193   Chana Rice Casserole

Group 1
1/2 cup chana dahl

Group 2
1 medium garlic, diced
1 small bay leaf
1 teaspoon ginger, diced
1 small onion, diced
1/4 teaspoon turmeric
2 1/2 cups water

1 (3-in) cinnamon stick
1/2 teaspoon cracked pepper
4 cloves
4 Tablespoons margarine
1 teaspoon salt

Group 3
5 cups rice, cooked
1/4 cup hot milk, whole

Wash Group 1 per section 13g (don't soak). Combine Groups 1 and 2 in pot, mix well, and bring to boil at "Medium High" heat setting. Boil 1-2 minutes. Reset heat to "Medium Low", cover, and simmer 45 minutes. Meanwhile, cook 3 cups extra long grain rice per section 23b. Reset heat to "Medium", remove cover, and evaporate Groups 1 and 2 to sizzling. Turn heat off. Add Group 3 to Groups 1 and 2, mix well, seal pot (see section 16a), bake 50 minutes at 325F, and serve.

194   Eggplant Supreme

Group 1
4 large eggs

Group 2
1 medium onion, diced
1 large garlic, diced
1 cup celery, diced
1 small green bell pepper, diced
1 medium tomato, diced
1 (6-oz) can, tomato paste
2 teaspoons sugar
1/2 teaspoon salt
1/2 teaspoon thyme flakes

1 cup water
2 Tablespoons olive oil
1/4 teaspoon pepper

Group 3
1 large eggplant, cut into 4 sections,
    lengthwise

Group 4
1/2 cup mozzarella cheese,
    shredded
2 Tablespoons Parmesan cheese,
    grated

Add Group 1 to 2-quart pot, boil, slice each egg into 4 slices, and set aside (see section 17f). Combine Group 2 in a 3-quart pot, mix well, and bring to boil at "Medium" heat setting. Boil 1-2 minutes, cover, and simmer 20 minutes. Mix occasionally. Meanwhile, prepare Group 3 in a 3-quart casserole bowl (with cover) and set aside. Preheat oven at 325F. Remove cover, evaporate Group 2 to sizzling, and pour over Group 3. Place Group 1 slices evenly over Group 2 sauce and sprinkle Group 4 evenly over the eggs. Cover the bowl, bake 45 minutes, and serve.

195　　Curried Potato in Yogurt Sauce**

Group 1
3 large potatoes, with skin,
　　cut each into 8 sections
Group 2
1/2 cup water
1 medium onion, diced
2 large garlic, diced
1 Tablespoon ginger, diced
2 medium fresh jalapeno peppers,
　　diced
1/3 teaspoon turmeric
1 teaspoon salt

4 Tablespoons oil
Group 3
1 cup plain yogurt
1/2 cup sour cream
2 Tablespoons fresh lemon juice
Group 4
1 Tablespoon mustard oil
Group 5
2 teaspoons black mustard seeds
Group 6
6 fresh curry leaves
2 dried red pepper, cut into halves

Add to 3-quart pot, Group 1. Add water to potatoes just enough to cover them. Bring to boil at "Medium High" heat setting. Boil 1-2 minutes, reset heat to "Medium Low", and simmer 15-20 minutes. Drain potatoes in colander and set aside Combine Group 2 in 4-quart pot, mix well, and bring to boil at "Medium High" heat setting. Boil 1-2 minutes. Reset heat to "Medium Low", cover, and simmer 20 minutes. Mix occasionally. Remove cover and evaporate to sizzling. Stir in Group 3, add Group 1, mix well, cover, and turn heat off. Meanwhile, fry Groups 5 and 6 in Group 4 (see section 19b), pour into Group 2, mix well, and serve.

196   Bitter Melon Country Style**

Group 1
1/8 teaspoon turmeric
1 medium onion, diced
2 large garlic, diced
1 medium tomato, diced
2 medium fresh cayenne
   peppers, whole
1/4 teaspoon crushed
   red pepper

1 teaspoon paprika
3 Tablespoons oil
1/4 teaspoon salt
1/2 cup water
Group 2
1/2 cup hot water
8 sprigs cilantro, cut in halves
2 large bitter melons,
   1/2-in slices

Add to 4-quart pot Group 1, mix well, bring to boil at "Medium High" heat setting. Boil 1-2 minutes. Reset heat to "Medium Low", mix, cover, and simmer 30 minutes. Meanwhile, prepare Group 2 vegetables and set aside. Remove cover, mix, and evaporate Group 1 to sizzling. Cover and let self saute 2 minutes. Reset heat to "Medium", add Group 2, mix well and bring to boil. Boil 1-2 minutes, reset heat to "Medium Low", cover, simmer 15 minutes, and serve. Add 1/4 to 1 cup hot water to pot for more sauce, if needed. Mix, salt to taste, and serve.

197   Vegetable Gumbo*

Group 1
3 Tablespoons oil
1 medium onion, diced
1 teaspoon paprika
2 medium garlic, diced
1 stalk celery, diced
2 large tomatoes, diced
1 medium fresh jalapeno
   peper, diced
3 sprigs parsley, diced
1 Tablespoon gumbo file`
1 small bell pepper, diced
1/4 teaspoon pepper

1 teaspoon salt
1/8 teaspoon cayenne pepper
   powder
1/2 cup water
Group 2
1 medium potato, cut into
   8 sections
   2 cups hot water
1 small zucchini, cut into 8 sections
Group 3
4 oz okra, whole or sectioned
1 Tablespoon gumbo file`

Combine Group 1 in pot. Mix well. Bring to boil at "Medium High" heat setting. Boil 1-2 minutes. Reset heat to "Medium Low", cover, and simmer 30 minutes. Mix occasionally. Remove cover and evaporate to sizzling. Reset heat to "Low", cover, and let self saute 5 minutes, mixing occasionally. Reset heat to "Medium", add Group 2, mix well, and bring to boil. Reset heat to "Medium Low" and simmer 20 more minutes. Mix occasionally. Add Group 3, mix well, cover, simmer 2-3 minutes, and serve. Add 1/4 to 1 cup hot water for more sauce if needed. Mix, salt to taste, and serve.

---

198   Potato Fritter on Cream Sauce

Group 1
1 medium potato, shredded
1 small onion, diced

Group 2
1 cup flour
2 teaspoons baking powder
2 teaspoons sugar
1/4 teaspoon MSG
1 teaspoon salt
1 teaspoon pepper

Group 3
2-3 Tablespoons water

Group 4
4 cups oil

Group 5
1 Tablespoon margarine
1/2 cup hot whole
   milk
2 (10-oz.) cans, cream of
   mushroom soup

Group 6
1 Tablespoon Parmesan cheese,
   grated

Shred potato with a shredder, combine with diced onion in 2-quart bowl, and set aside. Mix Group 2 well in 3-cup bowl. Meanwhile, heat Group 4 in 3-quart pot at "Medium" heat setting. Add one-half of Group 2 mixture to Group 1, mix well, add Group 3, mix well, and set aside. Reset heat for Group 4 between "Medium" and "Medium Low" setting. Scoop 1 Tablespoon of Group 1, roll in Group 2 mix, make a thin patty, and slide into Group 4 and fry until patty turns to tan color. Remove fried patty and drain on paper. Repeat same with the rest of the patties. Set them aside. Meanwhile, Combine Group 5 and mix well to disperse soup mix in 3-cup pot. Heat at "Medium" setting 3 minutes, mix often, pour over fried patties, garnish with Group 6, and serve.

199   Pepper Pizza

Group 1
2 (7-oz) flour packages,
    premixed for pizza
Group 2
2 Tablespoons corn oil
Group 3
12 oz pizza sauce
Group 4
1/4 teaspoon pepper
1 teaspoon garlic powder
1/4 teaspoon Italian seasoning
1/8 teaspoon salt
Group 5
1/2 cup cheese from pizza
    packages

1/2 cup mozzarella/provolone/
    Parmesan cheeses, premixed
Group 6
3 teaspoons cracked peppercorn
10 black olives, cut into halves
Group 7
1/4 teaspoon Italian seasoning
1/2 cup mozzarella/provolone/
    Parmesan cheeses, premixed
Group 8
2 Tablespoons sharp Cheddar
    cheese
1 Tablespoon Parmesan cheese,
    grated

Mix and raise crust mix (Group 1) per instruction on pizza package. Make pie crust and dress the pie as described in section 8 using the ingredient groups from this recipe. Bake per section 16b. Garnish with Group 8, section pizza, and serve.

200   Spicy Pink Lentil Soup*

Group 1
1 cup pink lentil
3 cups water
Group 2
1/8 teaspoon turmeric
1 teaspoon salt
1 medium fresh cayenne
    pepper, diced
Group 3
2 Tablespoons oil

1 large garlic, diced
2 teaspoons ginger, diced
1 medium onion, diced
Group 4
1 teaspoon cumin powder
2 teaspoons coriander powder
Group 5
1 medium dried red pepper,
    cut into halves

Wash pink lentil per section 13g. Combine Groups 1 and 2 in pot, mix well, and bring to boil at "Medium High" heat setting. Boil 1-2 minutes. Reset heat to "Medium Low" and simmer 30 minutes. Mix occasionally. Skimming white foam from boiling lentil is optional. Meanwhile, combine Group 3 in 2-cup pot, heat at "Medium High", and fry with frequent mixing until garlic starts to turn slightly tan color (see section 19j). Reset heat to "Medium Low", add to Group 3, Group 4 and fry 1 more minute. Add Group 5 to Groups 3 and 4 and continue frying until red pepper turns lightly brown. Remove pot from stove and pour fried ingredients (Groups 3, 4, and 5) into Groups 1 and 2, mix, and serve. Add 1/4 to 1 cup hot water if more gravy is desired, mix well, salt to taste, and serve.

---

201   Burmese Pink Lentil*

Group 1
1 cup pink lentil

Group 2
3 cups water
2 teaspoons ginger, diced
1/8 teaspoon turmeric
1/2 teaspoon salt
1 medium fresh cayenne
   pepper, diced

Group 3
1 oz bean sticks, cut in halves
8 curry leaves, fresh
1/8 teaspoon MSG

Group 4
2 Tablespoons oil
1 large garlic, diced
1 small onion, diced

Wash Group 1 per section 13g and then combine with Group 2 in pot, mix well, and bring to boil at "Medium High" heat setting. Boil 1-2 minutes. Reset heat to "Medium Low" and simmer 30 minutes. Mix occasionally. Skimming white foam from boiling lentil is optional. Add Group 3, cover, and simmer 15 more minutes. Meanwhile, combine Group 4 in 2-cup pot, heat at "Medium High", and fry with frequent mixing until garlic starts to get slightly tan color (see section 19g). Remove Group 4 from stove and pour entire content into Groups 1, 2, and 3, mix, and serve. Add 1/4 to 1 cup hot water if more gravy is desired, mix well, salt to taste, and serve.

202   Curried Sour Bamboo Shoots

Group 1
1 medium onion, diced
1 large garlic, diced
1 teaspoon ginger, diced
1 medium tomato, diced
1/8 teaspoon turmeric
1 teaspoon paprika
1 Tablespoon Madras curry
   powder

3 Tablespoons oil
1/2 cup water
no salt
Group 2
1 1/2 cups hot water
2 cups sliced sour bamboo shoots
1 teaspoon garam masala
1 medium fresh cayenne pepper,
   whole

Combine Group 1 in pot, mix well, and bring to boil at "Medium High" heat setting. Boil 1-2 minutes, cover, reset heat to "Medium Low", and simmer 20 minutes. Remove cover and evaporate to sizzling. Let self saute 2 minutes, reset heat to "Medium", add Group 2, and mix well. Bring to boil, boil 1-2 minutes, reset heat to :Medium Low", cover, simmer 15 minutes, and serve. Add 1/4 to 1/2 cup hot water to pot for more sauce, if needed. Mix, salt to taste, and serve.

203   Broccoli Delight*

Group 1
1 small onion, diced
1 small garlic, diced
3 Tablespoons margarine
1 large tomato, diced
3/4 teaspoon salt
1/2 teaspoon paprika
1/4 teaspoon oregano
1/4 teaspoon parsley flakes
1 small fresh jalapeno pepper,
   diced

1/4 teaspoon cracked pepper
1/2 teaspoon sugar
1/2 cup water
Group 2
2 hard boiled eggs, 1/2-in slices
Group 3
3 cups water .
2 stalks broccoli, cut into florets
Group 4
2 Tablespoons Parmesan cheese,
   grated

Combine Group 1 in pot. Mix well. Bring to boil at "Medium" heat setting. Boil 1-2 minutes. Reset heat to "Medium Low", cover, and simmer 30 minutes. Mix occasionally. Meanwhile, prepare Group 2 (see section 17f), cut into 1/2-in slices and set aside. Add to 2-quart pot Group 3, boil 2-3 minutes, drain in colander, put in 3-quart serving bowl, and set aside. Reset heat to "Medium". Remove cover and evaporate Group 1 to sizzling. Pour Group 1 sauce evenly over Group 3. Spread Group 2 slices over Group 1 sauce, garnish with Group 4, and serve.

---

204   Patrick's Pizza*

Group 1
2 (7-oz) flour packages,
    premixed for pizza
Group 2
2 Tablespoons corn   oil
Group 3
12 oz pizza sauce
Group 4
1/4 teaspoon Italian seasoning
1/4 teaspoon crushed red pepper
1/4 teaspoon cracked pepper
1 teaspoon garlic powder
1/8 teaspoon salt
Group 5
1/2 cup mozzarella/provolone/
    Parmesan cheeses,
    premixed

1/2 cup cheese from pizza
    packages
Group 6
1/2 small bell pepper, diced
10 black olives, cut in halves
1 small onion, diced
5 fresh mushrooms, each
    quartered
1 large pickled hot banana
    pepper, diced
Group 7
1/4 teaspoon Italian seasoning
1/2 cup mozzarella/provolone/
    /Parmesan cheeses, premixed
Group 8
2 Tablespoons sharp Cheddar
    cheese

Mix and raise crust mix (Group 1) per instruction on pizza package. Make pie crust and dress the pie as described in section 8 using the ingredient groups from this recipe. Bake per section 16b. Garnish with Group 8, section pizza, and serve.

205   Lentil and Vegetable Soup*

Group 1
1 cup pink lentil
Group 2
3 cups water
1/4 teaspoon turmeric
1 large potato, with skin, cut into
   8 sections
1 small tomato, diced
1 small zucchini, peeled and cut
   into 1-in slices

1 teaspoon salt
8 sprigs cilantro, diced
Group 3
3 Tablespoons oil
1 small onion, diced
2 teaspoons ginger, diced
1 large garlic, diced
Group 4
1 Tablespoon garam masala
3 medium dried whole red peppers

Wash Group 1 per section 13g. Combine Groups 1 and 2 in pot, mix well, and bring to boil at "Medium High" heat setting. Boil 1-2 minutes. Reset heat to "Medium Low" and simmer 30 minutes. Mix occasionally. Skimming white foam from boiling lentil is optional. Meanwhile, combine Group 3 in 2-cup pot, heat at "Medium" setting, and fry with frequent mixing until garlic starts to get slightly tan color (see section 19j). Reset heat to "Medium Low", add Group 4, and fry with mixing until cayenne pepper turns lightly brown. Remove pot from stove and pour contents into Groups 1 and 2, mix, and serve. Add 1/4 to 1 cup hot water if more gravy is desired, mix well, salt to taste, and serve.

206   Vegetarian Cream of Asparagus

Group 1
2 Tablespoons margarine
1 medium onion , diced
1 teaspoon sugar
1/4 teaspoon pepper
1/4 cup water
Group 2
1/4 cup hot water
18 stalks asparagus, tender parts
   only, each quartered

Group 3
2 (10-oz) cans, cream of asparagus
   soup
1 cup hot whole milk
Group 4
1 Tablespoon flour
Group 5
1/4 cup plain yogurt
1/2 cup sour cream

Combine Group 1 in pot. Mix well. Bring to boil at "Medium High" heat setting. Boil 1-2 minutes. Reset heat to "Medium Low", cover, and simmer 10-15 minutes. Mix occasionally. Meanwhile, prepare asparagus and set aside. Combine Group 3 and mix to disperse the soup well. Set aside. Remove cover and evaporate Group 1 to sizzling. Add Group 4 into sizzling margarine. Let self saute 3 minutes mixing occasionally. Reset heat to "Medium". Stir in Groups 2 and 3, mix well, cover, and simmer 5 more minutes. Add Group 5, mix, let simmer 3 more minutes, and serve. Add 1/4 to 1/2 cup hot water to pot for more sauce, if needed. Mix, salt to taste, and serve.

---

207   Casablanca Chana*

Group 1
1 cup chana dahl

1 teaspoon salt

Group 2

Group 3

3 cups water

2 Tablespoons oil

2 large garlic, diced

2 teaspoons black mustard seeds

2 teaspoons ginger, diced

8 fresh curry leaves

1 medium onion, diced

2 medium dried red peppers,

1/4 teaspoon turmeric

    cut in halves

Wash Group 1 per section 13g (don't soak). Combine Groups 2 and 1 in pot, mix well, bring to boil at "medium High" heat setting. Boil 1-2 minutes. Skimming white foam from boiling chana is optional. Reset heat to "Medium Low", cover, and simmer 90 minutes. Mix occasionally. Fry Group 3 (see section 19b), pour entire content into Group 1, mix, and serve. Add 1/4 to 1 cup hot water if more gravy is desired, mix well, salt to taste, and serve.

2.
PREPARING
AND
COOKING
TECHNIQUES

Tomato, *Lycopersicum esculentum*

The objective of this chapter is three fold. First is to describe the techniques for preparing ingredients. Second is to describe mechanics of the cooking techniques. Third is to promote safety awareness for more enjoyment and productive cooking.

Most preparing and cooking techniques details are described in this chapter. They include the techniques for trimming, cutting, and washing ingredients, mixing batter and corn starch mixtures, cooking rice, baking casseroles, simmer-sauteing, and so forth. Safety cautions are indicated when necessary. The techniques are intended to be used along with the cooking instructions described in each recipe; thus they are described for universal usage. For ready referencing the technique topics are arranged in alphabetical order and each is assigned with a unique number. The sub-techniques are assigned with the lowercase alphabets. For example, reference to making shrimp broth is cited as "see section 17c" in the recipes. Although the descriptions may be trivial to some readers, they could be essential for the beginners to grasp the elements of personal safety and reproducibility of the recipes. It is imperative that this chapter be at least skimmed through before the techniques are used.

Ingredient Preparations

Detailed preparation procedures for the ingredients, such as meats, herbs, vegetables, and so forth used in the recipes are described in the following sections.

1. Cans. Empty the can's content into a bowl or the pot. After emptying, scrape out the residual food into the pot, rinse the remaining contents with hot water into the pot unless specified otherwise in recipes.

2. Corn Starch, Mixture. Add the corn starch mixture (given in recipes for making the gravy) to 1-cup bowl. Add 2 Tablespoons cold water and disperse the mixture with a metal teaspoon scrubbing the mixture mass against the sides of the bowl with the bottom part of the teaspoon. Use 2 Tablespoons water at a time as the mixing progresses. Continue dispersing until the remaining water given in the recipe (usually 1/4 cup) is used. Mix until all the ingredients in the mixture are dispersed thoroughly to a smooth mixture. Set aside. Remix before use. See 20a for making corn starch gravy.

3. Fish. In most cases, fish fillets or nuggets are used to simplify cleaning or filleting the fish. The fillets are either used as whole or sliced into bite-size pieces and rinsed in cold tap water, unless specified otherwise in recipes.

    a. Catfish: Most farm raised channel catfish produce unusual amounts of broken down globular proteins on boiling. They are gelatinous and impart glutinous texture to the gravy. Aroma and flavor of the catfish variety is recognizably different from the common catfish variety most Asians are familiar with. However, when most of the gelatinous substances are removed, the flavor of the channel variety resembles closer to the Asian catfish. Most of the gelatinous materials are easily removed by preboiling the catfish and using it for cooking Asian catfish dishes. It may be noteworthy that most of the gelatinous substances are originated from the belly (catfish nuggets) and head parts of the catfish. To remove the gelatinous materials from the catfish meat, fillets or steak slices (with or without bones, skin, and head), cut to desired shape or sizes, may be boiled at "Medium High" heat setting for 10-15 minutes. The fish pieces are then removed from the boiling and used. The liquid is discarded.

4. Flour, Batter Mixture.

This basic mixture was developed myself to give you crispy, crunchy, and tasty coatings on vegetarian and non-vegetarian foods. It contains neither egg nor milk nor their derivatives. This batter will produce crusts with excellent AFTT, if not better than others, professional or otherwise. The basic mixture may be modified in recipes by adding herbs and spices to the mixture.

    Use the amounts of ingredients as given in recipes. Combine flour, baking powder, salt, black pepper, sugar, and MSG. Mix well. Set aside (Bowl 1). Measure the amount of the mixture given in recipes from Bowl 1 and disperse in cold water. Set aside (Bowl 2). In another bowl add flour. Set aside (Bowl 3).

    Most important thing about coating the batter on foods is to have the food surfaces dried. Otherwise, the batter crust will not adhere to the surfaces. Thus, it is necessary to wipe the food surfaces dry with paper towel and roll coat in the flour in Bowl 3. The dried coated food is then, dipped in Bowl 2, removed, and rolled coated in Bowl 1. The batter coated food is then deep fried per section 19a.

5. Marinating.

    a. Meat: Combine Group 1 ingredients given in recipes in an electric blender and blend for 30 seconds. Add to a double-layered nested

1-gallon plastic bags, blended Group 1 mixture. Add Group 2, close tightly, and mix well. Set aside for 3 to 4 hours at room temperature. Remove meat strips from the marinade. Cook as described in sections 21a, 21b, or 21c. Garnish with Group 3 and serve.

If marination is stored in refrigerator overnight, turn over the bag occasionally during the storage. Remove the bag from refrigerator and set aside at room temperature for 1 to 2 hours before cooking. Cook as described in sections 21a, 21b, or 21c. Garnish with Group 3 and serve.

b. Heated meat: Add to 3-quart pot, 1 quart water and bring it to a boil. Meanwhile, combine Group 1 ingredients given in recipes and blend in an electric blender for 1/2 minute. Add to a double-layered nested 1-gallon plastic bags, blended Group 1 mixture, and set aside. Add Group 2 (meat) to the boiling water. Boil 3-5 minutes. Remove meat, drain well, and add to Group 1 marinade mixture immediately. Mix well, close tightly, and set aside at room temperature at least 2 hours. Turn over the bag occasionally. Cook as described in sections 21a, 21b, or 21c. Garnish with Group 3 and serve.

6. Meat. All meat and poultry should be checked for their freshness before buying. Visual inspection for color changes and slimy liquid formation on the meat surfaces are insufficient. Punch a hole through the cellophane wrapping at any of the empty spaces in the package and take a quick sniff through the hole. Take the package if you don't detect any foul or rancid smell. If the content is not fresh return the package to the meat manager. Some fresh fish, meat, poultry, seafood, and shrimp displayed in see-through cases on crushed ice are intended to project unequivocal freshness of the items on the customer's mind. Our family had several unpleasant experiences with such items. So, have the salesperson let you smell the item of your choice for the freshness before the person weighs or custom dresses the items. See also "Smelling and Tasting", page 9. Because simmer-saute is limited to preparing stews, soups, stir fries, and casseroles, all cuts (shank, brisket, heel of round, etc.) of meat may also be used. Similarly, breast, leg, thigh, whole fryer, liver, and gizzard parts of chicken may be used with the simmer-saute cooking. The meat is rinsed with cold water to remove chemical preservatives and additives, if any. The meat is then drained. The rinsing is done in the cooking pot to keep dirty dishes to a minimum.

a. Beef: A boneless lean piece of beef is trimmed of its removable fat and sliced into 1 to 1 1/2 inch wide strips. Each strip is then either cut into 1 to 1 1/2 inch cubes or sliced into 1/4-inch slices, unless specified otherwise in recipes.

b. Chicken: Most recipes employ boned and skinned chicken white meat. They are readily available in most grocery stores. A boneless piece of white skinless meat is trimmed of its fat and sliced into 1 to 1 1/2 inch wide strips. Each strip is either cut into 1 to 1 1/2 inch cubes or sliced into 1/4-inch slices, unless specified otherwise in recipes.

c. disjointing: If a recipe uses disjointed chicken thighs/legs, the pieces may be disjointed and boned using the techniques described below. The effort avoids introducing bone splinters in the dish. Chopping the leg quarters through the bones could crush the bones into · small pieces at the chopping point and could produce sharp bone splinters in your chicken dishes.

To disjoint leg/thigh from the back bone first skin the chicken parts per section 6d. Cut through the meat at both sides of the thigh towards the joint. Hold the thigh/leg in one hand and the back bone in the other hand. The joint is placed in between your thumbs. Your remaining fingers from each hand should be pointing towards you. Then, bend the parts up in opposite directions while pressing the joint with both thumbs and dislocate the joint. Cut the remaining meat, if any, to free the thigh/leg from the back bone.

Separate the leg from the thigh by cutting through the joint where the parts are connected. You may locate the joint by holding the leg and the thigh with paper towels in each of your hands and flexing the parts at the joint and locate where the parts flex. This is the spot where you want to cut through to separate the parts. Often, you may not be able to cut through it if you miss the joint. In such case, after cutting at the joint, stretch the parts away from each other until the joint becomes visible and then cut through the joint. If you encounter some difficulty at your first attempt try again. Soon you will gain dexterity for disjointing at the joints. Similarly, you can also locate the joint at the base of the wing where it is connected to the breast, to cut through and separate the wing from the breast. The disjointed pieces may be used as they are.

d. skinning: The skin is removed by holding the skin in one hand with a paper towel and the part is held at the same place in the other hand with another paper towel. The skin is then peeled off by pulling the skin and the meat in opposite directions. Some recipes call for use of legs, thighs, breast, and wings. Most grocers carry chicken leg quarters and breasts.

e. types: Chicken of bantam varieties has tighter or tougher meat texture and tastes different. It may require 75-120 minutes

162

of cooking to make the meat tender. In Asia, bantam chicken are commonly used.

f. Chops, lamb, pork: Eight chops of any cuts are used as they are, unless specified otherwise in recipes.

g. Lamb: The piece of any lean cut of meat is trimmed of removable fat and sliced into 1 to 1 1/2 inch wide strips. Each strip is either cut into 1 to 1 1/2 inch cubes for stewing or sliced into 1/4-in thick slices, unless specified otherwise in recipes.

h. Pork: Slice a boneless lean piece of meat into 1 to 1 1/2 inch wide strips; cut each strip into 1 to 1 1/2-inch cubes or 1/4-inch slices, unless specified otherwise in recipes. All pork recipes use mostly fresh ham cuts because they are lean and contain less marbled fat. The meat is lean after skin and fat layers are removed. Use of butts and spare ribs are limited because fat on the cuts and their marbled fat are extremely difficult to trim. If one must use the cuts trim removable fat, boil the meat pieces for 10 minutes, and cool them down overnight in refrigerator or leaving them outside during winter days. The next day skim off the white frozen solid pieces, discard, and use the meat for your cooking.

i. Turkey: The leftover meat is used for making a variety of dishes. The meat is trimmed from the leftover carcass, such as breast, legs, and thighs. The parts are trimmed of fat and skin. Then, the meat is either carved from the parts with a sharp paring knife or peeled off by hand. The meat is then cut into bite-size pieces for use in your cooking. The wings, back bones, and neck bones may be used for making soups or broth.

7. Oil. Peanut, corn, or olive oil is used, unless specified otherwise. The amount of oil used normally in simmer-saute cooking, 3-5 Tablespoons, may seem excessive in relation to some low-fat cooking. The oil is needed for simmer-sauteing the ingredients in oil. However, if your dish has thick sediments of onion, tomato, etc., it may require more oil than I have indicated. But after cooking, if you prefer, you may serve the dish with as little oil as you wish by removing some of it. See also Purposes of Oil and Water in Chapter 4, "Simmer-Saute".

8. Pizza Dressing. Paint with Group 2 (ingredients given in recipes) evenly on the floor of pizza pan (16-inch diameter). Place Group 1 at the center of the painted pan. Flatten the dough by pressing it outward into a circular shape or any other shape. Patch any holes formed during spreading. Mix Group 3 and pour over the crust moving in circular motion as the sauce is poured. Hold the pan in two hands and shake the pan gently and/or rotate the pan tilting at a small angle to let the sauce flow over the blank spots. Sprinkle Group 4. Sprinkle Group 5. Place Group 6 evenly spaced. Sprinkle Group 7 and bake (see section 16b).

9. Rice. Extra long grain, long grain, precooked instant, jasmine, and brown rice may used, unless specified otherwise in recipes. Cook per instruction on the containers or per section 23b or use an automatic rice cooker. When jasmine rice is used, cook with about 10 percent less water than the other rice would require. There are several types of rice on the market today, including uncooked wild rice and brown rice. Some uncooked rice is enriched or fortified with vitamins such as vitamin A, Bs, C, and minerals. There are some special rice such as basmati, jasmine, sticky rice (black and white), and sweet rice. Saffron rice casseroles and pilafs (meat, vegetable or meat/vegetable) are prepared preferably with extra long grain or basmati rice. There are several precooked instant rice (brown rice, extra long grain rice, pilafs, wild rice, etc.) available.

10. Seafood. Oysters and clams are known to contain sand. Wash each piece under running tap water, scraping the sand off from in-between places. The juices may be saved for other uses by carefully decanting them into a bowl without disturbing the sand sediments settling on the floor of the containers.

11. Shrimp. Packaged frozen cooked shrimp may be used if you neither have the time nor the desire to clean shrimp. However, most of the water soluble nutrients and flavors of shrimp are removed during cooking for the packaging. Thus, shrimp will be more flavorful to use fresh and dress for yourself. To clean shrimp, peel shell, pluck legs, pull off heads and tails, and, peel off the veins. Then, rinse them in cold water and use whole or cut to sizes per recipes.

12. Spices. Black pepper is simply cited as pepper in the recipes. The black pepper, cayenne pepper, paprika, red pepper, turmeric, and white pepper are used in powder form, unless specified otherwise in recipes. In the case of curry, it is specified as curry or curry powder or curry mix.

13 Vegetables, Fresh. The vegetables in this section are grouped according to their similarity in the way I prepare them for cooking. Vegetables are washed in some cases before and in other cases after trimming, culling, and cutting. The washing is essential to rid of any residual pesticides and other chemicals for the consumption. After the rinsing or washing it is important to drain the vegetables well. Otherwise, you may be inadvertently introducing significant amount of water in your cooking in cases with the leafy vegetables, such as spinach, lettuce, bok choy, etc. Consequently, additional time and efforts will be needed to rid of the excess water to obtain the intended texture of your dish. Avoid unnecessary setting aside of vegetables soaked in water, peeled or otherwise, to prevent the lost of water soluble nutrients (minerals, vitamins, trace metals, etc.). Rinse the peeled vegetables (cucumber, potato, radish, etc.) just before cooking.

a. **Bean sprout, cilantro (or coriander leaves or Chinese parsley), curry leaves, mint leaves, spinach:** Put in an 8-quart pot filled with four quarts water, Scrub each leaf in the water to remove sand. Remove the vegetables by lifting them out from the water, and set aside in colander. Discard used water, rinse the pot free of sand, refill with water and repeat scrubbing the leaves in the clean water. Repeat the scrubbing at least one more time.

b. **Bitter gourd (or bitter melon), Bottle gourd (or bu-thee), cucumber, zucchini:** Trim both ends and cut along its vertical axis into two equal sections. Split each section into halves, lengthwise. Scrape out its core and seeds from each section. With bitter melon, each section is cut into 1/2-inch slices, widthwise, and the sections are used with skin. With others, each section is peeled and cut widthwise into 1/2-inch slices, unless specified otherwise in recipes. Rinse the slices just before use.

c. **Bok choy (or white mustard), celery, mustard green:** Detach each leave with its stem from the stalk. Wash them under running cold tap water by scrubbing each leaf and stem. Slice each into 1/2-inch slices, unless specified otherwise. Drain well in a colander.

d. **Broccoli, cauliflower:** Cut the lower end of the stem at about where the cluster of florets end. Cut the head into bite-size florets. Wash by dipping the florets in cold water several times, and drain well in a colander.

e. **Cabbage:** Peel one or two outermost layers of the leaves. Wash the head under running cold tap water and cut into 1/4-inch slices or four sections or as required in the recipes.

f. **Carrot, daikon (or Asian white radish), potato, radish (white):** Cut off 1/4 inch at each end, peel, wash, and cut into 1/4-inch slices, unless specified otherwise in recipes.

    g. Chana dahl, pink lentil, split peas (green or yellow): Wash in a 1-quart bowl. Drain after each washing. Repeat washing until water is clear (3 or 4 times). Soak 1 hour before use in the bowl unless specified otherwise in recipes.

    h. Eggplant, green beans, okra, tomato: Wash, cut off 1/4 inch at each end, and cut into 1/4-inch slices or cut into 2, 4 or 8 sections or as required in the recipes. Eggplant and tomato may be used with or without skin and seeds.

    i. Ginger, garlic, onion: They are to be peeled and diced or chopped or minced or pounded. Peel onion and remove residual stem from the onion by cutting it into halves along its vertical axis and wedging out the stem sections. Peeled and diced ginger is measured in teaspoon or Tablespoon, unless specified otherwise in recipes.
CAUTION: To peel garlic don't crush garlic by laying chef's knife or cleaver blade surface flat on the garlic clove and pounding on the blade surface with your fist as seen on TV shows, cookbooks, etc. The techniques are unsafe and uncalled for. There are many other safe alternatives such as pounding with a meat tenderizer. Accidents are unpredictable.

    j. Lemon/lime: Cut into halves widthwise. Squeeze the juice, remove seeds, and use, unless specified otherwise.

    k. Peppers (fresh), banana (fresh or pickled), bell (or green or red), cayenne (or red pepper), jalapeno: Hold the peppers with paper towel. Remove stem, wash, and use whole or diced and with or without seeds, unless specified otherwise. With dried cayenne or red pepper, it may be broken into halves or quarters after removing the stem.
CAUTION: Except for the bell pepper, handle the rest with care. Don't touch or rub your eyes or lips with your hands after touching them. They may cause painful burns to your eyes or lips. Wash your hands well with water after touching them.

    l. Scallion, chive: Trimmed or culled damaged or decayed parts, washed, and sectioned into 1/4 inch pieces, unless specified otherwise in recipes.

    m. Tamarind: Use one-half of a golf ball size tamarind. Add tamarind in a 2-cup bowl, add 1/2 cup hot water, and soak for 10-15 minutes. Disperse tamarind in the water, mix, remove the tamarind pulp, and use the juice.

14. Vegetables, Frozen. Most frozen vegetables - broccoli, carrot, corn, lima bean, okra, and so forth - are all packaged trimmed, washed, cut to bite-sizes, and ready to use. However, the frozen packages may require breaking them into smaller pieces and rinsing lightly under running tap water to rid of freezer odor. The pieces may be used without further thawing in your cooking.

15. Water and Broth, Hot. It is required in the recipes to sustain boiling and simmering tempos. If cold water is substituted, the cooking time will be prolonged since it will take additional time to heat the water. Broth, bouillon, and water are interchangeable under emergency situations. However, when bouillon are used as substitutes 1/4 teaspoon salt may have to be reduced from the recipes for every Tablespoon of bouillon substituted.

Cooking Techniques

Detailed mechanics of the cooking techniques used in this cookbook are described in this section.

16. Baking.

a. Casserole: Preheat oven at the temperature specified in the recipes. Stir in the ingredients. Mix well. Turn stove off. Remove pot from the stove. Seal the pot with aluminum foil by placing the foil over the pot then putting the cover snugly over the foil and folding down the edges against the side of the pot. Place the sealed pot in the oven and bake for the duration per recipe. Do not break the seal before the baking is completed unless specified otherwise in the recipe.

CAUTION: Always use gloves or pot holders when handling hot casserole pots and dishes.

b. Pizza: Preheat oven at 375F. Place pizza on the lowest oven shelf and bake 10 minutes uninterrupted. Put 1 to 2 Tablespoons oil on the pan around the outer edges of the dough. Reset the oven heat at 350F. Bake additional 5 to 10 minutes and check again. Check for the coloration at the pizza fringes. The edges should start to get light tan color. The mozzarella cheese should be white and melted. Otherwise, continue with the baking and check every 2 to 3 minutes from that point on. Remove pizza, garnish per recipe, section, and serve.

NOTE: Due to the differences in heating characteristics of the ovens no exact baking time is given in the technique.

17. Boiling.

a. Bones, beef/chicken/pork/seafood/shrimp: Beef, chicken, and pork bones and the stocks resulted from cooking seafood and shrimp are commonly used by restaurants for brewing the broths. The stocks are used for creating rich and robust flavors in the meat and seafood dishes (such as casseroles, sauces, soups, stews, and stir fries). The stocks are used in place of water in their cooking. Most restaurants have large heavy pots filled with bones and water brewing all day in their kitchens so that they can have ready and abundant supply of the broths. Neck bones and other bones leftover after carving out the meat are commonly used for brewing the beef and pork broths. Chicken breast, neck, and back bones are brewed for making chicken broths. For casual home cooking it may not be practical to brew bones all day in your kitchen. However, you may use the bones as a CI in your cooking and remove them after the cooking. You may make the broths as described below when you have time and feel like making them. The broths may be stored or frozen for later use.

Any of the meat broths (beef, chicken, or pork) may be substituted for the others. Alternatively beef or chicken bouillon may be substituted for the broths. Similarly, seafood and shrimp broths are interchangeable. Water may be used as a last resort substitute for any of the broths.

b. beef/pork broths: To prepare 4 to 5 cups beef or pork broth from neck bones and soup bones trim removable fat from the bones (3 pounds) and boil with 6 to 8 cups water in 6-quart pots and boil for 3 or more hours. Add hot water to compensate evaporation during brewing. Trim meat from the bones and combine with the broth.

c. chicken broth: To prepare 4 to 5 cups chicken broth from 1 to 2 pounds neck bones, breast bones, and backbones trim removable fat and boil with 6 to 8 cups water in a 6-quart pot and boil for 1 or more hours. Add hot water to compensate evaporation. Trim meat from the bones and combine with the broth. Discard the bones.

To separate fat remove the bones first to make the fat removal easier, then store the broths in a refrigerator (or in outdoor during cold weather). Skim the solidified fat on the top, discard, and save the broths. **NOTE:** Don't discard the fat in the sink save in a used can for disposal.

d. seafood broth: To prepare 4 cups clam stock scrub off sand from about 2 dozens clams and boil with their shells in 4 to 5 cups water in 4-quart pot. Boil for one or more hours, remove clam for some other use and save the stock.

e. shrimp broth: To prepare 4 cups shrimp stock rinse 2 pounds shrimp and boil with 4 to 5 cups water in 4-quart pot for 5 minutes. Remove shell, legs, heads, and tails from shrimp. Save the shrimp meat for some other use. Return shell, legs, heads, and tails to the pot and boil for one or more hours. Strain and save the stock. Discard the rest.

A variation to the stock making involves using a small onion (diced or quartered), 2 celery stalks (diced), and 1/4 teaspoon black pepper along with the meat bones or seafood and shrimp shells in the brewing.

f. Eggs, hard boiled: The most common problems in making hard boiled eggs are: difficulty in peeling the shell, eggs cracking during boiling, and forming green coloration in the yolk. One way to overcome the peeling difficulty is to obtain freshly laid eggs, age them in refrigerator for 3 days or more and hard boil them. Since most of us have to buy the eggs from the stores we can't be sure of their freshness. We just have to hope that they are fresh enough to make the hard boiled eggs that will peel easily.

The cracking of shell during boiling are caused by subjecting the eggs to a sudden change in temperature (a thermal shock). The shell will crack if the eggs are taken out from a refrigerator and heated rapidly to a boiling temperature. Thus, the cracking can be avoided if the eggs are brought to a boiling temperature by starting the eggs submerged in cold water and heating the water gradually to a boiling at medium heat settings ("Medium" or between "Medium" and "Medium High" settings).

Green coloration in the egg yolks are formed if the eggs are overcooked or boiled too long. The prolong cooking causes some of the sulfur containing proteins in the egg white to break down and form hydrogen sulfide gas. The gas is then attracted towards iron in the yolks and react to green colored iron sulfide compounds. Thus, the eggs are cooled down in cold water as soon as the eggs are cooked.

Hence, one way to make the hard boiled eggs is as follows: Put the eggs in a pot and add cold tap water just enough to cover the eggs. Turn heat on, heat at "Medium" setting, and set a timer for 20 to 25 minutes. Turn off heat and let stand for 5 minutes. Replace the hot water in the pot with cold water then shell and use as needed.

18. Broiling.

Clean the broiler pan and rack. Line the inside bottom and sides of the pan with aluminum foil so that it will be easier to clean after the broiling. Place the rack on the pan. Rinse the meat pieces (chops, kabob strips, steaks, etc.) of their chemical additives and preservatives under running cold tap water. Wipe dry with paper towels. Arrange the pieces on the rack so that they are positioned under the heating coils for efficient broiling. Adjust the oven rack to a proper height so that when the broiler pan is placed on it the meat pieces will be about 5 inches below the heating elements. If the chops should buckle during broiling, release the stress by making 1/2-in slits at the edges where the chops buckle and broil. The heating elements are usually exposed from the oven ceiling.

CAUTION: Most broilers are designed to broil with the oven door ajar. If your kitchen is equipped with an exhaust fan, it should be turned on while broiling. Otherwise, some fine carbon soot from your broiling may trigger a smoke alarm in your house. Always wear gloves or use pot holders when handling hot racks and broiling pan. Follow broiling instructions (using amount and type of ingredients, basting, turning, etc.) from the recipes unless specified otherwise.

19. Frying.

a. Battered food: Add to 3-quart pot, the amount of peanut or corn oil given in recipes. Heat the pot at "Medium" setting for 3 to 5 minutes. Add battered food, 3 to 4 pieces at a time, and fry until the coatings turn to light tan color. Turn the food pieces over, if necessary, and fry to light tan color. Remove the food, drain well, put in a bowl lined with paper towel, and serve. Leftover fried battered foods may be restored to their crispy and crunchy crust texture by refrying in hot oil for 2 to 5 minutes. The oil may be reused after filtering solid debris through cheese cloth. Store the filtered oil in refrigerator.

b. Curry leaves/black mustard seeds/red pepper (if used): Use the amounts of oil, curry leaves, black mustard seeds, and red pepper as given in recipes. Add to 2-cup pot, oil and heat at "Medium High" setting for 1 to 2 minutes (do not leave the pot unattended). Add mustard seeds, cover quickly, and allow the seeds to pop. When the popping subsides, turn off heat, remove cover, add curry leaves, and red pepper (if used) immediately while mixing continuously. Mix additional 45-60 seconds while the pot is still on the stove. Then, remove the pot from the stove. Use the fried ingredients per recipes.

c. Egg, hard boiled: Boil eggs (see section 17f), shell, and section each hard boiled egg into halves, lengthwise. Lay each section with its yolk side up in a heavy 10-inch skillet. Sprinkle ingredients, such as turmeric, salt, etc. on each section if recipe requires. Add oil to the skillet. Heat at "Medium High" setting. Reset heat to "Medium Low" when the oil gets hot, cover loosely, and fry undisturbed for 60 to 90 seconds. Flip each section over, cover, and fry the flipped sides undisturbed for 60 to 90 seconds more. Turn off heat, garnish if required, and serve or use for making other dishes. For healthfulness, discard the yolks from half of the sections.

CAUTION: The hard boiled egg sections have the tendency to pop and spit hot oil in the air during the frying. Hence, the skillet is covered loosely during the frying.

     d. Egg, omelets: For healthfulness, break half of the eggs and separate their whites into a bowl. Discard their yolks. Break the remaining eggs and add the whites and yolks to the bowl. Beat the mixture until the whites and the yolks are blended to yellow yoke color (an electric hand blender or an egg beater or a fork may be used for the blending). Set aside. Get the filling ingredients (cheese, nuts, onion, pepper, salt, vegetables and so forth per recipe), spatula, and a serving plate ready. Set them aside. Heat a heavy 10-inch skillet at "Medium High" setting for 60 to 90 seconds. Add the oil (corn, olive, margarine, etc. per recipe). Wait 15 to 20 seconds and add the beaten eggs to the skillet. Spread the filling ingredients evenly on the omelet immediately. When the bottom of the omelet has set, lift a portion of the edge of the omelet with the spatula, tilt the skillet towards the spatula, and allow the uncooked eggs and the oil to flow under the omelet. Remove the spatula and fry 10 to 20 seconds. When the omelet has set, lift a portion of the edge of the omelet and while lifting push the spatula further under the omelet towards the center until the omelet can be balanced on the spatula momentarily. Then, flip the omelet over quickly. Turn off heat. Fry the flipped side for 50 to 60 seconds. Garnish when required and serve or use for making other dishes.

     e. Egg, scrambled: For healthfulness, break half of the eggs and separate their whites into a bowl. Discard the yolks. Break the remaining eggs and add their whites and yolks to the bowl. Beat the mixture until the whites and the yolks are blended to yellow yoke color (an electric hand blender or an egg beater or a fork may be used for the blending). Set aside. Get the filling ingredients (cheese, nuts, onion, salt, vegetables and so forth), spatula, and a serving plate ready. Set them aside. Heat a heavy 10-inch skillet at "Medium High" setting for 60 to 90 seconds. Add oil (corn, olive, margarine, etc. per recipe). Wait 15 to 20 seconds. Add the beaten eggs and the ingredients to the skillet. Reset heat to "Medium Low" and scramble them immediately. Fry with mixing for

60 to 90 seconds. Garnish when required and serve or use for making other dishes.

f. Garlic: Use the amounts of oil and garlic (and turmeric if used) as given in recipes. Crush, peel, and dice the garlic. Add to 2-cup pot, oil, and heat at "Medium" heat setting for 1 to 2 minutes. Add garlic (and turmeric if used) and fry with frequent stirring until the garlic turns light tan color. Turn off heat and remove pot. Use the fried ingredient per recipes.

g. Garlic/onion: Use the amounts of oil, garlic, and onion (and turmeric if used) as given in recipes. Crush, peel, and dice the garlic. Peel and slice the onion into thin slices (same thinness will brown evenly). Add to an 8-inch skillet, oil and heat at "Medium" setting for 2-3 minutes, add onion and fry with frequent stirring until some slices begin to change to light tan color. Add garlic (and turmeric if used), and fry them together with frequent stirring until the onion begins to brown. Turn off heat and remove pot. Use the fried ingredients per recipes.

h. Garlic/ginger: Use the amounts of oil, garlic, and ginger as given in recipes. Crush, peel, and dice garlic. Peel and dice ginger. Add to 2-cup pot, oil, and heat at "Medium" setting for 1 to 2 minutes. Add garlic and ginger and fry with frequent stirring Fry until the pieces begin to turn light tan color. Turn off heat and remove pot. Use the fried ingredients per recipes.

i. Garlic/ginger/black beans: Use the amounts of oil, black bean, garlic, and ginger as given in recipes. Crush, peel, and dice garlic. Peel and dice ginger. Rinse black beans gently in cold water, dry on paper towel, combine with garlic and ginger and pound them lightly. Add to 2-cup pot, oil and heat at "Medium" setting for 1 minute. Add the ingredients and fry with frequent stirring for 30 to 60 seconds or until fragrance of the black beans is smelled. Turn off heat and pour the entire content over the food.

j. Garlic/ginger/onion: Use the amounts of oil, garlic, ginger, and onion as given in recipes. Crush, peel, and dice the garlic. Peel and dice the ginger. Peel and slice the onion into thin slices (same thinness will brown evenly). Add to an 8-inch skillet, oil, and heat at "Medium" setting for 2-3 minutes, add onion and fry with frequent stirring until some slices begin to change to light tan color. Add garlic and ginger to the onion and fry them all together with frequent stirring until the onion begins to brown. Turn off heat and remove pot. Use the fried ingredients per recipes.

k. Herbs/spices: Add to 1-cup pot, amount of oil given in

172

recipes, and heat at "Medium Low" setting. Heat 2 minutes, add amounts of spices per recipes, and stir constantly. Saute 60 to 90 seconds or until fragrances of the spices are smelled. Turn off heat and pour the entire content into the food immediately. Most herbs and spices that you will be using are dried. Thus, when they are fried or sauteed they burn readily. Therefore, you have to use heat settings at "Medium Low" or "Low" setting.

1. Onion: Use the amounts of oil and onion (and turmeric if used) as given in recipes. Peel and slice onion into thin slices (same thickness will brown evenly). Add to an 8-inch skillet, oil, and heat at "Medium" setting for 2-3 minutes. Add onion and fry with frequent stirring until onion slices begin to turn light tan color. Add turmeric if used and fry additional 30-40 seconds. Turn off heat and remove pot. Use the fried ingredients per recipes.

20. Gravy. One sure way to make a smooth textured gravy with the flour is to start with a cold gravy mixture (flour, water, and seasoning ingredients) and gradually bring it to a boil at "Medium" heat setting. The mixture is stirred frequently during heating. The thickening doesn't begin until the mixture begins to boil. Further mixing is needed while boiling to get to a smooth textured gravy. It may take about 8 minutes to make the gravy for four servings. Whereas, the corn starch starts thickening in much less time. It may require no more than 3 minutes of continuous mixing. Thus, the corn starch makes the cooking easier, faster, and less laborious. It is more user friendly than the flour. However, it is imperative that if the corn starch and flour solutions are added to the hot gravy with high heat setting, the corn starch will gel unevenly and the flour will coagulate into chunks instantly. Similarly, if they are added in their powder forms to a hot gravy or water, you will have a nice mess in your pot, the mess you cannot salvage. The globules and the chunks are extremely difficult to stir into a smooth textured gravy.

a. Corn starch: Prepare corn starch mixture as described in section 2. Reset heat to "Medium Low", add hot water (amount per recipe) to the pot, and mix. Wait 60 to 90 seconds. Then, remix corn starch mixture, stir into pot, and mix continuously until the gravy thickens to a smooth texture. If the corn starch gelled to a viscous mass while mixing, add 1 to 2 Tablespoons hot water at a time, with continuous mixing, until the gravy is thinner with a smooth texture. If more gravy is needed, add 1/4 to 2 cups hot water to the dish, mix well, salt to taste, and serve.

b. Flour: Add to a 2-cup pot, flour gravy mixture given in recipes. Add 1/3 cup cold tap water and disperse the ingredients by scrubbing the mass, with the bottom part of a metal teaspoon, against the sides of the pot. Disperse the flour globules as best as you can to get to a smooth thick mixture. Add another 1/3 cup cold water and repeat the process. Add your last 1/3 cup cold water and mix thoroughly until the ingredients are dispersed to a smooth mixture. Then, heat the mixture at "Medium" setting. Mix as frequently as you can during the heating until it begins to boil. Continue mixing while boiling until the mixture begins to thicken. Reset heat to "Medium Low" and continue mixing until the gravy thickens to a smooth texture. If thinner gravy is desired, add hot water in 2 Tablespoon installments and mix continuously until the gravy has a desired texture.

21. Kabob. To save work, kabob is cooked without the skewers. After cooking, the meat strips are cut into bite-size pieces, garnished, and served.

    a. Frying: Add to 12-in skillet (with cover), 3 Tablespoons peanut, corn, or olive oil, and heat at "Medium High" setting for 1 to 2 minutes. Add marinated meat, fry for 5 minutes, cover, reset heat to "Medium Low", and simmer for 10-15 minutes. Remove cover and evaporate to sizzling. Fry in the sizzling oil for 3 more minutes. Garnish and serve.

    b. Frying with vegetables:

Group A
marinated meat, cut into 1/4-in slices
Group B
1 small tomato, diced
1 small onion, diced

1 to 2 fresh cayenne or jalapeno peppers, diced
5 to 8 sprigs fresh mint leaves, diced

Heat 3 Tablespoons peanut, corn, or olive oil in 12-in skillet at "Medium High" setting for 1 to 2 minutes. Add Group A (marinated meat slices), fry for 5 minutes, cover, reset heat to "Medium Low", and cook for 10 to 15 minutes. Reset heat to "Medium", remove cover, and evaporate to sizzling. Mix occasionally. Add Group B and fry them in sizzling oil for 2 to 3 more minutes. Mix well. Reset heat to "Medium Low", mix well, cover, and let them cook for 2 minutes. Garnish and serve.

    c. Grilling: Place the marinated meat (strips or chops) on the grill. Use hot charcoal or gas flame. Grill each side of the meat until the surfaces are partially tanned. If the chops should buckle during grilling, release the stress by making an 1/2-in slit at the edges where the chops buckle and grill. Garnish and serve.

If your grill has a lid, place the meat on the grill, close the lid, and grill each side for 3-5 minutes at "Low" flame setting. Or grill each side until the surfaces are partially browned. Garnish and serve.

If your grill has a lid and an elevated rack, place the meat on the raised rack, close the lid, and grill each side for 5-8 minutes at "Medium" flame setting. Remove the meat and place them on the lower-level rack, close the lid, reset flame to "Low" setting, and grill each side for 2 minutes. Or, grill each side until the surfaces are partially browned. Garnish and serve.

22. Measuring Spoons.

Measuring spoons "Tablespoon" and "teaspoon" are intentionally spelled with an upper case "T" for the Tablespoon and a lower case "t" for the teaspoon measurements in the recipes. It is to avoid inadvertent mistakes in the recipes.

23. Rice.

a. About cooking: When you cook rice (long grain, extra long grain, brown, jasmine, and basmati) you may consider investing in an automatic rice cooker. We always have success with these cookers. You simply measure the rice with a measuring cup per instruction or with the cup that comes with the cooker. Add the recommended amount of water to the rice and close the lid. Press the button and the rice will be cooked automatically and perfectly. More expensive models will cook your rice and keep it warm if needed. Some will allow you to cook pilafs or similar dishes automatically. However, most cookers are not designed for cooking precooked or instant rice automatically. Jasmine rice is cooked with 10 to 15 percent lesser water than the rice cooker instructions call for if fluffy cooked rice is desired.

Directions for cooking commercially processed precooked rice are printed on the packages. Our family has used many types of them. In few cases we have to do our own final touches to the rice to have them come out just right. Thus, regardless of what the directions on the packages say, I feel that you should know something about cooking rice.

To cook rice for four servings, as a rule of thumb you need to cook anywhere from 1 to 5 cups of non-instant rice depending on how much rice the people you are cooking for can eat. Roughly an Asian consumes 2 to 4 times more rice than the Westerner.

The pot size for cooking non-instant rice is very important. You will have a real mess if the pot is too small for the number of servings you are cooking for. Since the cooked rice swells to about twice its uncooked volume, you will need a correct sized pot. As a rule of thumb you will need a 5-quart pot with a tight fitting lid (for efficient steaming) to cook five cups of extra long grain non-instant rice for four copious servings (four Asian guests).

Next, the amount of water needed for cooking the rice is critical. The cooked rice would be soggy, sticky, and gluey if you use too much water or is overcooked. With too little water, the rice could be hard or undercooked. There is no exact amount of water I can spell out for you. It depends on the type of rice, the amount of heat used, and how long it is cooked. However, in general, the ratio of the amount of water to the amount of rice used for cooking the rice is about one 6-oz cup of water to one 6-oz cup of rice with an initial heat setting of "Medium High".

b. Cooking: For your convenience I would recommend you use precooked instant rice or an automatic rice cooker to prepare your rice. However, if you would prefer to cook from scratch here is our family secret for cooking the rice. The secret is to start out with a lesser amount of water than what it needs for the cooking, using a "Medium High" heat setting; that is to use a water level with a depth to the first digit of your forefingers over the leveled rice surface. This is done because an undercooked rice can be managed easily by adding 1/8 to 1/2 cup of hot water to the rice during steaming. Bring the rice to a boil at "Medium High" heat setting with frequent stirring. Let it boil until the water level over the rice has boiled down to about an eighth of an inch. Then, the heat is turned down to a setting between "Low" and "Medium Low". Cover the pot tightly and allow it to steam for 15 minutes. Then, the rice is checked for doneness by picking out a couple of rice grains with a fork or spoon and squeezing and rubbing them at the same time between your thumb and forefinger. See if the rice grains still have some uncooked rice particles. If the rice is done the squashed grains should be clear without any residual uncooked rice particles (opaque-white granular) left on your fingers. If the rice seems not done and looks wet, cover and steam for 15 more minutes and check again. If the rice seems not done and looks dry sprinkle 1/8 cup of hot water evenly over the entire rice surface. Cover, and let it steam again for another 15 minutes. Then check again and repeat sprinkling water if the rice is dry until your rice is cooked and fluffy. It is quite laborious.

Cooking rice this way is an art. But you can develop the skill by practice. It may need a few tries. When you have mastered the technique you are well equipped with cooking most types of rice dishes (pilafs, casseroles, etc).

c. Cooking with marinated meat: The amount of rice and spices per recipe are boiled with water as described in section 23b. When the water level over the rice has boiled down to about 1/8 of an inch, turn off heat, and leave it on the stove for 1 to 2 minutes. Remove the pot from stove. Transfer three quarters of the rice into a bowl and set aside. Level the remaining rice in the pot. Add spices and marinated meat in the center of the rice bed. Cover them with one-half of the rice saved earlier. Sprinkle with seasoning ingredients on the rice, if used, per recipes. Repeat the same with the remaining rice on the top. Seal the pot with aluminum foil by placing the foil over the pot. Then, put the cover snugly over the foil and fold down the edges against the side of the pot. Place the sealed pot in the oven and bake for the duration and at the temperature per recipe (see also section 16a).

d. Cooking with spices: The amount of rice and spices per recipe are boiled with water as described in section 23b. When the water level over the rice has boiled down to 1/4 to 1/8 of an inch, stir in the remaining seasoning ingredients per recipes. Cover, and steam per section 23b.

24. Roasting.

a. Nuts: Almond, cashews, peanuts, pecans, etc. may be roasted or toasted in a toaster oven. Preheat the toaster oven at 300F. Put 1/2 cup of the nuts on a roasting pan and roast in the oven for 20 to 40 minutes or until the fragrances of the nuts are smelled.

b. Spices: Cardamon pod, coriander, cumin, cloves, peppercorn, and so forth may be roasted over the stove at a heat setting between "Medium" and "Medium High". Put 1/4 cup of the spices in a 2-cup pot and roast, mixing frequently. Roast them until their coloration change, usually within 2 to 3 minutes. You should also be smelling their roasted fragrances or aromas. Remove them immediately and set them aside in a bowl. Use a small coffee grinder. if grinding is desired. Grind about 1 to 2 Tablespoons of roasted seeds at a time. Transfer in a cleaned, dried, and airtight dark container. Store in a cool place. Reseal after each use. They retain their fragrances and freshness more than a year if stored and used properly.

25. Simmer-Saute. The technique is used in place of the traditional

precooking (sauteing) for preparing casseroles, sauces, soups, stews, and stir fries. The technique is consisted of simmering, evaporating, and self-sauteing in the sequence.

a. Heat setting: In simmer-saute the heat setting is changed three or four times using "Medium High", "Medium", "Medium Low", in between (the "Medium Low" and "Low"), and the "Low" settings. The purpose of this maneuvering between the first three settings is to speed up the initial boiling for the simmering, to assure that water is always present during the simmering, and to evaporate the residual water for the subsequent self-sauteing. The settings between the last two are to control the self-sauteing at a moderate rate of sizzling in oil so that the ingredients can be self-sauteed for at least 10 minutes, if necessary, without burning.

The heat settings used in the recipes are obtained from the use of our family electric range. The "Medium Low" setting on the range produces a moderately aggressive bubbling during the simmering in a covered pot. I could self-saute under the conditions for about 5 minutes without burning the ingredients. Using the same covered pot at lower settings, between the "Medium Low" and "Low", a less aggressive moderate bubbling could be accomplished for the simmering. I could do the self-sauteing for 7 to 8 minutes with the same results. And, at the "Low" setting the simmering takes place with no bubbling. The self-sauteing could be done for 10 to 12 minutes without burning the ingredients.

Nevertheless, it is essential to warn you that you may or may not get the same results at the same settings with your stove. A different range would produce either the same or different bubbling speeds during simmering at those same settings. Similar variations exist between the larger and the smaller burners on the same electric range. However, you will need the larger burner to cook for the four servings. We may expect no lesser variations between the electric and gas ranges on the rate of bubbling for the same settings. This is the way it is because it is unnecessary to design home kitchen ranges that are precise and accurate to control its heat energy output, so that the ranges can be set at the same setting and yield the same heat output on all different makes and models. The intent of the design is to avoid investing in the feature which is not absolutely essential for the home cooking.

To get around this problem I have a simple procedure built in the detailed simmering instructions described in the last section 25f, "Simmering". That procedure is intended to compensate for the variations in the heat settings for the simmering. It instructs you to check your simmering occasionally and to replenish with 1/4 cup hot water installments when your simmering starts to get dry. This compensates for the water lost during the more aggressive simmering at your "Medium Low" or "Low" setting. However, if your simmering is left with too much water at the end of your simmering, corrective procedures are also built in the two detailed sections below, "Evaporating" and "Evaporating/Sauteing". These procedures instruct you to evaporate the residual water to sizzling in oil under different simmering conditions. Thus, the corrective procedures are sufficient to ensure that the simmering is always done with some water and that they are sizzling in oil without scorching the ingredients at the end of the simmering.

It may be necessary for you to select a setting by trial between your last three markings on your range control knobs, "Medium Low," in between the "Medium Low" and "Low", and "Low" settings that will allow you to self-saute at least 10 minutes with the same results. If your range doesn't have the same designations as my range for these settings you may choose the last three or four successive graduation marks on your control knobs for the experiments.

b. Evaporating: At the end of the simmering, reset heat at "Medium Low", remove cover, and simmer until ingredients are dry and sizzling in oil. Mix often and don't leave the pot unattended. To hasten evaporation use "Medium" or "Medium High" setting and reset back at "Medium Low" when ingredients sizzle in oil.

c. Evaporating/Sauteing: At the end of the simmering reset heat at "Medium", remove cover, and simmer until the ingredients are dry and sizzling in oil. Mix often and don't leave pot unattended. At the end of evaporation, push some ingredients (usually the meat) aside in the pot and make room for the ingredients given in recipes (usually garlic and ginger). Add them in the oil and saute only the ingredients (don't mix with the other ingredients) to a light tan color, anywhere from 1 to 8 minutes. Mix often during sauteing, scraping any scorched ingredients on the floor of the pot. The combined instructions are used in preparing most Asian stir fries and stews.

d. Self-Sauteing: After the evaporation to sizzling in oil reset heat to "Medium Low", cover, and allow to self-saute (sizzling in oil) for the period as specified in recipes, usually 3 to 10 minutes. Mix occasionally. Turn off heat and remove pot from stove. A one-step dish is now ready for either serving or continuing to preparing casseroles, salads, soups, stews, and stir fries using the simmer-sauteed ingredients.

179

e. Self-Sauteing, alternate: After the evaporation to sizzling in oil reset heat to "Low", cover, and allow to self-saute for the period as specified in recipes. Mix occasionally. Turn off heat and remove pot from stove. This alternate technique is used when a long self-sauteing, usually 5 to 15 minutes, is desired to develop flavor of the dishes containing ingredients that burn or brown easily, such as tomato, paprika, and so forth.

f. Simmering: Add meat (given in recipes usually from Group 1) to 5-quart pot with cover. Rinse meat with cold water and drain. Add remaining Group 1 ingredients. Mix well. Heat ingredients to a boil at "Medium High" setting. (**CAUTION:** Don't leave pot unattended when the high heat setting is used; it is a potential fire hazard. See also safety caution on page 182.). Stir to mix. Allow to boil 1 to 2 minutes. Reset heat at "Medium Low". Cover and simmer for the duration specified in recipes, usually 15 to 120 minutes. Mix occasionally. (**NOTE:** During simmering don't let the ingredients go dry. If they need water, add 1/4 cup hot water at a time and continue simmering. The simmering is always used in preparation for the evaporating, sauteing, and self-sauteing of the ingredients in the simmer-saute cooking).

26. Steaming.

a. Homemade steamer: If you already have a steamer use either technique 26b or 26c below. Otherwise, you can either buy a commercially made steamer or make one as follows: Take a small can, such as an empty 8-ounce pineapple can or a 6-ounce tuna can, remove the bottom, leaving only the ring and wash it thoroughly. Place the hollow can in the center of an 8- to 10-quart pot and add water to just below the top rim of the can. Place the bowl (uncovered) on the tuna can. Cover the steamer and steam the foods as in 26b. See safety on page 182.

b. Fish, meat, poultry, vegetables: Arrange Group 1 ingredients (given in recipes) in a heat proof bowl. Put MI first in the bowl and the remaining ingredients on the sides, around, and on top of the MI. Put water in the steamer, place the bowl on the tuna can in the steamer (uncovered), cover the steamer, and bring it to boil at "Medium High" setting. Boil 1-2 minutes. Reset heat to "Medium Low" and let the steamer simmer undisturbed for the time given in recipes. Add SIs and GIs, if used in recipes, and continue with steaming per recipes. Turn off heat. Remove the bowl from the steamer using pot holders, empty the steamed food into a 3-quart serving bowl, garnish if required, and serve.

c. Soup making: Divide the ingredients given in recipes equally in two cleaned empty one-pound coffee cans. Place Group 2 first in the cans. Place cleaned meat pieces (Group 1) on top of Group 2 in the cans. Place the cans (uncovered) in a steamer (an 8- to 10-quart pot with cover). Fill each coffee can to 1/3 full with hot water. Add about 2 to 3 quarts water in the steamer. Cover and bring the steamer to a boil at "Medium High" setting. Boil 2 minutes and reset heat to "Medium Low'. Steam undisturbed for the duration given in recipes. Add SIs if used. Cover and steam again undisturbed for the duration given in recipes. Turn off heat. Remove the cans with pot holders from the steamer and empty the food into a 3-quart serving bowl. Garnish if required and serve.

27. Stir Frying. Simmer-saute technique is used to simplify Chinese stir frying. Two basic stir-frying techniques are used for preparing traditional authentic Chinese dishes. Detailed instructions of the technique is described below.

 a. Meat: Add Group 1 usually (meat given in recipes) to 5-quart pot with cover. Rinse meat with cold water. Drain and add the remaining Group 1. Mix and heat to a boil at "Medium High" setting. (**CAUTION:** Don't leave pot unattended when the heat setting is used; it is a potential fire hazard). Stir to mix. Allow to boil 1 to 2 minutes. Reset heat to "Medium Low". Cover and simmer for the duration specified in recipes, usually 15 to 120 minutes. Mix occasionally. (**NOTE:** During simmering don't let them go dry. If they need water add 1/4 cup hot water at a time and continue simmering). Meanwhile, prepare corn starch mixture per section 2. Reset heat to "Medium". At the end of simmering, remove cover and evaporate until ingredients sizzle in oil. Add the ingredients per recipe (usually garlic, ginger, scallion, etc.), cover, and let the ingredients self-saute until lightly tanned as required in recipes. Reset heat to "Medium Low" or "Low". Remove cover, add hot water per recipe, and mix well. Remix corn starch mixture and add to pot with continuous mixing until the gravy thickens to a smooth texture (see section 20a). Turn off heat. Remove pot and transfer foods into 3-quart serving bowl. Garnish with ingredients per recipe, and serve.

 b. Meat/Vegetable: Add Group 1 (usually meat given in recipes) to 5-quart pot with cover. Rinse meat with cold water. Drain water. Add the remaining Group 1. Mix and heat to a boil at "Medium High" setting. (**CAUTION:** Don't leave pot unattended when the heat setting is used; it is a potential fire hazard). Stir to mix. Allow to boil 1-2 minutes. Reset heat to "Medium Low". Cover and simmer for the duration specified in recipes, usually 15 to 45 minutes. Mix occasionally. (**NOTE:** During simmering don't let them go dry. If they need water add 1/4 cup hot water at a time and continue simmering). Meanwhile, prepare vegetable per recipe. Drain well. Prepare corn starch mixture per section 2. Set them aside. At the end of simmering, reset heat to "Medium". Remove cover, and evaporate to sizzling. Mix well. Push a few meat pieces aside, add the ingredients per recipe in the oil (usually garlic, ginger, scallion, etc.), let self-saute for 30 seconds, and then mix. Add hot water, mix well, and bring to a boil. Add vegetable, mix, cover, and cook for 2 minutes. Reset heat to "Medium Low" or "Low." Remove cover, remix corn starch mixture, and add to pot with continuous mixing until the gravy thickens to a smooth consistency (see section 20a). Turn off heat, remove pot, and transfer the food into 3-quart serving bowl. Garnish with group ingredients per recipe and serve.

SAFETY CAUTION: When using the cooking techniques, slow cooking, steaming, simmering, boiling, and pressure cooking, protect yourself against steam burns. Use pot holders or insulating gloves when placing or removing pot cover, stirring, adding ingredients into the pot during cooking, placing or removing food from steamer, and so forth. Steam vapors are very deceiving and burn you when they are least expected.

3.
THE
ART OF
RECIPE
VARIATION

Cucumber, *Cucumis sativus*

This chapter focuses on the art of recipe variations. Derivation and modification of recipes are illustrated. Relationships between the American and Asian recipes are explored.

Recipes

Some paleoanthropologists could place the beginning of the use of fire for cooking by the Peking Man to about 400,000 years BP (before present). The human species are gifted with anatomical features and structures (brain, fingers, oral faculty, etc.) to develop and advance intelligence. These led to creatively mixing various favorite foods and inventing many varieties of dishes. This creativeness is one of the basic differences between the human and the animals. Humans also must have then learned to reproduce the AFT of their favorite foods. They shared, exchanged, and traded their techniques of reproducing their favorites (recipes) with other members of the family and friends. Thus, it is reasonable to speculate that the concept of recipe must also have been conceived around that period.

As our ancestors developed skills for their survival, their desire to cure pains, to poison enemies, and to preserve eternal youth had become their common obsessions. The wealth, influence, power, and social standing of possessing these skills were so great that many people devoted their lives pursuing these skills. At that time, there were no written languages. When someone discovered substances for curing pains or poisoning enemies or preserving youth (for deception), the person would guard the recipes for making the potions by establishing secret ceremonial rituals surrounded with supernatural mystic powers. These rituals were formulated with meticulous care so that selection of the ingredients (type and quality), proportions of the ingredients, conditions, and techniques for making the secret potions would be accurate and reproducible. These rituals were known only to the very close family members and were intended to be passed on from generation to generation. There were no chemical formulas or equations known then. When the ceremonies were carried out with highly trained disciplines, the making sequences were fixed to produce their secret potions with the consistent quality and characteristics the creator of the rituals had intended. These rituals were another forms of recording secret recipes. Thus, we can appreciate the significance of the recipes.

Today, food manufacturers, among others, jealously guard their recipes in the form of material standards and process engineering specifications. Most are locked up in personal safes. However, fundamental concepts and theories of scientific and technological discoveries are now being recorded in international public domain documents (such as technical books, periodicals, literatures, publications, etc.) and information databases for academic interests.

In cooking, we use our recipes for recording essential variables to fix the methods of reproducing our favorite dishes. Therefore it is important to include the four key parts in the recipes: ingredients, amounts of the ingredients, sequences of the procedures, and special instructions when essential (such as folding egg roll skin, skinning chicken meat, safety, and so forth). A well-written recipe fixes important sequences of the cooking steps and excludes unnecessary special ingredients, procedures, utensils, and accident-prone steps. One of the primary purposes of a recipe is then to help users reproduce its intended AFTT safely.

Some of the attributes of the recipes in this cookbook include the use of simple and inexpensive ingredients, avoidance of laborious and complicated techniques, the use of minimum number of cooking utensils, and the promotion of safety awareness. Thus, the recipes are ideal for casual cooking by the busy people to prepare their delicious and healthful meals safely with little or no prior cooking experience.

Basic Beef Stew. I find the ingredients used in a basic Beef Stew recipe are commonly used in other traditional dishes such as Chili Con Carne, Curry, Goulash, Gumbo, Spaghetti Sauce, Stroganoff, and many other dishes. Therefore, the Beef Stew recipe will be chosen as a basis for the discussions, though the stew may not be the progenitor of the other dishes. The discussions will focus on modifying, relating, and converting the stew to other American and Asian dishes.

A traditional Basic Beef Stew Recipe Ex 1 (Example 1) is shown below. This is one of our favorites and is one of the earliest recipes we have collected from our friends. Although, we have forgotten who gave us the recipe, it is shown as received with the exception of the ingredients labels (Main Ingredients, Core Ingredients, etc.). Some of the ingredients, the Core Ingredients, used in the recipe are also commonly used in other popular American dishes such as Meat Sauces, Meat Vegetable Soups, Gumbos, and so forth. Therefore, the recipe is named as Basic Beef Stew and chosen as a basis for discussing modifying recipes and relating and converting the stew to some American and Asian dishes. The ingredients are grouped and arranged for the discussions. They are not in the order of their uses in cooking.

Ex 1   Basic Beef Stew

Main Ingredient
32 oz beef, 1-in cubes
Core Ingredients
3 Tablespoons oil
1 large onion, diced
1 medium garlic, diced
1/2 teaspoon sugar
1/4 teaspoon pepper
1 teaspoon salt

2 cups beef broth
Secondary Ingredients
3 large carrots, 1/4-in slices
2 Tablespoons burgundy wine
1/4 cup frozen pearl onions
3 large potatoes, each
    quartered
Garnishing Ingredient
1/4 cup flour

Sprinkle salt and pepper on meat cubes. In a 5-quart pot heat the oil and brown meat cubes well, turning on all sides. Remove the browned meat and set aside. Saute the onions and garlic until soft and tender in the pot. Add the browned meat, beef broth, sugar, and broth. Cover and simmer for 1 1/2 hours. Add wine and all the vegetables and simmer for additional 30-40 minutes. Disperse flour to a smooth paste in 1/4 cup water and stir into the stew with constant stirring until it thickens.

Ingredients

Ingredients are one of the key components of a recipe. They are the seasoning and flavoring ingredients of the foods we enjoy everyday. They could be naturally occurring fruits, herbs, fish, meats, poultry, spices, vegetables, etc. Or, pre-processed seasoning and flavoring mixes such as catsup, cheeses, curry powders, pickles, soup mixes, soy sauces, wines, and so forth. The types and proportions of the ingredients used in a recipe characterizes the AFTT of a dish. The AFTT is a collective contribution from all the ingredients used in the preparation. For instance, in the above Beef Stew recipe all the ingredients (beef, onion. carrot, flour, etc.) contributed to its characteristic AFTT. The two ingredients, salt and water, are considered as trivial ingredients in all dishes. However, the non-trivial ingredients may be subdivided arbitrarily into four categories: Core Ingredients, Main Ingredients, Secondary Ingredients, and Garnishing Ingredients. The classification and grouping are convenient for discussing foods, cooking, cooking techniques, recipe variations, etc. Their implications are described in the following subsections in order of their use in most cooking.

Core Ingredients (CIs). An AFTT of a dish is developed collectively by all the ingredients used in the cooking. However, each dish has its own identity. For instance, the Beef Stew shown above has its own characteristic flavor which is distinguishable from other stews such as Chicken, Egg, Fish, Turkey, Lamb, Pork, Seafood, and Vegetable stews. Nevertheless, in each of the stews there is a group of ingredients oil, onion, garlic, sugar, pepper, and broth that is commonly present in the stews (see in the above Beef Stew). These ingredients in the group are referred in this cookbook as Core Ingredients (CIs).

Variations to the CIs of the Beef Stew are commonly made for creating different versions of the stew, such as Irish Beef Stews, Old Fashion Beef Stews, and so forth. The CIs are usually thoroughly digested, pulverized, and extracted of their cooked AFT in preparing most dishes. Thus, the CIs are usually cooked from the beginning to the end of the cooking.

Main Ingredients (MIs). A dish or the recipe is given a name usually to indicate its type of dish or its cooking method and the name of its featured MI. Examples of the names of the dishes are Oyster Stew, Chicken Curry, Vegetable Soup, Grilled Cheese, Barbecue Ribs, and so forth. Names of the ingredients (Oysters, Chicken, Cheese, etc.) of the dishes are the featured ingredients of the dishes. These ingredients are arbitrarily classified as the MIs of the dishes. Characteristic flavor of a MI is an integral part of the overall AFT of the dish. Thus, the MI, beef, is a member of the stew CIs. This classification is useful to discuss the MI variation of a recipe. Thus, the same basic ingredients and the same cooking technique of the Beef Stew recipe may be used with another MI, lamb, to make a Lamb Stew.

The MIs are also usually cooked along with their CIs from the beginning to the end of the cooking because the cooking is usually carried out until the MIs are cooked to their tenderness. However, the soft textured MIs, such as boned chicken, egg, fish, vegetables, shrimp, etc., are often brought into the cooking either at the middle or end of the cooking to avoid pulverizing or overcooking them.

Secondary Ingredients (SIs). They are the secondary flavoring and/or seasoning ingredients of a recipe. In the Beef Stew recipe, carrot, onion, potato, and wine are the examples of the SIs. The solid ingredients (carrot, onion, and potato) are not allowed to pulverize but to retain their shapes, sizes, and colors in the cooking. Their individual cooked flavors are intended to punctuate their individual AFTs at the time when the ingredients are chewed. The liquid (wine in this case) punctuates its identifiable flavor to the overall AFT of the dish. Often, one or more of the CIs are repeated in the same recipe as part of the SIs. For instance, chopped onions are used as one of the CIs and the pearl onions are used as a SI in the beef stew. In such cases, the intent is to emphasize the cooked flavor of the pulverized onion in the broth and the solid onion pieces when you chew them. Sometimes, the SIs are also used as garnishing ingredients.

The SIs are not used at the beginning of the preparation to avoid overcooking them. They are usually introduced into the cooking at about the midway of the cooking. The ingredients are usually used in the cooking at about the same time.

Garnishing Ingredients (GIs). The ingredients are usually introduced at about the conclusion of the cooking or during the serving. Flour is the garnishing ingredient in the above Beef Stew recipe. It contributes its partially cooked flavor as an added external flavor to the beef stew (similar to the flavor of butter on a piece of bread). It also imparts a thicker texture to the stew.

In Asian cooking, one or more of the CIs and/or SIs (such as pepper, onion, garlic, etc.) are repeated as GIs in the same recipes. However, they are usually prepared differently from the main dish fried, toasted, partially cooked, uncooked, etc. to add their contrasting flavors and give impetus to the flavor of main dish. For example, in some Burmese stews garlic is used as one of the core ingredients. Then, just before serving a couple of cloves of garlic are crushed and garnished the stew to punctuate a strong fresh garlic flavor to the stew (sometimes crisply fried garlic and its oil are used in place of the uncooked garlic).

The type of garnishing ingredients used in a recipe sometimes reveals the creator's favorite ingredients in the recipe. The term "Garnishing Ingredient (GI)" is used in this cookbook with additional meanings and implications than the conventional usage of the word in cooking.

Recipe Variations

Cooking is an art. There are many variables in cooking such as types of ingredient, proportions of the ingredients, cooking technique, color, texture, etc. to manipulate for the variations. Thus, there are infinite ways you can vary the recipes to create dishes with similar or widely differing AFTTs and colors.

Most recipes are derived from some traditional basic recipes. They are derived by making changes to their ingredients (MIs, CIs, SIs, and GIs), cooking technique, etc. In some cases different names of dishes are created out of the same dish with slight minor changes to the ingredients or the cooking techniques. For example, Meat Stews, Pot Roasts, and Pot Pies are essentially the same dish. They are just another meat stew served in different forms using the same ingredients. Thus, the Pot Roasts (Beef, Pork, Lamb, etc.) may be prepared the same way as the basic stew, with the larger pieces of the meats and vegetables. Similarly, the Pot Pies (Beef, Chicken, Fish, Turkey, Seafood, Vegetable, etc.) may also be the same stews cased in pie shells. They are essentially the same as serving the stews on biscuits. They may be made by first preparing the stews in thicker gravies using smaller pieces of the meats and vegetables. The pie crust shells are then filled with the stews and baked in the oven. Similarly, numerous dishes are created by varying their cooking techniques. Thus, some stews are prepared by simmering over the stove and some are baked in the oven. Different types of dishes, such as Pickles, Salads, Soups, Casseroles, Kabob, and numerous other dishes, may be created by changing their CIs, MIs, SIs, or GIs and their cooking techniques.

Beef Stew Variations I. It is quite common for some food enthusiasts to make changes to a Beef Stew recipe by replacing some ingredients in the recipe with their favorites. I have done this myself to many dishes. In these subsections, variations of the MI and variations of the SIs and GIs are discussed, while keeping the CIs unchanged.

MI variation: A common and simple variation to the basic stew recipe may be made by replacing the MI (beef) and its broth with a MI of your favorite, such as chicken, lamb, pork, or vegetable and its corresponding broth. The same CIs, SIs, and GI, in the same proportions, may be used for your variation. The same cooking technique may also be used with a minor change in the cooking time. Thus, the basic recipe may be used for generating the Chicken Stew, Lamb Stew, Pork Stew, and Vegetable Stew respectively.

SIs/GIs variations: A general approach to creating the dishes similar to the beef stew are illustrated in Diagram 1 below. The Diagram excludes proportions of the ingredients, their cooking instructions, and their trivial ingredients (water and salt). Incomplete recipes as such are

189

referred to as "Stripped Recipes" in this cookbook. The MI (beef) is incorporated among its CIs because the same MI is used in all the variations.

The following variations involve only making changes to the SIs and GIs of the basic stew. The CIs of the stew are used unchanged. Thus, the diagram shows only one CIs block belonging to all the stripped recipes. The SIs and GIs of the beef stew and the new dishes (Stroganoff and Goulash) are shown. The blocks are arranged from the top to bottom.

The CIs, SIs, and GIs of the Beef Stew are shown. If we start from the Beef Stew recipe, we can convert the stew to a Hungarian Beef Goulash by using the same CIs of the stew and replacing its SIs (potato, carrot, onion, and wine) with the paprika, bell pepper, and tomato. The bell pepper is repeated also as a GI, replacing the flour.

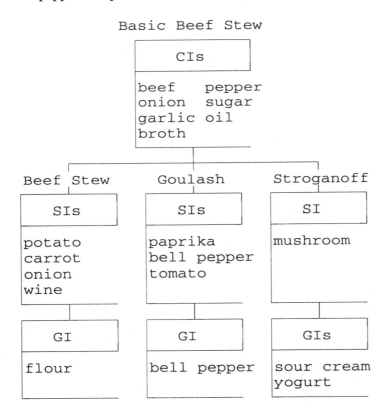

Beef Stew Variations I
Diagram 1

190

Conversion to a Beef Stroganoff would involve using the stew CIs and replacing the SIs of the beef stew with the mushroom. The stew GI is replaced with the sour cream and yogurt. We may note that although the Goulash and the Stroganoff are called differently, they are merely different versions of the beef stew.

Many other versions of the Goulash would use spices such as bay leaf, cloves, caraway, marjoram, lemon grind, sauerkraut, sour cream, and so forth. Similarly, variation to the Beef Stroganoff recipe would include the use of bay leaf, cloves, nutmeg, sweet basil, heavy cream, wine, etc.

You will notice that the ingredients of the dishes differ only in their SIs and GIs. The use of different types of SIs and/or GI in the Beef Stew recipe could produce dishes that closely resemble the stew. Thus, we can relate the Beef Stew to many other American dishes, such as Swedish Meat Balls, Beef Vegetable Soup, Oyster Stew, and so forth.

Beef Stew Variations II. In the following subsections, variations of the stew's two ingredient groups (CIs and SIs) are discussed for creating three different versions of the beef stew. The stripped recipe variations are illustrated in the following Diagram 2. The variations of the CIs are done by adding additional ingredients to the CIs of the Basic Beef Stew Version 1 (V1) recipe. The V1 blocks are arranged with its SIs block on top of the CIs block and its GI on the left side of the SIs block. The order of the remaining blocks for V2, V3, and V4 are arranged from the tops to the bottoms.

CIs/SIs variations: Many versions of the Beef Stew, such as American, English, Irish, Old Fashion, Country Style, Grand Mother's, and so forth, are being offered in many cookbooks. They are merely variations of the CIs and SIs of some beef stews. A general approach to the CIs/SIs variations of the Basic Beef Stew V1 to Beef Stews versions V2, V3, and V4 will be discussed.

version V1: In Diagram 2, the basic stew is shown as a version V1. The CIs of V1 involvement in CIs of the other three versions are clearly marked as V1 CIs in V2, V3, and V4. Although we have no knowledge of the progenitor stew among them, it is reasonable to assume that V2, V3, and V4 are built from V1 because V1 CIs are the simplest and are utilized in the other versions (variations of the V1 CIs). It should be noted that the CIs of the three new versions contain additional ingredients on top of the V1 CIs.

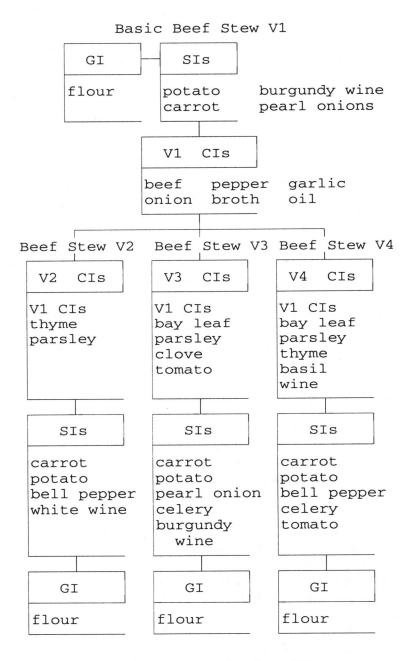

Basic Beef Stew V1

GI

flour

SIs

potato   burgundy wine
carrot   pearl onions

V1   CIs

beef   pepper   garlic
onion   broth   oil

Beef Stew V2

V2   CIs

V1 CIs
thyme
parsley

SIs

carrot
potato
bell pepper
white wine

GI

flour

Beef Stew V3

V3   CIs

V1 CIs
bay leaf
parsley
clove
tomato

SIs

carrot
potato
pearl onion
celery
burgundy
  wine

GI

flour

Beef Stew V4

V4   CIs

V1 CIs
bay leaf
parsley
thyme
basil
wine

SIs

carrot
potato
bell pepper
celery
tomato

GI

flour

Beef Stew Variation II
Diagram 2

version V2: Comparison of the versions V1 and V2 will show that V2 recipe was developed from V1 by adding a hint of seasoning ingredients, thyme and parsley, to the V2 CIs. The intent is to give a mild touch of spiciness to the blended stew flavor. Thus, the CIs of V2 include V1 CIs, thyme, and parsley. Lastly, pearl onions of the V1 SIs are omitted and a white wine and bell pepper are substituted for the burgundy wine in V2. The GI of V1 is retained in V2.

version V3: In this version, its CIs contain the V1 CIs, bay leaf, parsley, clove, and tomato. The intent is to impart tomato flavor and some spiciness to the basic beef stew. V3 SIs contains celery in addition to the V1 SIs. Putting the celery in the cooking at this later stage will no doubt give the fresh celery flavor punch among others when you chew into the pieces. The GI of V1 is also retained in V3.

version V4: There are quite a few CIs used in creating V4. Wine is used from the beginning of the cooking to assist in the cooking and to instill its subtle flavor to the AFT of the stew. Moreover, the wine, in combination with the oil and water, extracts many more kinds of substances (such as fragmented fats, proteins, carbohydrates, organic salts, etc.) during the simmering. These extracts will no doubt contribute their AFTs to the overall stew's flavor. Seasoning ingredients bay leaf, parsley, and thyme are also used in the CIs to integrate their spicy zest to the stew. Green bell pepper, celery, and tomato are used in addition to potato and carrot in its SIs. Pearl onions are omitted from the SIs. V4 and V3 are very similar except that V4 uses green bell pepper to punctuate the pepper's dominating flavor in the stew. Thus, V4 is intended to resemble more like an Italian stew.

Recipe variations are subjective. They reflect the creator's preferential taste. For instance, the versions V1 and V3 use quartered onions and pearl onions as their SIs respectively. The reason is to emphasize the flavor of the onions in their variations. The onions that are used as CIs in the V1 and V3 are pulverized along with their other CIs and add bulk and flavors to their gravy sediments. The SIs, pearl onions and quartered onions, are meant to punctuate the onion flavors at the time when you chew them. Therefore, additional onion flavors in the stews are to please the taste buds of the onion lovers. The creator could have gone further with the onion by adding fried onion and scallion as garnishing ingredients in the two versions.

Each of the above dishes is being modified to many more versions. For example, some stews use Worcestershire sauce, some use caramel, some use pre-blended beef stew mix, etc. with their CIs and/or

SIs to produce different beef stew versions.

Often, we improvise our food as we eat by garnishing with our favorite ingredients, such as catsup, mustard, black pepper, onion, and so forth. My mother's favorite was fiery hot-toasted crushed red pepper. She would garnish her favorite snack, a Burmese national dish "moat-hinn-gar" (a stew of fish, onion, garlic, ginger, red pepper, chickpea flour, and fish sauce served on noodles made of fermented rice flour, see Recipe #92), with one heaping teaspoonful of the red pepper (no exaggeration). The reaction of the pepper was almost immediate. Her eyes glittered with tears and her nasal passages filled with drips. She would wipe them off frequently as she ate and would breathe out through her mouth as a means of cooling her tongue and mouth. Don't feel sorry for her; that was the way she expressed her complete contentment and enjoyment of the snack. These red peppers were her most favorite garnishing ingredients. Naturally, they were also the favorite of everyone in the family, too. We kept the red peppers in glass jars at home on the dining table. Whenever we got bored with the main dish of the day, we would sprinkle the red pepper on our foods to kick-start our taste buds. This is quite common with most Southeast Asian families.

Beef Stew Variations III. In the variations, additional ingredients are added to the V1 CIs. However, some of these are Asian herbs and spices which are different from the Western types (see Table 4) used in the above Beef Stew Variations II. Hence, many different types of dishes, such as Chili Con Carne, Curry, Gumbo, Spaghetti Sauces, etc. may be derived and related to the Basic Beef Stew V1 recipe.

CIs/SIs variations: In the following stripped recipe Diagram 3, the blocks are configured with the V1 CIs at the top of the configuration to show the V1 relationships to the Beef Gumbo, Beef Chili Con Carne, and Beef Curry. The V1 CIs are also shown in V5, V6, and V7 CIs. Thus, the blocks are positioned to emphasize that the CIs of V5, V6, and V7 use the V1 CIs as bases for the conversion of the stew to Beef Gumbo, Beef Chili Con Carne, and Beef Curry.

version V5: The Beef Gumbo V5 recipe may be created from the stew CIs by adding some new ingredients such as cayenne pepper, white pepper, bell pepper, tomato, celery, and gumbo file to the stew V1 CIs. Its SI block consists of only okra. GI is optional.

Basic Beef Stew V1

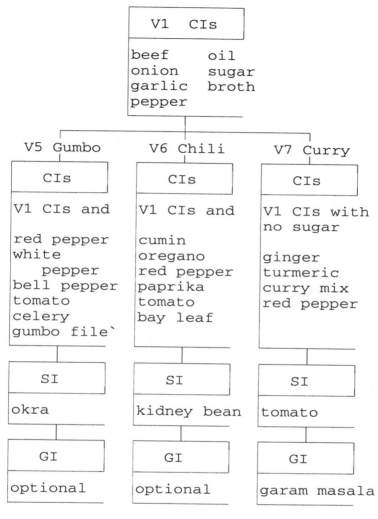

Beef Stew Variations III
Diagram 3

version V6: Similarly, Beef Chili Con Carne V6 may be derived from the beef stew by adding some new CIs such as cumin, oregano, red pepper, paprika, tomato, and bay leaf to the beef stew CIs. Kidney bean is used as a SI. GI is optional.

195

version V7: In the same manner, the Beef Curry V7 may be created by replacing sugar and adding ginger, turmeric, curry mix, and red pepper, to the V1 CIs. Sugar is removed from V7 CIs because most curry dishes don't use sugar. However, there are Chinese and some Indian curries that use sugar. The curry may be prepared with or without the broth. Tomato is used as SI. Garam masala, a milder curry mix, may be used as a GI. These dishes have their own AFT which are distinctly different from the Stroganoff, Goulash, and other dishes of Western origin.

The Gumbo V6 and Chili Con Carne V7 use mixed spices of different geographic origin, East and West. The CIs red pepper and white pepper in the gumbo are the Asian spices. Similarly, the CIs cumin and red pepper in V6 are also Asian spices. The combination of cumin and oregano in V6 is the basic flavor of the chili con carne seasoning mixes and they are the spices of East and West respectively (see Table 4). Thus, the Gumbo and Chili Con Carne employ mixed herbs and spices of Asian and Western origin. These dishes have their own AFTs which characterize them as a cross between the Western and the Asian flavors. Many such crossed-flavor dishes have taken roots in countries all over the world. There are many more to come. Many Western professional chefs are experimenting with the Asian herbs and spices and creating many such new crossed-flavor dishes such as grilled salmon marinated in ginger sauce and so forth. Thus, the use of fresh ginger, saffron, turmeric, fenugreek, cilantro, etc. are common among Western chefs today. We are no doubt witnessing a paradigm shift in Western culinary art.

The additional ingredients added to the V7 CIs are all Asian herbs and spices. Thus the dish has all the characteristics of an Asian curry. Creation of the Beef Curry V7 from the Basic Beef Stew V1 reveals how they may be derived and related.

In the above variations we have seen the modifications of the basic Beef Stew V1 to different versions of the Beef Stews, V2, V3, and V4. We have also seen the conversions to different types of dishes (Stroganoff, Hungarian Goulash, and Spaghetti sauce). However, the seasoning herbs and spices used in all the ingredients exchanges for the variations originated in the Western countries. Consequently, these modifications of the Western stew lead only to different versions and different types of the Western dishes. When one or more of the Asian spices replace the Western ingredients from the stew CIs, a cross between Asian and Western dishes such as Gumbo, Chili Con Carne, etc. may result. But when all the additional ingredients of Asian herbs and spices

196

are added to the V1 stew CIs, the stew may be transformed into an Asian curry dish.

Comparison of Asian and Western Stews

The technique used for preparing the Asian dish is basically the same as the way Americans would prepare chili, gumbos, soups, spaghetti sauces, stews, and others. The Asian and Western dishes are different only in the types of the CIs used. However, a unique thing about the Asian cooking is that fresh ginger root is used as one of the CIs. Whereas, use of the fresh ginger in the Western dishes is almost unknown. Only recently some contemporary creative chefs are beginning to use ginger in marinades and salads. Dried ginger powder and ginger extract are, however, occasionally used in small amounts as flavoring ingredients in the Western confectioneries, baked foods and soft drink beverages. Similarly, pickled meats, fish, vegetables, etc. are not commonly used in Western cooking (with the exception of the use of sauerkraut in some pork dishes). The pickles are, however, served commonly as hors d'oeuvres and relishes. Whereas, the pickled foods are frequently used as relishes and as a MI and/or SI in preparing many Asian main course dishes (curries, soups, stews, stir fries, etc.).

Now I would like to discuss how two different ethnic foods can be related by modifying their CIs. As you already are aware, the Asian foods have distinctively different AFT from most of the American foods that were derived from the Europeans, such as stews, roasts, casseroles, etc. To look into these differences I would like to compare two similar dishes used by the Americans and Asians. An Asian dish that resembles closest to the American Beef Stew V1 would be a basic Asian Beef Curry.

The following Table 1 lists the basic CIs of these two beef dishes. They are broken down into three CIs subgroups G1, G2, and G3 for the comparison (trivial ingredients, salt and water, are excluded in the table). The two dishes are prepared by the same cooking techniques (sauteing and simmering) and cooked for the same amount of time, 1 1/2 to 2 hours.

Ingredients in the subgroup G1, beef, garlic, and onion, are used in both the curry and the stew CIs.

In subgroup G2, the CIs are substantially different from each other. Black pepper is common to both dishes. When the pepper is excluded from both the CIs, there are 11 Asian herbs and spices used in the beef curry and only three mild common ingredients are used in the beef stew. This difference is the main reason for their differences in the AFTs of the two dishes. In some other beef stews, flour and sugar may be used in prebrowning the beef. The robust flavors of the browned crusts are unlike the flavors of the curry ingredients. The curry flavors are blatantly pungent, spicy, and hot.

TABLE 1. Comparison of the Asian Curry and the American Stew CIs

Asian Beef Curry	American Beef Stew V1	
beef garlic onion	beef garlic onion	G1
black pepper cardamon cinnamon clove coriander cumin fenugreek ginger mace nutmeg red pepper turmeric	black pepper broth sugar	G2

oil
(butter,
  clarified butter,
  crude sesame,
  crude peanut,
  mustard, corn,
  etc.)
	oil
	(butter
	  refined
	  vegetable,
	  olive,
	  crude olive,
	  etc.)
		G3

The subgroup G3 consists of the oils used by the two recipes. As you can see these oils are of two different types. The oils used in the beef curry are crude or unrefined. Whereas, the beef stew recipe uses refined oils. When either of the two unrefined oils is used in the curry, it contributes its natural peanut or sesame flavor to the curry, which are distinctly noticeable. Although the crude oils are not spicy, the curry prepared by using one of the crude oils can easily be distinguished from the curry prepared by the other crude oils. The same observations are also made when the peanut and sesame oils are used in the stew dish.

In the case of the refined oils (corn, peanut, cotton seed, vegetable, etc.), they are odorless and their contributions to the AFT of the stew are so subtle you cannot readily identify which of the oils is used. The flavors of the refined oils may also be not readily distinguishable from one another when used in the curry.

When butter is used in either dish, the curry or the stew, its flavor is noticeable in the dishes. Thus, either the curry or the stew prepared with the butter is distinguishable from the flavors of the dishes prepared by the refined oils.

Some beef stews use spices to break the mild blended flavor of the basic stew by adding seasoning ingredients such as, basil, bay leaf, parsley, thyme and so forth. The results of these modifications do make the stews spicier and more flavorful; however, the overall AFT of the stews are still entirely different from the beef curry. Obviously, they are of different spiciness.

The same subgroup 1 CIs from the beef stew are used in most other ethnic meat and vegetable recipes. Similarities between all ethnic recipes end after the subgroup 1 CIs. From that point on, the AFT of the ethnic recipes branches off to many different directions. They use additional flavorings, seasonings, and seasoning mixes in their basic core ingredients.

Asian Beef Stew Variations. Similar improvisation of a popular recipe is a common practice in other ethnic cooking. Country-style Burmese Beef Stew is a popular dish among the rich and poor people in Burma. There are countless variations to it. Some examples of the variations to the stripped recipes are illustrated below in Diagram 4. This dish is chosen for the discussion for the following reasons. The ingredients used in the dish are simple and they are the basic group of ingredients used in numerous popular Burmese dishes. The texture and the cooking technique used in its preparation are practically a clone of the Basic Beef Stew V1. I classified this Burmese beef dish as a stew because it is served as a main dish and prepared like the American stews. The texture of it is variable; however, most other characteristics are similar to the American stew dishes. It is called Burmese Beef Stew because the dish is a Burmese version of the beef stew.

199

Basic Burmese Beef Stew V8

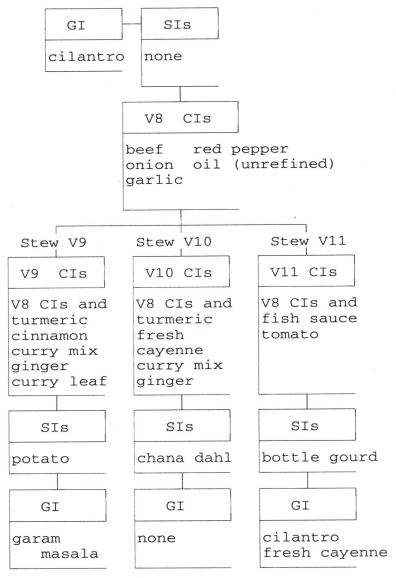

**Variations of Burmese Basic Beef Stew V8
Diagram 4**

The Burmese name of the V8 is "ah-mare-thar yeh-gyo" (ah-mare-thar means beef, yeh means water, and gyo means stewed, brewed, or cooked). The blocks are configured to show the improvisations of the basic Burmese Beef Stew version V8 to the Burmese Beef Stews versions V9, V10, and V11.

Version V8: Beef Stew V8 is one of the simplest versions of the Burmese stews. Its CIs consists of a combination of Asian seasoning ingredients (onion, garlic, red pepper, and unrefined peanut oil). These CIs are also used in many other Burmese main dishes such as chicken in coconut sauce, fish dishes, pork dishes, mutton dishes, vegetable dishes, and so on. They are similar to the Western Stews, Stroganoff, Gumbos, Spaghetti Sauces, and so forth. Cilantro is traditionally used as a GI in many Asian dishes. It is used at about the end of the cooking. In the stripped recipe variations in Diagram 4, variations of the version V8 are shown where, the CIs of the Burmese Beef Stew versions V9, V10, and V11 are built from the V8 CIs. Thus, the CIs group of V8 are shown in the CIs blocks of the versions V9, V10, and V11.

Version V9: Beef Curry V9 is a mere improvisation of the basic recipe V8. V9 is closer to the Indian curries than V10 and V11 are. The V9 is prepared by adding turmeric, cinnamon, curry mix, ginger, and curry leaf to the CIs of V8. Potatoes are added to V9 as a SI. Additionally garam masala is used as a GI at the conclusion of the cooking. This later improvisation makes the dish spicy and mildly hot.

Version V10: It is a typical Burmese Beef Curry stew. A very popular dish. Chana dahl, a family of chickpea similar to the American yellow and green split peas, is used as a SI. Most Burmese people love this combination of chana dahl and beef curry. V10 CIs is a modification of the V8 CIs by adding turmeric, fresh cayenne pepper, curry mix, and ginger to the V8 CIs. No GI may be used.

Version V11: Beef Stew V11 CIs is a simple variation of the V8 CIs. In addition to V8 CIs a fish sauce and tomato are used as CIs. Use of the fish sauce in such meat stew is a typical provincial Burmese way. The fish sauce has a saltiness and fishy taste to it, but it enhances the overall flavors of meat, poultry, shrimp, seafood, and vegetable dishes. The fishy taste is no longer noticeable in the dishes. Thus, it enhances the robustness of the Beef Stew flavor. The SI is a tropical squash called "bu-thee" in Burmese or "bottle gourd" in English. This vegetable is somewhat similar to zucchini. Unlike zucchini it has a flavor that is almost neutral but very subtle. Asians love this vegetable and use it in many dishes such as soups, sauces, stews, stir fries, and battered fries.

201

The GIs, fresh coriander leaves (cilantro) and fresh hot cayenne pepper, are commonly used as GIs in the Southeast Asian cuisines. Such kinds of GIs are not used in the Western main dishes. This bottle gourd beef and chicken stew dishes are among the favorites of the Burmese people (see Recipe #27).

Variations in Chinese Short Order Cooking. Most Chinese short order dishes such as Beef Broccoli, Chicken with Chinese Vegetables, Sweet and Sour Pork, Beef With Tofu, and so forth are prepared very similar to each other. They use the same CIs (oil, garlic, ginger, corn starch, rice wine, soy sauces, oyster sauce, MSG, broth, etc.) and GIs (scallion, black pepper, white pepper, etc.). Only the MIs (beef, chicken, pork, shrimp, vegetables, etc.) and SIs (broccoli, bok choy, bamboo shoot, etc.) may be varied. Most dishes are prepared practically the same way. Thinly sliced MI is quickly stir fried in a very hot wok along with some of the CIs (garlic, ginger, scallion, etc.). Then, SIs such as Chinese vegetables are added to the MI and the frying is continued for about 2 minutes. Broth is added to the frying and then the remaining CIs (cornstarch, oyster sauce, rice wine, sugar, MSG, etc.) are added to conclude the preparation. The dish is garnished with black pepper, white pepper, scallion, and a few drops of toasted sesame oil, then served.

Chinese dishes can be very involved and complex. There are numerous CIs that are used in Chinese cooking. Most of these ingredients are, however, in the form of sauces such as soy sauces, oyster sauce, Hoisan sauce, etc. These sauces are usually made of soybean derivatives. Other pre-processed ingredients used in the cooking include vegetables, meats, fish, poultry, and seafood that are seasoned with soybean derivatives, fermented or pickled and/or dried. The preserved ingredients, tastes range from salty, sour, and sweet to hot and spicy.

Comparison of Asian Curries

Among the Asian stews discussed above, the Indian/Pakistani curries (beef, fish, lamb, pork, poultry, and vegetable) are the most widely used and modified by the other Asians (Burmese, Cambodian, Chinese, Filipino, Indonesian, Japanese, Korean, Laotian, Malaysian, Thai, Vietnamese, etc.). However, among this uncountable variety of curries, the Indian/Pakistani and the Chinese versions define the boundaries of the spectrum of the curry variations.

The other Asian curries fall in between these two boundaries. Variations of the Asian curries CIs are compared in Table 2.

TABLE 2. **Variations of CIs among Asian Curries**

Basic Asian Curry CIs		
Indian and Pakistani	Other Asians	Chinese
All the Asian herbs and spices listed in Table 4	All the Asian herbs and spices listed in Table 4 and commercial curry mixes	commercial curry mixes* corn starch* garlic soy sauce* rice wine MSG*, sugar

*Asian ingredients available in supermarkets

Most Indian/Pakistani families blend their own complex curry mixes. Indian/Pakistani housewives usually blend their curry mixes for each preparation. They hand grind onion, garlic, ginger, red pepper, fresh cayenne pepper, curry leaf, cumin, coriander, etc. into a paste. They are fried in woks in a very hot oil. Then, MI is added and simmered for 1 hour or so before SIs (vegetables, chana dahl, etc.) are added and cooked. Whereas other Asians don't usually formulate their own curry mixes as involved as the Indian/Pakistani curry mixes, they instead use pre-blended commercial curry mixes (such as curry powders, garam masala, meat masala, curry paste, etc.) and may use additional Asian spices and herbs from Table 4. Or, ten or fewer herbs and spices from the list are used in place of the commercial curry mixes. In addition, the Asians may use some Chinese flavoring ingredients such as fish sauce, MSG, shrimp paste, soy sauces, preserved vegetables, etc. in their curries. These Chinese ingredients are not used by most Indian/Pakistani in their curries. This is a main difference between the curries of the Indian/Pakistani and the other Asians and places the other Asians curries in the middle of the curry spectrum. At the other end of the spectrum are the Chinese curries. The Chinese prepare their curries differently from the remaining Asians and use the CIs consisting of strong commercial curry powder, MSG, corn starch, rice wine, soy sauce, and sugar. These CIs, except the soy sauce, are not used in the Indian/Pakistani and the other Asians curries. These Chinese ingredients are the basic CIs commonly used in many other Chinese dishes, including stir fries. This clearly illustrates the way the Chinese put local touches to the curry recipes imported from India and Pakistan.

Most curries are prepared similar to the American stews. The CIs (onion, garlic, ginger, and curry mix) are sauteed in oil and simmered with MIs and SIs (if used) to the desired textures. The dish is then garnished with the GIs and served. The overall AFTs of the curries are the hybrid blend of the cooked ingredients. However, the Chinese prepare the curries in a wok using their traditional stir frying technique. Because the technique quickly cooks the ingredients with an intense heat for a short time, the ingredients (MIs and SIs) are used thinly sliced. Thus, the ingredients are cooked mostly on their outer layers. Furthermore, the technique necessitates the use of the curry CIs (cornstarch, curry powder, soy sauce or soybean paste, rice wine, MSG, and sugar) at the conclusion of the stir frying as the GIs to avoid burning them. Hence, the AFTs of the Chinese curries are, unlike the rest of the Asian curries, the mixed flavors of the ingredients cooked on their outer layers and the flavors of the corn starch mixture. Hence, the overall flavors of the Chinese stir fried curries are analogous to the mixed flavors of the stir fried meats smothered with a barbecue sauce on it.

All the Asian curries bear the characteristic curry AFT. It is because one of the CIs (curry powder) used by the Chinese and the other Asian contains most of the spices used in the Indian/Pakistani homemade curry blends such as cardamon, cinnamon, clove, coriander, cumin, and so forth. In addition, the remaining CIs, such as garlic, ginger, oil, and onion, are commonly used in all the curries.

Asian Spices

The type of spices and seasoning mixes used in Asian cooking has a certain pattern. The ingredients used by the Chinese and the Indian/Pakistani cooking define the two ends of the Asian spice spectrum. The other Asian foods lie in between these two boundaries. Some are closer to the Chinese (such as Japanese, Korean, and Vietnamese). The other remaining Southeast Asians (such as Burmese, Cambodian, Filipino, Indonesian, Laotian, Malaysian, and Thai) use both Indian/Pakistani and Chinese ingredients.

Most ingredients used in the Indian/Pakistani cooking are not used in the Chinese cooking (except curry powder) and vice versa. Whereas the other Asians use both in their cooking. The differences are outlined in Table 3. Group G1 ingredients are used in all Asian cuisines. Group G2 is not used by the Chinese, and used only by the

204

Indian/Pakistani and the other Southeast Asians. Group G3 ingredients are not used by the Indian/Pakistani but used only by the Chinese and the other Southeast Asians.

TABLE 3. Some Asian Herbs, Spices, and Seasoning Ingredients

Indian/ Pakistani	Other Asians	Chinese	
cinnamon	cinnamon	cinnamon	
clove	clove	clove	
curry mix	curry mix	curry mix	
garlic	garlic	garlic	G1
ginger	ginger	ginger	
cayenne	cayenne	cayenne	
etc.	etc.	etc.	
asafoetida	asafoetida	–	
curry leaf	curry leaf	–	
black	black		G2
mustard	mustard	–	
etc.	etc.		
–	black bean sauce	black bean sauce	
–	fish sauce	fish sauce	G3
	Hoisin sauce	Hoisin sauce	
–	oyster sauce	oyster sauce	
	pickled tofu	pickled tofu	
–	etc.	etc.	

I used to go hunting small game (deer, wild fowls, wild pigeons, etc.) with my boyhood friends in small villages surrounding Yangon (Rangoon) in Burma. We would then make arrangement with the local folks to cook our meals with the game we had gathered in our hunting. I would watch the husband and wife, who undertook the cooking, clean the game and prepare the meals. While, the husband cleaned the game the wife made the CIs mix (onion, ginger, garlic, red pepper, and fresh cayenne pepper), pounding the ingredients together in a heavy grindstone mortar and pestle by the outdoor wood fire made for the cooking. The husband would cut the cleaned meat to bite-size pieces, washed them, and massage the pieces by hand with salt, turmeric powder, and the CIs mixture his wife had prepared. The wife then put the meat in cold-pressed unrefined peanut oil, added water, then cooked the meat stew. The stew was served on steamed rice. We all would sit on the floor around a round table and enjoy the meal.

Many such experiences lead me to conclude that the seasoning CIs used by the country folks must represent a typical group of ingredients that is provincial and identifies with their ethnic character. The kind of seasoning ingredients usage broadens with the urban folks. Although there are variations to the kind of the ingredients used by the people from different regions of Burma, the variations are, nevertheless, maintained within the group of the Asian spices and herbs listed in Table 4. My experiences with the other Asian foods have also lead me to identify them also with the same group of the core ingredients.

My similar experiences with the Western cooking have also led me to similar conclusions for the Western ingredients listed in the same Table 4. The spices commonly used in the Western cooking were unknown to me before I came to the Untied States in the fall of 1954 to study at the University of Wisconsin, Madison. I stayed at one of the University's dormitories, Jones House. There I met and became very good friends with Paul Conant, Dave Gray, late John Licking, and Jim Wimmer. Jim and John were Freshmen then. Jim came from Wisconsin Dells. He graciously invited me to spend a night with his family. Jim took me in his family boat for an unforgettable wonderful sightseeing trip to see the river-carved sandstone formations in the Dells. Dave, John, and Paul came from Ripon. Dave and Paul were Sophomores then. I was invited by Dave to visit his family. John and Paul were also visiting their families that weekend. That night they took me for pizza at the "Jess & Nick's Pizza" on the Main Street in Oshkosh. They ordered a large pizza with cheese and Italian sausage on it. I had one of my most memorable feast that night. That was my very first experience with the Western spices (oregano, sage, thymes, and parsley). I was very impressed and developed a love for pizza. Now, I will eat pizza at every opportunity I get. I was also introduced to other American foods bratwurst, spaghetti, chili con carne, peanut butter, and so forth during my stay in Wisconsin.

Asian and Western Ingredients Comparison

Some of the ingredients commonly used in Asian and Western cooking are compared in Tables 4, 5, and 6 below. Use of these different kinds of ingredients are the main reasons for their basic differences in AFTs between the Asian and the Western foods.

TABLE 4. Common Herbs and Spices Used as CIs

Asian		Western	
Spices	Herbs	Spices	Herbs
anise*	cayenne*	all spice	celery
asafoetida	fresh	basil	chives
bay,leaf*	chives*	celery	garlic
caraway*	cilantro*	chervil	lemon
cardamon*	curry leaf	dill	onion
cayenne*	garlic*	marjoram	parsley
cinnamon*	ginger*	oregano	pepper,
clove*	lemon*	paprika	bell
coriander*	lemon grass	rosemary	
cumin*	lime*	sage	
curry,leaf	onion*	savory	
curry,mix*	tamarind	sassafras	
fennel*		tarragon	
fenugreek		thyme	
horseradish*			
mace*			
masala,garam			
masala,meat			
mustard,black			
mustard,white*			
nutmeg*			
pepper,black*			
pepper,red*			
pepper,white*			
poppy*			
saffron			
turmeric*			

*Asian ingredients available in supermarkets

Some of the seasoning mixes commonly used in the Asians and Western cooking are listed below. Indian/Pakistani use mixes such as chutnies, curry pastes, etc. other than those listed under Asian. The seasoning mixes are formulated using the ingredients from their respective groups of herbs and spices shown in Table 4 above.

TABLE 5. Some Commonly Used Seasoning Mixes

Asian	Western
barbecue sauce,Chinese	all spice
black bean sauce	barbecue sauces
black bean/garlic sauce	Beau Monde
fish sauce	bouillon
five spice,Chinese	catsup,tomato
Hoisan sauce	cheeses
oyster sauce	chili
pickled tofu	gravy mixes
pickled tofu,red rice	Italian seasoning
shrimp pastes	mayonnaise
shrimp sauces	mustard sauce
soy bean,fermented	poultry seasoning
soybean paste	soup mixes
soy sauces*	tomato paste
	wines
	worcestershire

*Asian ingredient available in supermarkets

208

Cooking Oils. Although there are many varieties of oils used in preparing foods, most commonly used oils in cooking Asian and Western dishes are listed below in Table 6. Oils play a major role in developing the basic AFTTs of all kinds of prepared foods. Thus, use of such different types of oils is a main factor contributing to the differences in the basic AFTs of the Asian and Western dishes. See "Purposes of Oil and Water" section in Chapter 4 for the roles play by the oils and water in cooking.

TABLE 6. Most Commonly Used Cooking Oils in Asian and Western Cooking

Asian	Western
animal fats	animal fats
butter	butter
coconut oil,crude	corn oil,refined
ghee,clarified butter	hydrogenated oils
ghee,clarified	margarine
vegetable oil	olive oil,crude
mustard oil,crude	olive oil,refined
palm oil,refined	partially
peanut oil,crude	hydrogenated oils
rice bran oil,refined	peanut oil,refined
sesame oil,crude	vegetable oils,
	refined (soybean,
	sunflower,etc.)

Asian Grocery Lists

Asian Grocery Stores. Following lists show where you can obtain Asian ingredients for preparing the recipes given in this cookbook. Western ingredients are not listed since they are commonly available in all supermarkets.

The lists are not intended to be exhaustive. However, they are the ingredients I am familiar with. They are available at Asian stores and some American supermarkets. Ever-increasing varieties of Asian ingredients are becoming available in your local supermarkets as well. When I immigrated to the U.S. in 1959, I was first located in Buffalo, New York. At that time, the only Asian ingredients I could buy from my local supermarkets were some soy sauces and curry powders processed by the American food manufacturers. There was a small Asian grocery store in downtown Buffalo owned and operated by a Chinese man, Mr Lee. He was my good friend. Even at his store, I could occasionally buy a few Asian ingredients such as fresh ginger root, sour bamboo shoots, oyster sauce, and the soy sauces processed in Hong Kong. Sometimes fresh coriander leaves were available. I had to visit the nearby larger cities Chicago, Detroit, New York City, and Toronto (Ontario, Canada) for other common Asian ingredients. But times have changed since then. Nowadays, the number of Asian grocery stores has exploded in the U.S. They are so numerous and overwhelming that they are no longer viable to identify them by their store names and addresses in this cookbook. Even Kansas City, where I now reside, has many Asian grocery stores owned and operated by the Chinese, Indian, Pakistani, Korean, Laotian, Thai, and Vietnamese. In addition, supermarkets are also carrying a respectable inventory of the Asian items, such as bamboo shoots, bean sprout, bitter gourd (or melon), bok-choy, bottle gourd, cilantro, diakon, fresh ginger root, and so forth, which were not available before.

You have a ready compiled list for shopping Asian ingredients if you wish to stock your pantry. The ingredients are summarized in three groups. Each group identifies the stores where you can have larger varieties and selections of the items.

Chinese Ingredients. Complete line of the ingredients are available in most Chinese, Korean, Thai, and Vietnamese stores. The ingredients used in the recipes are listed below.

TABLE 7. Chinese Ingredients Used in the Recipes

bamboo shoot, in water
bamboo shoot, sliced sour
barbecue sauce, Chinese
black bean in soybean oil
curry powder
curry paste
fish sauce
garlic/black beans/red pepper
Hoisin sauce
Kim Chee
mackerel, salted, in peanut oil
mushroom, Chinese dried
noodle, instant Oriental
oyster flavored sauce
red snapper, salted, in peanut oil
rice, extra long grain

rice wine, cooking
sesame oil, toasted
shrimp pastes or shrimp sauces, fine or coarse
soy bean dried, fermented
soy bean paste
soy bean sauce
soy sauces, light, dark, black, and thick
tofu, fresh
tofu, fried
tofu, pickled in rice wine
tofu. pickled in rice wine, hot
tofu, pickled/red rice/ wine
tofu, pickled/red rice/wine, hot
vegetables, pickled in rice wine

Indian/Pakistani Ingredients. The ingredients used in the recipes are shown below. They are readily available in Indian, Pakistani, and in some Chinese, Korean, Thai, and Vietnamese stores.

TABLE 8. Indian/Pakistani Ingredients Used in the Recipes

black mustard seeds	flours (gram chick pea, rice)
black pepper, powder and peppercorn	garam masala
cardamon, seeds and powder	mango chutney
cinnamon, powder and sticks	mango pickle in oil,
clove	meat masala
coriander, seeds and powder	lentils (pink, moong, toor, chana)
cumin, seeds and powder	red pepper whole, crushed,
curry leaf or sweet neem,	and powder
(fresh and dried)	rice, extra long grain, in 25 to
curry powder	100-pound bags
curry paste	saffron strand (Spanish or Syrian)
fennel seeds	sambar, instant
fenugreek	tamarind

Garam masala: Several garam masala brand names are readily available only in the Indian/Pakistani grocery stores. They are manufactured in India, Pakistan, and in the U.S. Several different brand names were used for developing the recipes.

Madras curry powder: One of the curry powder brand names used for developing the recipes is identified below with the permission from the manufacturer. The curry mix used in Recipe #22, "Golden Curry Mix" is also manufactured by the same company.
"S&B" Oriental Curry Powder and Golden Curry Mix
S&B Shokuhin Co., Ltd.
Nihonbashi, Chuo-ku, Tokyo 103

Meat masala: The following meat masala was used for developing the recipes included in this cookbook. Several meat masala brand names are readily available only in the Indian/Pakistani grocery stores. They are manufactured only in India and Pakistan. The name brand is included with the permission from the company.
MDH Meat Masala
Mahashian Di Hatti (P) Ltd.
9/44, IND. Area
Kirtinagar, New Delhi-110 015, India.

212

Instant sambar mixes: There are only three brand names I have experiences with. They are commonly available in most Indian/Pakistani grocery stores. The mixes are also produced only in India. Please note that the recipe 173 "Sambar" uses only the instant sambar mix not the sambar powder which is also available in the stores.

Fresh Asian Vegetables. These are readily available in most Asian stores. They carry more varieties and selections. Large supermarkets in metropolitan cities carry most of these vegetables as well.

TABLE 9. Asian Vegetables Used in the Recipes

bean curd or tofu, fresh	daikon or Asian white radish
bitter gourd or bitter mellon	eggplant, Asian
bok choy or white mustard	green mustard leaves
bottle gourd	snow peas
cayenne pepper, fresh	spinach, Asian
cilantro or coriander leaves	

Chili, Chilli, and Cayenne Pepper. Fresh and dried cayenne or red peppers are used extensively in Asian cooking. But, the peppers are known only as chilli (or chili) among the Asian in English. So, when I first came to the U.S. in 1954, I had a disastrous experience with the word. I was completely unaware of the ingredient chili powder which is used for making a popular chili con carne in the U.S. So, when I went to the grocery stores for chili (or chilli) the only chili powder I could find on the spice racks were, of course, the chili powder seasoning mix. I saw the cayenne and the red pepper powders on those racks, but I was unaware that they were the ones I was looking for. I had no idea of what they are used for. Thus, I dared not use them because I was so afraid of messing up my Burmese dishes. I opted for the chili powder instead, and used in all my cooking.

The Burmese dishes that I cooked with the chili tasted everything but the Burmese flavors that my mother used to cook for the family. Of course, when you use the chili inadvertently as red pepper in Asian dishes, the AFT of the dishes are changed. In fact that was exactly what I was trying to avoid in the first place, and it lead me to avoid the use of the cayenne and red peppers I saw on the racks. I am most certain that there are many Asians who are experiencing the same with the word chili at least on their first arrival in the U.S.

Such confusion would also be true with most Americans who

reside in the Asian countries. Some would even misconstrue the word chili as the chili seasoning mix and use in their chili dishes. If that is the case, I can assure you that this mistaken identity would be one of their most memorable rude awakening experiences when they taste their chili con carne much much hotter than usual. Similarly, they would also have great difficulty in finding cayenne pepper powder there because, the word cayenne pepper is not commonly understood.

Even today, you will find the word chilli used on Chinese, Indian, Pakistani, and Thai food package labels. These labels should be understood as the cayenne pepper or red pepper, not as chili seasoning powder.

Storing Spices. Most of the dried herbs and spices are hygroscopic (absorb moisture readily). Hence, we don't dispense the spices directly from their containers (bottles or cans) holding them above the pot during the cooking. Instead, we would measure all the needed spices into a cup, reseal the containers, and empty the cup into the cooking pot. This technique is used to avoid collecting moisture, given off from the cooking, in the containers. The moisture if collected in the containers would cake and culture fungi on the spices during their storage. Store them in cold, dry, and dark places. Don't store them in spaces above or next to your stove; they get hot during cooking and accelerate their spoilage. Proper storage will preserve your spices, especially coriander, cumin, curry, and turmeric powders, and they last at least a year. Paprika could lose its red color with age, if this happens replace it.

We used to store newly acquired caraway, coriander, and cumin seeds in our kitchen cupboards. When we opened the containers (jars or the sealed bags) for the first time, we found these seeds in clusters, damped, and covered with molds. We lost several new packages in the past due to such contaminations. Somewhere along their way to the store shelves, the spices were obviously stored inadequately in damp and warm places. Thus, allowing the airborne microorganisms to contaminate the seeds. When we stored the newly purchased seeds in the freezer the problem disappeared completely. They may be stored for two to three years in the freezer.

We were also having problems storing enriched rice in our closet. We often found baby moths flying out from our rice bags. Somehow, during the storage, either in our closet or at the grocery stores, the mother moths laid eggs on the rice bag to feed their newborns after they hatched from their eggs. We also overcame this problem when we stored our newly purchased rice bags in the freezer. We buy two 25 pounds rice bags at a time or more when they are on sale. We have stored our rice bags in the freezer sometimes for 3 months or more. However, we had to store a newly opened bag differently for daily use. We store the opened 25-pound rice bag in a large polyethylene bag and they are placed in a garbage-can-sized plastic container. The container is then covered with another plastic sheet over its opening and the lid is placed over the sheet and sealed.

4.
SIMMER–SAUTE

Onion, *Allium cepa*

Why are You not Cooking?

Economical, technological, and social advances are continuously changing with time, thus affecting every aspect of our daily lives. Thus, the scope of our daily subsistence obligations are widening. This means fitting our daily chores into a 24-hour time frame, with less time to attend to each chore. Among these, keeping up our good health is of primary importance. Maintenance of our good health depends upon, among others, eating healthful, flavorful, and satisfying meals. A sure way to ascertain such meals is to cook for ourselves. Eating processed foods (canned foods, frozen meals, fast foods, restaurant meals, etc.) cannot always assure us of healthful meals. Descriptions of the ingredients and nutritional contents of some foods on their packaging labels and menus of some restaurants are inaccurate and often misleading. It is difficult to know what we are eating just from reading them. Therefore, it is unwise to consume processed meals in excessive quantities and frequencies. Most of us get so exhausted from a long stressful day at work that we have no ambition left to do anything when we return home. But, we sense that we still have to fulfill our daily obligations for ourselves and our families. There are many people who want to cook but don't know how. We also have many who know how but cannot find time to cook. There are some who just hate to cook; they are turned off because their subconscious sense that the cooking is complex, intimidating, and time consuming. They may also believe that cooking is a special skill and needs talent.

Precooking techniques (presauteing and prebrowning) are the basis for preparing at least 85 percent of our everyday cooking. These traditional techniques are generally considered as the critical steps for developing the AFT bases for the dishes. Thus, they are traditionally used in conjunction with the basic techniques such as baking, boiling, broiling, frying, steaming, etc. For example, when a beef pot roast is prepared, its flavoring and seasoning ingredients (beef, black pepper, flour, salt, and sugar) are prebrowned. Then, they are simmered with the remaining ingredients. Similarly, other popular dishes such as casseroles, curries, soups, stir fries, etc. are also prepared in the same manner. Nevertheless, prebrowning and presauteing are labor intensive and time consuming. They demand organization, preparation, skill, patience, and time to use them effectively and safely. A good nine-tenths of our manual labor over the stove is expended in attending to these precooking steps. For instance, many classic cookbooks recommend 10-20 minutes for prebrowning the ingredients in preparing the beef pot roast. Those minutes are the most strenuous and stressful time you have to invest (flipping, mixing, poking, stirring, scraping nonstop) to prepare the roast. But they are worthwhile if you are motivated and have stamina and time for cooking. Otherwise, you lose all your enthusiasm just by thinking about the hard work that you will have to go through. Eventually, you end up postponing enjoying the dish for some other time. This chapter intends to help you overcome these conflicting obstacles. The Simmer-Saute (S-S) is an answer for you.

Clarifying Presauteing

The word is used extensively in this cookbook. It's a special case of sauteing. The word implies sauteing of the core ingredients ahead in preparation for the main cooking event. It's one of the precooking techniques intended to soften and develop the basic aroma, flavor, taste, and texture of the ingredients for preparing the dishes.

Simmer-Saute

I would like to introduce you to a cooking technique that is extensively used in Burma. It is called "pyote-kyaw" in Burmese. Its equivalent translation in English is "Simmer-Saute". The technique is generally used for preparing beef, chicken, chicken parts (gizzard, heart, and liver) and shrimp dishes. The dishes are also referred to as "pyote-kyaw" collectively. A typical Burmese provincial way of preparing these dishes is by combining a MI with an oil (usually an unrefined cold-pressed peanut or sesame), turmeric powder, salt, and water and bringing them to a boil. The MI is boiled until it is cooked. At the conclusion of the cooking the remaining water, if any, is evaporated until the ingredients sizzle in the oil. There are numerous geographical variations to preparing these dishes. My mother used this technique often as I was growing up. When I came to this country, I found myself using this technique most of the time after modifying it, because it is extremely simple to use and gave me ample time during the simmering to do my homework. This fitted in with my busy graduate school schedule as well. Moreover, these dishes are tasty, satisfying, healthful, and inexpensive.

I use the S-S technique as a substitute for prebrowning, presauteing, and simmering wherever it is applicable. Thus, it is adapted with some modification for preparing various types of American, Burmese Chinese, Indian, and Pakistani dishes. They include stir fries, stews, salads, curries, soups, casseroles and so forth . The technique is also used for precooking meats and vegetables for use in combination with other basic cooking techniques such as baking, broiling, grilling, roasting, smoking, and

218

steaming. For example, it is used for precooking meats for preparing meat salads and kabob. The technique uses any cut of meat and allows you to cut to any size including bite-sized pieces. It is a very useful and versatile method. When I am under stress or short of time and not in the mood for cooking, I resort to this technique. I can assure you that this technique will soon become your favorite for preparing healthful and delicious meals when you are exhausted and not motivated for the cooking.

Anatomy of Simmer-Saute Technique. Most recipes included
in this cookbook employ the S-S technique. Various simple traditional American and Asian dishes are prepared with the technique. The cooking sequences that constitute the S-S technique are summarized in the following Diagram 5.

Boiling->Simmering->Evaporating->Self-Sauteing-> (One-Step Dishes)
  SQ1   SQ2   SQ3   SQ4

Simmer-Saute Cooking Sequences
Diagram 5

In sequence 1 (SQ1), the method combines a MI (beef, chicken, fish, or pork, etc.), CIs (celery, garlic, oil, onion, spices, etc.), and water in a pot and bring them to a boil. In SQ2, the heating is reset and they are covered and simmered with occasional mixing until they are cooked partially or completely (this is my first modification to "pyoat-kyaw"). In SQ3, residual water in the cooking is evaporated until the ingredients sizzle in the oil. In SQ4, the sizzling of the simmered ingredients in the oil is carried out for a few more minutes (this is my second modification to "pyoat-kyaw" and is called self-sauteing). Then, the cooking is either concluded here, with the one-step dishes ready to serve, or continued with the one-step dishes (simmer-sauteed ingredients) to making other types of dishes: casseroles, curries, salads, sauces, soups, stews, and stir-fries (this is my third modification to "pyoat-kyaw"). The one-step dishes are the key intermediates to preparing the other types of dishes.

Basic Beef Stew Recipe #Ex 1 was described in Chapter 3, page 186. The cooking procedure of the stew is summarized under Conventional Cooking Procedure below. The procedure will be adapted to the simmer-saute technique to illustrate the simplicity and labor-saving features of the S-S technique.

Conventional cooking procedure of Recipe# Ex 1:

1. Sprinkle salt and pepper on meat cubes.
2. Add to 5-quart pot the oil and brown meat cubes, turning on all sides.
3. Remove the browned meat and set aside.
4. Add to the pot onion and garlic, then saute until soft and tender.
5. Add the browned meat, sugar, and beef broth. Cover and simmer for 1 1/2 hours.
6. Add wine and all the vegetables, secondary ingredients, and simmer additional 30-40 minutes.
7. Disperse flour to a smooth paste in 1/4 cup water and stir into the stew with constant stirring until it thickens.

Since the meat was prebrowned and onion and garlic were presauteed cooking the stew for a total of 2 hours or more is counterproductive. Moreover, the mixture of water, oil, and wine used in the cooking is a powerful combination of solvents. Thus, the ingredients could be thoroughly cooked, pulverized, and extracted of their soluble substances within 75 to 90 minutes. Hence, main intent of the recipe could be accomplished without sacrificing much of its browned nutty flavor by leaving out the steps 1, 2, 3, and 4 of the recipe and using the S-S technique as described below.

To adapt Ex 1 to the S-S cooking the ingredients are regrouped and rearranged in order of their cooking sequences. Water is included in the listing for simmer-sauteing and making flour mixture. The modification is shown in recipe Ex 1A below.

Ex 1A   Basic Beef Stew (regrouped)

Group 1
32 oz beef, cut into
   1-in cubes
3 Tablespoons oil
1 large onion, diced
1 medium garlic, diced
1/2 teaspoon sugar
1/4 teaspoon pepper
1 teaspoon salt
1/2 cup water
Group 2
1/2 cup water

1/4 cup flour
Group 3
2 cups hot beef broth
2 medium onions, each
   quartered
4 large potatoes, each
   quartered
3 large carrots, cut into
   1/4-in slices
2 Tablespoons burgundy
   wine

Simmer-saute cooking procedure:

Prepare beef per section 6a. Combine Group 1 and add to 5-quart pot. Mix well and bring to boil at "Medium High" heat setting. Boil 1-2 minutes. Reset heat to "Medium Low", cover, and simmer 60 minutes. Mix occasionally. Meanwhile, prepare Group 2 mixture per section 20b and set aside. Remove cover, evaporate Group 1 to sizzling, cover, and let self-saute 5 minutes. Reset heat to "Medium". Add Group 3, mix, and bring to boil. Boil 1-2 minutes. Reset heat to "Medium Low", cover, and simmer 30 minutes. Remix Group 2, add to pot with continuous mixing until the gravy thickens to smooth consistency, and serve.

You can see in the simmer-saute procedure the redundant steps from the conventional technique are avoided. The cooking is simplified and the time spent over the stove, about 15 minutes, is avoided.

Preparing Various Types of Dishes

Typical recipes illustrating the adaptations of the basic S-S technique to preparing one-step dish, stir fried, stew, soup, and casserole are described below. In addition experimenting new ingredients with the S-S technique is also illustrated.

One-Step Dish. A distinguishing feature of the one-step dishes is that they have only one group of ingredients listed in their recipes. Thus, during their preparations no other ingredients are introduced in their cooking. The cooking is concluded after completion of the four basic simmer-saute sequences described in Diagram 5. All other dishes are derived from their respective one-step intermediate dishes. A recipe that illustrates the adaptation of the technique to preparing a one-step dish, Ex 2 New Orleans Pork, is described below.

Since all the ingredients are used together at the same time in the cooking they are grouped together in Group 1. The ingredients may be added to the pot in any order.

Ex 2   New Orleans Pork*

Group 1

32 oz pork, cut into 1-in cubes	1/8 teaspoon white pepper
3 Tablespoons oil	1/4 teaspoon pepper
1 1/2 cups water	1/4 teaspoon basil flakes
1 medium onion, diced	1 teaspoon salt
1 large garlic, minced	1/2 teaspoon thyme flakes
1 medium tomato, diced	1/4 teaspoon parsley flakes
1 medium jalapeno pepper, diced	1/4 teaspoon crushed red pepper

Combine Group 1. Mix well. Bring to boil at "Medium High" heat setting. Boil 1-2 minutes. Reset heat to "Medium Low", cover, and simmer 60 minutes. Mix occasionally. Remove cover and evaporate to sizzling. Cover, let self-saute 5 minutes, and serve. Add 1/4 to 1/2 cup hot water to pot for more sauce, if needed.

Many such simple recipes that use canned and packaged American and Asian foods (such as soups, pre-blended seasoning mixes, seasoned meats, pickled vegetables, and so forth) are included in this cookbook.

Stir-Fries. Traditional Chinese stir frying needs skill and practice, especially when meats are required to be sliced almost paper thin. In addition, frying the ingredients to a proper tenderness, by manipulating the heating, is a very tricky skill. These difficulties are inherent in Chinese stir frying. However, the Chinese technique may be simplified using the simmer-saute technique to reproduce authentic Chinese dishes. In general, the simplified version would first simmer the meat (sliced to 1/4 inch thickness or to any other thicknesses, no skill required) to right tenderness and sauteed with garlic and ginger. The simmer-sauteed ingredients are then mixed with a corn starch seasoning mixture consisting of corn starch, soy sauce, oyster flavored sauce, sugar, MSG, and Chinese rice wine, etc. The dish is garnished with black pepper, white pepper, and toasted sesame oil. Many stir fried meat/vegetable combination dishes are created by adding fresh or precooked or preserved vegetables to the simmer-sauteed ingredients. A popular traditional Chinese stir fried recipe Ex 3 is described below. The new technique is used for preparing the dish. The intent is to illustrate how little time you have to spend over the stove and how little stressful it is to prepare the dish. After enjoying this dish you will be pleasantly surprised and convinced that you have prepared such an exotic dish with ease. Now, you can prepare such healthful Chinese dishes at home any time you want.

Note that the recipe ingredients are grouped in five separate groups and are arranged in order of their use in the cooking to adapt to the S-S technique.

Ex 3   Ginger Chicken in Oyster Sauce

Group 1
32 oz chicken white meat cut
    into 1/4-in slices
3 Tablespoons oil
1 cup water
Group 2
3 Tablespoons corn starch
1/4 cup water
2 Tablespoons oyster sauce
1 Tablespoon soy sauce
1 Tablespoon rice wine
1/2 teaspoon sugar

1/4 teaspoon MSG
no salt
Group 3
1 Tablespoon ginger, diced
1 large garlic, diced
Group 4
1 1/2 cups hot chicken broth
Group 5
4 stalks scallion, diced
1/4 teaspoon sesame oil
1/4 teaspoon pepper
1/8 teaspoon white pepper

Prepare chicken per section 6b. Combine with the remaining Group 1 in pot. Mix and heat to boiling at "Medium High" heat setting. Boil 1-2 minutes. Reset heat to "Medium Low," cover, and simmer 20 minutes. Mix occasionally. Meanwhile, prepare Group 2 per section 2. Set aside. Reset heat to "Medium", remove cover, and evaporate to sizzling. Add Group 3 in sizzling oil. Do not mix. Let self-saute 30 seconds. Add Group 4 and mix. Reset heat to "Medium Low". Remix Group 2, add to pot, mix immediately, and stir continuously to a smooth consistency per section 20a. Garnish with Group 5 and serve.

Stews. Many types of Western stews are prepared by first simmer-sauteing a meat with seasoning ingredients. When the ingredients self-saute themselves in the sizzling oil, corn starch, potato, and water are added, and they are simmered until the ingredients are tender. Asian curries and stews are also prepared in the similar manners.

Ex 4   Lamb Stew

Group 1
32 oz lean lamb, cut
   into 1-in cubes
1 cup water
1 medium bay leaf
1/8 teaspoon oregano
1 medium garlic, minced
1/8 teaspoon pepper
1/8 teaspoon white pepper
2 Tablespoons beef
   bouillon
1/4 teaspoon salt
3 Tablespoons oil
1 teaspoon sugar

Group 2
1/4 cup water
2 Tablespoons corn starch
1 Tablespoon Worcestershire
   sauce
Group 3
2 cups hot water
Group 4
2 large carrots, cut each into
   8 pieces
2 large potatoes, each quartered
2 medium onions, each quartered
Group 5
1/4 teaspoon pepper

Combine Group 1. Mix well. Bring to boil at "Medium High" heat setting Boil 1-2 minutes. Reset heat to "Medium Low", cover, and simmer 60 minutes. Mix occasionally. Mix Group 2 per section 2 and set aside. Reset heat to "Medium". Remove cover and evaporate to sizzling. Reset heat to "Medium Low". Add Group 3, mix well, remix Group 2 and add to pot. Mix continuously until gravy thickens to smooth consistency per section 20a. Reset heat to "Medium". Add Group 4, mix well, cover, and simmer about 20 minutes. Mix occasionally. Garnish with Group 5 and serve.

Soups. A multitude of healthful and delicious soups are prepared with the S-S method. When a meat vegetable soup is prepared, the meat is first simmer-sauteed to partial tenderness with the core ingredients (onion, celery, tomato, bouillon or broth, oil, black pepper, sugar, herbs and spices, etc). Then secondary ingredients (vegetables such as carrot, potato, green bean, bell pepper, as well as rice or macaroni and so forth) are added and simmered until the vegetables are cooked. See Ex 5 below.

Ex 5   Rinaldo's Beef Vegetable Soup

Group 1

8 oz lean beef, cut into 1-in cubes
1 cup water
3 Tablespoons olive oil
2 Tablespoons beef bouillon
1/2 teaspoon sugar
1 teaspoon pepper
1/4 teaspoon white pepper
1/2 teaspoon salt

Group 2

3 cups hot beef broth
2 large onions, each quartered
2 celery stalks, diced
2 large carrots, cut into
    1/2-in slices

2 large tomatoes, each quartered
1 (8-oz) can kidney beans
1 large garlic, diced
1 teaspoon paprika
1/4 teaspoon crushed red pepper
1/4 teaspoon sage
1/2 teaspoon thyme
1/4 teaspoon oregano
1 teaspoon parsley flakes

Group 3

15 green beans, cut into halves

Group 4

2 Tablespoons Parmesan cheese,
    grated

Combine Group 1. Mix well. Heat to boil at "Medium High". Boil 1-2 minutes. Reset heat to "Medium Low", cover, and simmer 30 minutes. Mix occasionally. Remove cover, reset heat to "Medium", and evaporate to sizzling. Cover and let self saute 2 minutes. Mix occasionally. Add Group 2, mix, reset heat to "Medium Low", and simmer 30 minutes. Add Group 3, mix well, and simmer 2 minutes. Garnish with Group 4 and serve. Add 1/4 to 1 cup hot water to pot for more sauce, if needed.

Casseroles. They are one of the best ways to use your leftovers. Here also you will notice how little effort you need to invest over the stove and prepare such an involved and time-consuming dish with ease. The dish is prepared by simply simmering and sauteing a mixture of meat, seasoning ingredients, oil, and water. Then, the simmer-sauteed ingredients are mixed with vegetables, noodles, pasta, or steamed rice. The pot is sealed and baked. A traditional popular American casserole recipe Ex 6 Broccoli Beef Rice Casserole is shown below to illustrate the adaptation of the simmer-saute technique.

Ex 6   Broccoli Beef Rice Casserole

Group 1
16 oz beef, 1/4-in slices
3 Tablespoons oil
1 cup water
Group 2
3/4 cup hot water
Group 3
1/2 cup 2% milk
2 Tablespoons margarine

1/2 teaspoon salt
1 (10-oz) can, cream of chicken
  soup
1/4 teaspoon pepper
Group 4
5 cups cooked rice
8 oz broccoli, frozen
4 oz American cheese, diced

Combine Group 1. Mix well. Heat to boiling at "Medium High" setting.
Boil 1-2 minutes. Reset heat to "Medium Low", cover, and simmer 20-25
minutes. Mix occasionally. Reset heat to "Medium", remove cover, and
evaporate to sizzling. Add Group 2 and mix. Add Group 3 and mix.
Reset heat to "Medium Low", cover, and simmer 5 minutes. Preheat oven
to 350F. Remove cover, add Group 4, and mix. Remove pot from stove,
seal, bake 45-50 minutes, and serve.

Experimenting New Ingredients. One of the most useful
attributes of the simmer-saute technique is for exploring basic AFTT of
unfamiliar seasoning ingredients. You can get some preliminary idea
about the new ingredients quickly and effectively with the method. You
can test the seasoning mixes with many kinds of MIs (meat, poultry,
seafood, shrimp, and vegetable). You may further develop your
preliminary results obtained in your previous experiments by
incorporating some additional ingredients, such as onion, garlic, ginger,
tomato, and so forth. Typical vegetarian (Ex 7) and non-vegetarian (Ex
8) recipes are shown below as examples for your experiments with a
Kansas City (KC) barbecue sauce. Use 2-quart pot with cover for all
experimental cooking.

Ex 7   Zucchini with Barbecue Sauce

Many other kinds of Group 1 MIs and Group 2 seasoning ingredients may be used with this recipe. The recipe is for one serving.

Group 1
1 small zucchini, cut
   into 1/2-in slices
1 Tablespoon oil
no salt

1/4 cup water
Group 2
2 teaspoons KC
   barbecue sauce

Prepare zucchini per section 13b. Combine with the remaining Group 1 in 1-quart pot. Mix well. Bring to boil at "Medium" heat setting. Boil 1-2 minutes. Reset heat to "Medium Low", cover, and simmer 10 minutes. Mix occasionally. Remove cover and evaporate to sizzling. Add Group 2, mix well, cover, let self-saute 3-5 minutes, and serve.

Ex 8   Beef with Barbecue Sauce

Group 1
4 oz lean beef, cut
   into 1/4-in slices
1 Tablespoon oil
no salt

1/4 cup water
Group 2
2 teaspoons KC
   barbecue sauce

Prepare beef per section 6a. Combine with the remaining Group 1 in 1-quart pot. Mix well. Bring to boil at "Medium" heat setting. Boil 1-2 minutes. Reset heat to "Medium Low", cover, and simmer 30 minutes. Mix occasionally. Remove cover and evaporate to sizzling. Add Group 2, mix well, cover, let self-saute 3-5 minutes, and serve.

A list of Asian seasoning mixes is shown below for you to experiment with the simmer-saute technique. Substitute one of these ingredients for the KC barbecue sauce in the above Ex 7 and Ex 8 recipes. Use only 1 to 2 teaspoons of the ingredients for your small scale experiments. Most of these foods are hot, salty, spicy, pungent, sour, and delicious..They are excellent with the simmer-sauteed pork, beef, chicken, shrimp, and fish. They are readily available in Chinese, Korean, Thai, and Vietnamese Asian grocery stores in most large metropolitan cities in the U.S. The ingredients shown in the list are also described in the Glossary section.

List of Asian Seasoning Mixes for Experiment
Tofu Sauce.
Chinese Preserved Vegetable.
Braised Bamboo Shoot.
Preserved Radish with Red Pepper Sauces.
Black Bean/Garlic/Red Pepper Sauces.
Black Bean in Soybean Oil.
Shallot/Garlic/Ginger in Oil.

There are also many Thai pre-processed foods using shrimp, fish, and vegetables. They may also be used for your experiments. Similarly, you may also wish to experiment on a small scale with some Western seasoning sauces, such as Cajun sauces, spaghetti sauces, Taco sauces, steak sauces, tabasco sauce, etc. other then the KC sauce used in Ex 7 and Ex 8.

Modular vegetarian and non-vegetarian recipes, using a Tofu Sauce as examples, are shown below to prepare for four servings with any of your favorite Asian and Western seasoning sauces listed above. Since, taste is subjective, you need to experiment yourself to find the one that will please your taste buds.

Ex 9   Tofu Sauce on Zucchini*

Group 1

1 large zucchini, cut
   into 1/2-in slices
3 Tablespoons oil
no salt

1/2 cup water
Group 2
3 Tablespoons Tofu Sauce
   (see glossary)

Prepare zucchini per section 13b. Combine with the remaining Group 1 in pot and bring to boil at "Medium High" heat setting. Boil 1-2 minutes. Mix well. Reset heat to "Medium Low", cover, and simmer 10 minutes with occasional mixing. Remove cover and evaporate to sizzling. Add Group 2, mix well, cover, and let self-saute 3 minutes, and serve. Add 1/4 to 1/2 cup hot water to pot for more sauce, if needed. Mix, salt to taste, and serve.

228

Ex 10   Pork with Tofu Sauce*

Group 1

32 oz lean pork, cut
  into 1/4-in slices
3 Tablespoons oil
no salt

1/2 cup water

Group 2

3 Tablespoons Tofu Sauce
  (see glossary)

Prepare pork per section 6h. Combine with the remaining Group 1 in pot and bring to boil at "Medium High" heat setting. Boil 1-2 minutes. Mix well. Reset heat to "Medium Low", cover, and simmer 45 minutes with occasional mixing. Remove cover and evaporate to sizzling. Add Group 2, mix well, cover, and let self-saute 3 minutes, and serve. Add 1/4 to 1/2 cup hot water to pot for more sauce, if needed. Mix, salt to taste, and serve.

    In addition several stripped recipes are included in the glossary section to experiment with above recipes Ex 7, Ex 8, Ex 9, and Ex 10.
    There are hundreds of pre-processed vegetarian and non-vegetarian ingredients, such as relishes, appetizers, hors d'oeuvres, and seasoning mixes are used all over the world. They are already seasoned, fermented, dried or pickled. Although most are salty, sour, spicy, and hot, we can use them in cooking with a little imagination. They are convenient, simple, inexpensive, and less laborious to use. Furthermore, it is an effective way to prepare authentic ethnic dishes. It is ideal for casual cooking using the simmer-saute technique. However, it may impose some problems for those who suffer from chronic medical conditions, such as hypertension, diabetes, and so forth to enjoy these dishes. Read the labels carefully before use. Many recipes that use canned and packaged American and Asian foods, such as soups, pre-blended seasoning mixes, seasoned meats, dried and fried fish, pickled vegetables, and so forth are included in Chapter 1.

Gravy Thickeners

One of the purposes of prebrowning meats coated with thickening starches such as, flour, corn starch, tapioca, etc., is to provide a base for producing tasty and flavorful gravies at the end of cooking. Thus, when you prepare a pot roast you prebrown the meat with flour for 20 minutes and simmer them for 2-3 hours. At the end of the cooking the browned flour contributes rich robust flavors to the pot roast gravy.

Flour. Similarly, you can also obtain a robust browned gravy base using simmer-saute. There are three ways you can obtain this gravy base. They only differ in when you put the flour in the cooking; that is, using the flour about the beginning, about the middle, or at the conclusion of the cooking.

In the beginning of cooking: In such cases, the flour is used as one of the core ingredients. First, simmer the meat with the oil, salt, sugar, and a small amount of water (about 1/4 cup) to dryness. This dryness stage should be attained within 10 minutes or so at "Medium" heat setting. Then, add flour to the oil and let them self-saute in the oil with occasional stirring until the flour is lightly browned. Then, add hot broth or water, cover, and simmer the mixture until the meat is tender. It is almost like cooking the browned flour with the meat from the beginning to the end of the cooking. The flavor of the browned flour is integrated into the overall flavor of the dish. When the cooking is completed you will have a tender meat in a robust brown gravy.

In the middle of cooking: In the second case you can simmer the meat with the salt, sugar, oil, and water for 20-30 minutes. The water is then evaporated to dryness. Then, the flour is added to the sizzling oil. Let them self-saute as above until the flour is browned. Hot broth or water is then added and the simmering is continued to the end of cooking. This second method simmers the browned flour only through part of the cooking. In such cases, flour is used as one of the secondary ingredients SIs in the cooking. The flavor of the browned flour is also integrated into the overall flavor of the dish. When the cooking is completed you are left with a brown gravy base.

At the end of cooking: In this case, the flour is used as a GI at the end of the cooking. The flour is mixed with other seasoning ingredients, if used, and made a mixture in a broth or water. The flour is mixed until it is dispersed well in the mixture. The mixture is set aside. At the end of the cooking, hot broth or water is added to the sizzling ingredients. Then the flour mixture is stirred in. The stirring is continued until a smooth textured gravy is obtained. The flour is not browned like in the previous first two cases. Therefore, it contributes its normal color and subtle taste to the gravy. The flavor of the flour in this case is unlike in the previous two cases it just merely added its flavor to the overall hybrid flavor of the dish. Similar to the taste of bread and butter where the flavor of the bread and butter are separately identifiable. Such uses are common in making some beef stews, stroganoff, chili, pot pies, Chinese stir fries, etc. It is a matter of preference which of the three methods one would like to use. The first two methods produce a similar tasty brown gravy. Thus, the simmer-saute is a viable alternative to the traditional prebrowning technique for making the gravy bases.

Corn Starch. Corn starch can develop a similar texture and flavor of flour. The corn starch is, in fact, more user friendly than the flour. The starch gets swollen and thickened as soon as it is heated with water, whereas the flour requires you to bring it to a boil and cook it for about 1-2 minutes to start the thickening process. You traded off very little, if any, of the robust flavor of the flour with the corn starch in these types of cooking. Thus, using the corn starch makes the cooking simpler, faster, and lesser work. However, it is rather important to disperse the starch thoroughly in a cold water or in a cold seasoning solution mixture. Make sure there is enough liquid in the pot to make the gravy. Otherwise, add some hot water to the pot, reduce heat to "Medium Low" or "Low" setting, and wait for 15-20 seconds before adding the starch mixture. Then, add the corn starch mixture to the gravy gradually and stir briskly immediately. Stir continuously until the gravy thickens to a smooth textured gravy. If the corn starch solution is added to the gravy with high heat setting, the solution mixture will jell and cook unevenly making, the mixture difficult to get to a smooth textured gravy. Similarly, if the corn starch powder is added to the gravy by itself, the starch will change instantly into many small chunks. The starch globules and the chunks are difficult to stir back into a smooth textured gravy.

Purposes of Oil and Water

Presauteing is done in a hot oil at a much higher temperature than boiling water. The intent is to soften the ingredients in a shorter time than boiling and to extract the hot oil soluble substances from the ingredients.

After the sauteing the ingredients are simmered. This simmering is done in the gravy (hot mixture of oil and water). The gravy plays an important role in the cooking. It extracts the substances of aroma, color, flavor, and taste from the ingredients. However, some of these substances are extracted only with the oil and some are only with the water. Thus, only the oil soluble components of the ingredients may be extracted by the presauteing, whereas both the oil and the water soluble substances are extracted during the simmering. For instance, the colors and some of the flavoring components of paprika and turmeric are readily soluble in oil;

231

other components are soluble in hot water. The residues (such as fiber, if any) of the spices contribute to the gravy sediments. Thus, most of the flavoring and seasoning components of the ingredients can be extracted in hot oil and water mixture during the simmering. Therefore, when these ingredients are simmered in the mixture for one or more hours, the ingredients are thoroughly pulverized and extracted of their flavors.

The presauteing purposes are accomplished in the simmering process. Thus, the presauteing technique may be substituted with the simmering in the cooking. Although the simmering takes longer than the sauteing to cook, it requires much less supervision and effort over the stove. Moreover, the sauteing is less safe.

Is Rubbing Spices on Meat Important?

I am sure, you are quite familiar with the sprinkling, rubbing, or massaging of salt, pepper, garlic, herbs, spices, and so forth on the surfaces of the meats just a few minutes before cooking such as baking, frying, grilling, or roasting. These cooking techniques do not use water. After the cooking, the flavors developed by the seasoning ingredients are the outcomes of the reactions between them and the meat on the meat surfaces. Such pretreatment techniques cannot assist these reactions to take place throughout the meat even after the cooking. For example, oven broiled lamb chops sprinkled with seasoning ingredients (salt, pepper, paprika, turmeric, curry powder, MSG or sugar, and garlic powder) would develop the combined flavors. The flavors that you taste would be the combined flavors of the cooked spices, cooked meat, and the products of the reactions between the spices and the meat on the meat surfaces. However, the flavor of the cooked meat predominates beneath the layer of the coated surfaces. There wasn't enough time given for the reactions to react throughout the meat. None of the spices penetrated inside the meat. If your intent is just for the flavor enhancements on the surfaces, like shaking salt and pepper on the foods, then this technique is justifiable. If you choose to cook the meats by boiling, simmering, or steaming (involving water), most of the coated seasoning ingredients on the surfaces of the meats are washed or rinsed into their drippings during the cooking. If your intent is to impart the cooked flavors of the ingredients throughout the meat, all the efforts you put in such pretreatment are wasted.

The following preparation steps of a Pot Roast recipe illustrate nonproductive pretreatment of the beef with the seasoning ingredients:

232

1. Rub all sides of beef with seasoned salt, pepper, and paprika
2. Combine the seasoned beef with the remaining ingredients in a 5-quart pot, cover, and simmer for 5-6 hours.
3. Remove cover, evaporate to sizzling in oil, and serve.

A case in point in the above recipe is that you can cook the Pot Roast without rubbing the meat with the seasoning ingredients. The recipe would be simpler and would save the unnecessary labor if the step 1 in the cooking instruction is omitted. The AFT of the dish would be the same either way.

My mother always believed that to prepare the provincial Burmese fish and meat dishes the seasoning CIs (fish sauce, garlic, ginger, onion, red pepper, salt, and turmeric) must be massaged and squeezed into the meat tissues by hand before the sauteing to bring out their robust and satisfying flavors. Although, my mother was a great cook I will have to disagree with her on this point as explained below.

To affect the reactions of the meat with the CIs at the room temperature, the MIs (meats, fish, shrimp, etc.) are marinated with the seasoning ingredients. Such reactions between them are so slow that they must be marinated for at least three hours or more in the marinade with the ingredients containing organic acids such as vinegar, lemon juice, yogurt, etc. Sometimes you may wish to marinate the meats in the mixture at the refrigerator temperature overnight. Thus, the marination reactions are slowed down to allow you to cook the foods later at your convenience.

Alternatively, when you are in a hurry, you can precook the meat for at least 15 minutes (just to heat through the meat) before the marination. During this time the meat expands forcing out volatile substances from the meat. When this heated meat is put directly into the cold marinade mixture, the marinade is absorbed by the contraction of the meat as it cools down in the mixture. The meat is then marinated further for two hours or more in the mixture at the room temperature. Meats marinated this way can even be boiled, simmered, or steamed for one hour or more without affecting the AFT of the marinated foods. Some recipes that employ the marination are included in this cookbook for your enjoyment.

Cutting Ingredients

It is rather difficult to get different kinds of ingredients browned or cooked at the same time. Some are browned and cooked sooner than the others. This is because the ingredients are of different chemical substances and textures. Nevertheless, these differences are compensated when they are cut to different thicknesses, shapes, and sizes. Thicker, bigger, and smaller surface area ones take a longer time to brown than the thinner, smaller, and larger surface area ones.

For example, potato chips are fried to crispiness in much less time than french fries because the chips are thinner and have larger surface areas than the french fries pieces. Similarly, cutting the ingredients to certain shapes that have larger surface areas reduces the browning time. Thus, serrated french fries pieces are cooked faster than non-serrated ones. For the same reason, some knives are made with serrated cutting edges to cut through the objects easier and faster. The serrate edges are designed to have larger cutting surface area than the conventional non-serrated knives.

Ingredients should be prepared so that they will be browned or cooked to the same extent at about the same time. Otherwise, some of them may be undercooked and others may be overcooked or burnt. Meat should be cut to approximately the same size and thickness to have them cook about the same time. Meats are like any other ingredient: the size determines how long they will take to cook. Smaller and thinner meat cooks faster than the larger and thicker pieces. For instance, 1/4 inch thick stewing beef slices will cook faster than the 1 inch cubes. Thus when you don't want to presaute the seasoning ingredients you may cook them together with the larger pieces of meat cubes from the beginning of your cooking. This way the ingredients will get pulverized and the meat pieces will get cooked with the ingredients together. If you wish to prepare a meat dish in a shorter time you may use the thinner meat slices and presaute or prebrown the meat and the seasoning ingredients together. The meat dish will be done in a few minutes. This is how the Chinese stir fried short order dishes are prepared.

Many recipes call for physical destruction of the texture of the seasoning ingredients (such as onion, ginger, garlic, red pepper, herbs, spices, etc.) by grinding, pounding, electric blending, chopping, dicing, slicing, and so forth for cooking. Of course, such pretreatment helps reduce the time of softening, pulverizing, and cooking the ingredients. Chopping, dicing or slicing should not change the flavor and the taste of the ingredients. However, pounding, grinding or electric blending of the ingredients together could result in some chemical reactions between the pulverized ingredients. These reactions could possibly contribute to the overall flavor of the cooked dish. Such compounded effects may be noticeable in some cases. In most other cases, they would hardly make much difference in their aromas, authenticities, colors, flavors, and tastes, regardless of the physical destructive techniques used in their preparations. Some recipes employ boiled small diced potato pieces for making mashed potatoes to expedite the preparation. However, for the same reason, more nutrients in the potatoes could have been salvaged during the boiling if larger, quartered or halved potato pieces were used in the preparation.

Simmer-Saute vs Precooking Techniques

Essential difference between the conventional precooking techniques (prebrowning and presauteing) and the simmer-saute method is in the simmering and sauteing sequences. In the conventional techniques, the ingredients are sauteed first and then they are simmered. That is, simmering the sauteed ingredients, whereas in the simmer-saute method the ingredients are simmered and then they are self-sauteed. Or, you are sauteing the simmered ingredients. The sequences in the precooking methods are the reverse of the simmer-saute method. When you use the conventional techniques you have to stir the ingredients continuously in the pan while it is being sauteed or browned. This is laborious, time consuming, unsafe, and needs some skill. In the simmer-saute, you get to the self-sauteing stage by itself with only occasional stirring. This stage of cooking is accomplished with safety and simplicity. Although both the methods take the same amount of time to cook the ingredients, the simmer-saute technique requires practically no supervision. Thus you spend very little time over the stove and it allows you to do other things during your cooking.

Seasoning and flavoring ingredients such as celery, garlic, ginger, onion, herbs, spices, etc. (I will refer to these as core ingredients) are usually used in cooking to provide a basis of aroma, color, flavor, taste, and gravy sediments to the dishes. The intents of the core ingredients can serve their purposes best only if they are thoroughly pulverized and extracted of their AFT by the cooking processes (presauteing, prebrowning, and simmering). The combined processes such as presauteing and simmering, prebrowning and simmering, or simmering by itself do perform that task.

In the conventional techniques the ingredients are subjected to higher temperatures (sauteing) at the outset, while the ingredients are still raw. Then they are simmered at lower temperature (simmering). In the simmer-saute method the processes are reversed. The ingredients are first subjected to simmering at lower temperature and then they are sauteed at the higher temperature. Theoretically, these could lead to different fragmentation and reactions of the food molecules. Consequently, they could possibly lead to different tasting dishes from the conventional techniques. Or are they really different? Because aroma, flavor, and taste are subjective, I personally find the differences insignificant, if any. Even if one finds some differences in their flavors and tastes, the inherent benefits of the simmer-saute (simplicity and safety) should outweigh the differences. Hence, if you are under stress and/or short of time, patience, and stamina to cook your daily healthful meals, you may like to resort to the simmer-saute.

Prebrowning. Most Asians prebrown their CIs and GIs in cooking their curries, whereas the technique is rarely used in the Western cooking except, prebrowning of flour coated meat for preparing some pot roasts. The intent of prebrowning the ingredients in any cooking is to impart toasted nutty flavor of the browned ingredients to the overall AFT of the dishes. At the beginning of the prebrowning, the ingredient surfaces are subjected to intense heating which quickly cooks and hardens their surfaces. This hardening retards the heat penetration to their inner layers. Eventually, the surfaces are browned and coated with the reddish brown crispy crusts while the cooking gradually progresses to the inner layers of the ingredients. On long simmering, these crusts are dispersed and dissolved in the gravy. Thus the meat and vegetable dishes attain their characteristic robust and satisfying tastes.

In preparing meat dishes, it is a common practice in all ethnic recipes to call for:
a. prebrowning the core ingredients to a browned or burnt texture and then, simmering them with the meat; or
b. prebrowning the core ingredients and the meat together and simmering them; or
c. prebrowning the ingredients separately and simmering them together.

There is only one basic flavor you can have when the meat dishes are prepared using the above three alternatives. Either one of these techniques can be used for preparing Asian meat curries with the browned curry flavors. If you prefer the browned flavors there is no other way but to prebrown the core ingredients. All the three techniques develop the same curry flavors. However, the techniques (b) and (c) are more laborious than (a) and they are redundant and complicate the recipes. When the ingredients are simmered for 60 minutes or more in each case, the browned flavors of the meat developed by the techniques are indistinguishable in the overall flavor of the dish. Therefore, flavorwise, there is no additional benefit from prebrowning the meat as in (b) and (c) except to shorten the meat cooking time by about 5 minutes. The simmer-saute method may be used to simulate the flavors and tastes developed by the above three techniques. The simulation may be accomplished by extending the self-sauteing sequence longer in the simmer-saute method. You may prefer the method over the traditional prebrowning when you don't want to labor over the stove mixing and scraping continuously, or you may altogether prefer the flavors of the self-sauteed meat curries. Of course, when you have the time, patience, and motivation you may prefer one of the techniques to prepare the meat curries.

Does prebrowning seal flavors?: It is a widely held opinion, once including myself, that the prebrowning of the meat seals the natural meat flavor and juices in the meat. It is also a belief that such a sealing is responsible for the deliciousness of the meat. The brown crispy crusts are usually formed on the surfaces of the ingredients during baking, broiling, deep frying, pan frying, broiling, grilling, and sauteing of the foods. These cooking are done in absence of water and at the temperatures much higher than boiling.

The reddish brown crusts are usually formed on foods that contain carbohydrates and proteins. These crusts are the result of a series of not-well-understood organic reactions, known as Maillard reactions, between the two classes of organic compounds, amino acids and sugars. The amino acids and the sugars are formed during the cooking from fragmentation of proteins and carbohydrates respectively. These two classes of compounds are reacted to form amine/sugar complex salts (the reddish brown crusts) during the frying. They are soluble in water and insoluble in oil. As these compounds are formed during the frying they are deposited on the hardened surfaces of the foods. Some are formed in the frying pan because these solids are insoluble in the oil. The solids are scorched during the frying and form the reddish brown crunchy crispy crusts on the food surfaces and in the frying pan.

Widely held opinion about the sealing ability of these crusts on the food surfaces, during simmering in water for more than one hour, are questionable. Some of these crusts will be at least dispersed by the boiling water bubbles (hydrodynamic pressures) and others will be dissolved by the hot water in the simmering process. Thus on prolonged boiling or simmering, these crusts cannot seal in the natural juices in meats and vegetables. However, when these foods are subjected to frying, baking, broiling, grilling, toasting, etc. (in absence of water and at higher temperatures), the hardened scorched crusts on the surfaces of the foods could possibly inhibit oozing of their natural juices more effectively than during the simmering and the boiling.

Presauteing. This technique is used traditionally in most Western cooking because we all feel that the technique is one of the most critical parts of the cooking to develop the AFTT of meat dishes (sauces, stews, soups, etc.).

Hence, most recipes call for either one of the following techniques:
a. presauteing the core ingredients and then, simmering them with the meat; or
b. presauteing the core ingredients and the meat together and simmering them; or
c. presauteing the ingredients separately and simmering them together.

The normal flavors, without the browned nutty flavors, are developed by these techniques. The intent of the presauteing is to shorten the cooking time and to extract the substances of AFTs from the ingredients by the hot oil. The simmering processes subsequently pulverize the ingredients and extract their AFTs by the gravy (mixture of hot oil and water). Similarly, in the simmer-saute method, the softening, pulverizing, and extraction processes can be accomplished simultaneously by simmering the meat and the CIs together from the beginning of the cooking. At the end of the simmering, the residual water may be evaporated to the sizzling to allow the extraction of the AFTs of the simmered ingredients by the hot oil. Thus, the hot oil extraction in the simmer-saute is on the cooked ingredients, whereas the extraction in the presauteing technique is on the fresh ingredients before simmering. This difference is a very subtle one which could lead to a slightly different tasting dish. This may be a subjective difference. Otherwise, the presauteing technique duplicates the objectives of the simmer-saute method. Therefore, the presauteing technique may be replaced with the simmer-saute technique.

Little supervision is required by the technique during the simmer-saute sequences. The colors and AFTs produced by the two techniques are practically the same. Although the simmer-saute takes a little longer than the presauteing technique to cook the CIs, the overall time for cooking the dish is not changed in any case because the overall time for the cooking depends only on the time it takes to cook the meat to tenderness.

The overall cooking time may be shortened by about 5 minutes if the MI and the CIs are presauteed and simmered as described in techniques

(b) and (c). Nevertheless, the presauteing itself is a time-consuming and strenuous technique. It demands continuous personal attention over the stove. You want to avoid this hard labor when you don't have much time for the cooking. Therefore, you would not mind sacrificing the 5 minutes advantage over the technique that requires less effort to use.

Some recipes may call for presauteing the herbs and spices with no other ingredients. This technique may be avoided if you wish to simplify your cooking. The new technique would simply simmer-saute the herbs and spices with the rest of the ingredients from the beginning of the cooking. Alternatively, the spices may be added to the sizzling oil after the evaporation sequence and extending the self-sauteing time of the ingredients in the hot oil by 1-5 minutes. The aromas, authenticities, colors, flavors, and tastes of the dishes prepared by the presauteing and the simmer-saute will be very close to each other.

Soft textured MIs and simmer-saute: Presauteing of the CIs becomes an essential technique when dishes of boned chicken, egg, fish, shrimp, steak, vegetables, etc. are prepared. These ingredients require much shorter cooking time than their CIs. These MIs are soft textured and are usually cooked in 20 minutes or less. If the MIs are cooked together with their CIs from the beginning of the cooking, they can be either overcooked or pulverized. Therefore, presauteing or prebrowning the CIs is essential so that the CIs will be at least softened when the MIs are cooked. However, if you prefer to use the simmer-saute method, the CIs with the oil and water are simmer-sauteed first for at least 15 minutes. At the end of its self-sauteing sequence, the MI is added to the cooking and simmered with water; or alternatively, continue with the self-sauteing in the oil until the MI is cooked. Of course, when you have the time, patience, and motivation for the cooking or if you are a professional chef, you may use the presauteing in your cooking out of necessity.

Simmer-Saute vs Slow Cooking/Steaming

Slow Cooking. The cooking is similar to the simmer-saute. The resemblance between them is that they combine all the ingredients and cook them in gravy until the ingredients are cooked to tenderness. Both are simple to use and require little supervision during the cooking. Their resemblances end there. They are two entirely different techniques.

For example, the simmer-saute is carried out at water boiling temperature, whereas the slow cooking is done at temperatures lower than the boiling. Consequently:

a. Most simmer-saute cooking is completed within 90 minutes with little supervision. The slow cooking takes anywhere from 4 to 10 hours, unattended.

b. It is rather important in slow cooking to arrange the ingredients (vegetables, meat, seasoning herbs and spices, etc.) in a certain sequence in the stoneware pot to avoid uneven cooking of the ingredients. The simmer-saute requires no such sequential arrangement.

c. To sustain the slow cooking at the lower temperature, insulated stoneware pots are used to minimize the heat lost. They are also heated from the sides of the pot for even heat dispersion and distribution. No such special cooking pots are needed for the simmer-saute.

d. Heat conduction is very slow with the stoneware materials, therefore activities that could lead to sudden drastic changes in temperature (thermal shock) are restricted. Thus the slow cooking is done with the pots covered until the cooking is completed. However, when more water is needed for some reason, boiling water is used in the cooking. Similarly, removing excess water in the slow cooking is a long, tedious, and laborious process. Use of frozen foods in the stoneware are absolutely prohibited to avoid permanent damages to the stoneware pot. None of these restrictions are applicable to the simmer-saute cooking.

e. A most distinguishing feature of the simmer-saute from the slow cooking is its flexibility and versatility. Because the pot is heated from the bottom in the cooking, self-sauteing of the ingredients in the sizzling oil can be accomplished at the end of the cooking. Many different types of dishes are created after the self-sauteing sequence. Thus, the simmer-saute can be readily used for preparing casseroles and stir fries. The slow cooking method cannot be used readily for preparing these dishes. The simmer-saute can do everything that the slow cooking can do. The slow cooking cannot reciprocate.

Steaming. Steaming technique is also similar to the slow cooking and the simmer-saute. These techniques cook all the ingredients together from the beginning to the end. Their resemblances to the simmer-saute end there. Steaming is much closer to the slow cooking than to the simmer-saute. Although the steaming is done at about the same temperature as the simmer-saute, their differences are practically the same as the differences between the slow cooking and the simmer-saute described earlier.

Processed Foods

Fast Food Services and Restaurants. Whatever your reason for dinning out or picking up some fast foods, you are doing the right thing as long as they are done in moderation (quantity of the foods you eat at a time and frequency of the visits you make to the services). In fact, sometimes, it may be a necessity, especially when you and your family have been living on self-cooked healthful meals. We very well know that most healthful foods are not the best tasting foods. It is just like what Murphy's Law said, "What tastes good is not good for you". It is not unusual for some fast food stands and restaurants to use rich ingredients in their foods. Their intent should be clear: to attract their customers to return to them. We have practically no control over what goes into the foods prepared by them. There are many uncertainties with some of the food services. We cannot take things for granted. Eating these foods once in a while would be your best way to cope with these uncertainties. So, enjoy them in moderation. But, the best policy for us is to prepare our own meals whenever practical, so that we have more control over what goes into our bodies.

Food Manufacturers. There are times we use commercially processed foods (such as frozen foods, pre-blended seasoning mixes, prepared salad dressings, sauces, soups, and so forth) in our home cooking for convenience, savings, simplicity, and variety. Using the processed foods can make your cooking easier and save significant time of cooking. It is also one of the easiest ways of preparing authentic ethnic foods because most of these foods originated and are processed in their native countries by the natives using their native ingredients. Several recipes in this cookbook use some American and Asian pre-processed foods such as condensed soup mixes, sauces, gravy mixes, pickled vegetables, seasoning herbs, spices, and mixes, etc. However, as explained above, use them in moderation with controlled frequency.

5.
TECHNIQUES
VERSUS
FLAVOR

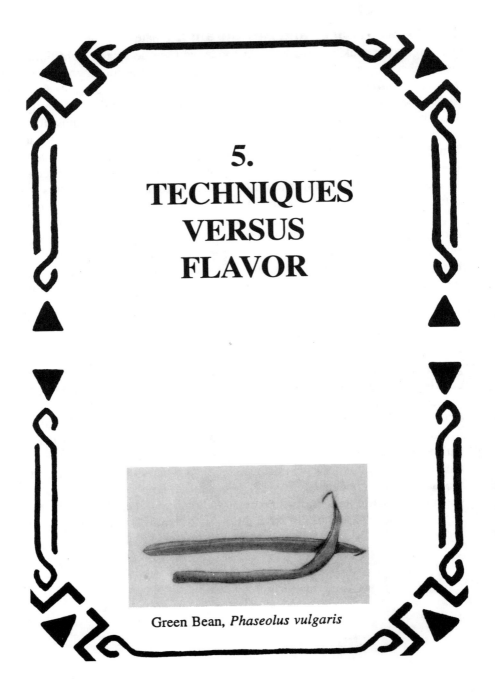

Green Bean, *Phaseolus vulgaris*

In this chapter, various home preparing and cooking techniques will be surveyed. Physical and chemical changes affected by the techniques on foods will also be discussed. An attempt will be made to correlate the techniques with the AFTTs of the foods developed by the techniques. The correlation will be used for selecting alternate preparation and cooking techniques.

Temperature and Time are the Keys

Biological molecules undergo different reactions that are dependent on the temperature of their environment. For example, a fertilized egg will be preserved longer at refrigeration temperatures 4C (4 degrees Celsius) or 40F (40 degrees Fahrenheit. Leave the egg at room temperature 13-30C (55-85F) for several days, and you get a spoiled egg. Incubate the egg at a constant temperature of 43C (110F) for four weeks, and you get a baby chick. Place the egg in boiling water, 100C (212F), for two minutes and you get a soft-boiled egg and for 15-20 minutes and you get a hard-boiled egg. Prolong boiling of the egg may generate hydrogen sulfide gas. Or raising the temperature to above 177C (350F) and you can fry up an omelet. A little longer frying makes your egg turn brown and eventually would burn to a carbon mess. These observations are repeatable as many times as you wish with the same set of variables (fertilized chicken egg, time, and the ambient conditions). They will yield the same results. Thus, directions of the biological reactions are controlled by the temperature and the time of exposure to it.

In our cooking we also deal with the biological molecules. Therefore, temperature and time of cooking are also the keys to control the kinds of AFTT you wish to have with a given recipe. In other words, you can vary the AFTT of a recipe by changing the cooking technique within the same temperature range or at different temperature ranges. Thus, you may be able to select alternate techniques to meet your special circumstances, needs, and safety.

Preparing and Cooking

The word "preparing" in this book implies concoction of ingredients with or without applying additional heat to the foods. Thus, the preparations are not only limited to the temperature range, from freezing to room temperatures. At these low temperatures mostly the physical changes (icing, shrinking, discoloring, etc.) and slow microbiological chemical changes (molding, decaying, etc.) affect the ingredients. Whereas in cooking, additional heat is applied to the ingredients. The cooking activities are usually limited to the temperature range, beginning from slow cooking to grilling. During the cooking, the ingredients undergo nonreversible physical and chemical changes producing substances with their own characteristics AFTTs and colors.

When a food is cooked, the chemical composition of the food is changed. The uncooked and the cooked foods have their own chemical identities, and they are of different chemical substances with different AFTs. In most cooking we use a multitude of pre-processed foods. Most of these foods such as corned beef, pickled herring, salted mackerel, etc. were prepared without cooking. However, they no longer have the same chemical compositions and flavors as their respective non-pickled foods (raw beef and fish). Hence chemically, making the pre-processed food by pickling is analogous to cooking, although they were not cooked by heating. When we boil the corned beef and a fresh beef brisket they produce different tasting beef. It is because the cooked beef was prepared from different chemically constituted beef. In the case of boiling the corned beef, the beef was subjected to two different series of chemical changes. One of the series was accomplished during its pickling and the other was during boiling, whereas the beef brisket was subjected only to one series of chemical changes during the boiling. For the same reasons, different tasting chicken meats are obtained by grilling fresh chicken meat and marinated chicken meat.

Let us take a look at basic home preparation and cooking techniques. These techniques may be classified broadly into five groups. This classification is based on the temperature range at which they are used. These techniques include freezing, refrigerating, preparing at room temperature, cooking in the boiling temperature range, and cooking at temperatures higher than the boiling.

Choosing a technique, among those that use heating such as baking, boiling, broiling, frying and so forth, depends very much upon the type of AFTT you wish to have in your food. Some of these techniques are simpler, some are quicker, and some are safer than the others. Some require special utensils. Sometimes, your choice of a cooking method may be dictated by the amount of time you want to spend in your kitchen.

Our family does most of our cooking at the boiling water temperature range, that is, simmering, boiling, and steaming. Most home cooking is also done at this temperature range. These techniques are simpler to use and are used often as a stand alone or in combination with other cooking techniques, such as baking, frying, etc. We used to use pressure cooking often. Now, we very seldom use it. The pressure cooking cooks about two to three times faster than other techniques, hence, you can use less expensive meat cuts. Nevertheless, the technique is cumbersome for safe handling. We also use baking, roasting, grilling, and broiling often. However, we would use the oven in our kitchen less often in the summers to save our air-conditioning cost. Thus, you can pick a cooking technique depending on your needs.

Preparing at Freezer Temperature. At this -18C (0F) temperature, food preparations are limited to making ice, ice creams, frozen salads, and frozen desserts. In these preparations the liquids are changed to solids by freezing. There are very little chemical changes, if any, involved in these preparations because, the flavor and taste of each ingredient in the food is still identifiable in its solid phase.

The primary use of a home freezer is, of course, for food storage so that microorganisms (including bacteria, molds, and yeasts) that are responsible for most food spoilage are either killed or become dormant. All biological species, including human, are being attacked continuously by these microorganisms of all forms and all types that coexist with us. The biological species have immune systems to cope with these attacks while their metabolism is functioning (that is while living). When the biological species die, their immune systems also die, allowing the microorganisms to recycle the chemical elements of the dead species (carbon, oxygen, hydrogen, nitrogen, phosphorous, and so forth) to the environment as ecological balancing. Thus our foods (meats, vegetables, and so on) get spoiled as a consequence of attack by these microorganisms. When we store the foods in the freezer, the activities of these microorganisms are at least slowed down significantly. The effectiveness of this preservation of foods depends on the temperature of the environment. The lower the temperature of the storage, the slower the activities of these microorganism. Thus foods are preserved for longer periods in the freezer than in the refrigerator than at the room temperature. The foods cannot be stored for unlimited periods in the home freezers.

Preparing at Refrigeration Temperature. The refrigeration temperature is used mostly for chilling beverages because their tastes and flavors are enhanced when they are cold. Marinated foods are stored at the refrigeration temperature before cooking to slow down the marination

245

to a slower rate. This allows you to plan to cook the foods at your convenience. Many salads are prepared ahead and stored for later use. Fresh dairy foods, eggs, meats, vegetables, and so forth are stored for a short period to prolong their freshness. Fruits are stored at this temperature to slow their rate of ripening. This cannot be accomplished by freezing because, the fruit's texture may be destroyed. Sometimes your milk gets sour sooner than at other times because either the milk was very old or you left the milk out of the refrigerator longer than at other times.

Preparing at Room Temperature. Curing, fermenting, germinating, mixing, pickling, and soaking are the most commonly used preparing techniques that are carried out at room temperature. These techniques are mostly used in conjunction with baking, boiling, frying, grilling, and so forth.

In general, similar types of chemical reactions take place in the above preparations. The room temperature heat has sufficient energy to cause some food molecules to undergo simple acid-base type reactions: esterification, hydrolysis, and neutralization. Some less reactive molecules can also react at this temperature when appropriate reaction conditions and time are prevailing. Such type of the room temperature reactions may prevail in the following techniques:

Curing: Curing is a process for preserving foods. It includes salting, pickling, and smoking. Vegetables, meats, fish, and so forth are usually preserved by pickling. Pickling employs spices, rice flour, vinegar, salt, and so on. When the foods are pickled, a high concentration of salt is usually used in the pickling solution along with the pickling spices. This high salt concentration dehydrates the food cells by osmosis. Over some period of time, the spices gradually react among themselves and with the dehydrated food cells producing pickles. Curing by smoking is discussed in Broiling, Grilling, and Smoking section.

Fermenting: Fermentations are generally used for making wine, raising dough, making batters, and so forth. In the case of wine making and dough raising, yeast microorganisms are employed to break the food molecules to simpler molecules at room temperature. Thus soybean is fermented for making Oriental soybean cake (tofu), soybean paste, soy sauce, and many other soybean derivatives for food flavoring. This microbiological fermentation reaction characteristically gives off carbon dioxide and water as by products.

Germinating: Germinations are usually used for sprouting seeds (beans and peas). The seeds soak up water and swell, peeling their skins. The growth is then followed by the formation of roots. The germinated seeds are more tender and cook faster. Thus, some peas and beans are sprouted for easier steaming and boiling. Sprouting changes the chemistry of the seeds to yield AFTT different from the non-germinated seeds. The sprouted peas and beans make a variety of delicious snack foods (battered fried peas, Indian pancakes "dosa", Burmese steamed garden peas, *Pisum sativum* or in Burmese sadaw-pe, "pe-pyoate", etc.) and main dishes casseroles, soups, stews, and stir fries. Moong beans and soybeans are sprouted to make bean sprouts. They are used extensively for making variety of snack foods (egg rolls, sandwiches, spring rolls, etc.) and the main dishes.

Marinating: When we marinate our foods, we actually soak them with the spices, herbs, salt, sauces, sugar, oil, wine, water and the ingredients containing weak organic acids (vinegar, citrus fruit juices, sour cream, yogurt, and so forth). Most of our foods contain animal fats, carbohydrates, minerals, proteins, saturated fats, vitamins, etc. Use of an oil and wine are mostly for flavoring and to serve as solvent media for the marinating reactions between the foods and the ingredients. In most marination weak organic acidic substances are needed to react by acid-base type hydrolysis, esterification and/or neutralization reactions. Hence, vinegar, citrus juices (of lemon, lime, and orange), sour cream, yogurt, etc. are used as the source of weak organic acidic substances for the marination. Marination is a slow chemical process and requires more than one hour for the effective marinations. However, there are several parameters to vary the marination time to fit with your schedules. You can either hurry the marination to one hour or stretch it to 24 hours to cook the marinated ingredient later at your convenience. For a given recipe, you can vary the marination time with the size of the ingredient, marinating temperature (at room or refrigeration temperature), and using the ingredient raw or boiled. Boiling the ingredient, 10-15 minutes, for the marination has several advantages. It expands the ingredient immediately, expelling the matrix substances from the food tissues. When it is immersed into the cold marinade it contracts (absorbing the marinade into the ingredient texture), heats the marinade mixture, and contributes some fluidity for the marination. Thus, the fastest marination would use a smaller-size ingredient, boiled, and marinating at room temperature. Similarly, to prolong marination, for use later, would require using larger ingredient pieces, raw, and marinating at refrigeration temperature. Many other combinations of the parameters can be used for in-between marination time.

Mixing: Mixing is commonly employed in creating vegetable and/or meat salads and salad dressings; breading of meats, shrimp, seafood, poultry, fish, and vegetables; making dessert toppings, cocktail drinks, just to name a few. Similar types of reactions between the food molecules are likely to take place, such as in marination, if the mixed foods are given enough time to react.

Pickling: Use of pickled meats and/or vegetables in preparing main dishes is a distinguishing characteristic of Asian culinary from Western cooking. The pickled foods are typically salty, sour, and pungent. In Southeast Asia vegetables and fish of various kinds are pickled with cooked rice and salt.

Soaking: Soaking of rice, peas, lentils, vegetables, and so forth is usually done in water. During soaking water is absorbed and incorporated into the molecular framework of the foods tissues causing the foods to swell and loosen the chemical bonds that gave rigidity to the framework. Thus making the foods textures softer and easier to cook to their tenderness.

Cooking at Boiling Temperature

Water, a Key Role. Now, let us focus our attention on some of the important roles of water in our everyday cooking. Most of our daily cooking is done around the temperature of boiling water. The methods used for preparing our daily meals at these conditions include slow cooking, steaming, boiling, and pressure cooking. These methods are commonly used for preparing boiled eggs and vegetables, rice, cereals, sauces, soups, and stews. Water plays the central role in these cooking methods. Some properties of pure water that are important in our cooking are the following:

1. Pure water is very stable. It does not break down or decompose during cooking. Thus, it does not contribute any acidity, basicity, color, odor, or taste of its own to the cooking.

2. It serves as a medium for extracting, mixing, reacting, transferring heat from burner to the foods, and distributing heat evenly to all the ingredients during cooking.

3. At around its normal boiling point, at sea level, it provides sufficient heat energy to cause chemical and physical changes to the ingredients. It also sterilizes the foods from most microorganisms, such as Clostridium

botulinum toxin, Staphylococcal enterotoxin, etc.

4. Pure water is considered a universal solvent because it dissolves inorganic salts, such as sodium chloride as well as some organic substances such as vinegar, alcohol, sugar, and water soluble enzymes, vitamins, and proteins. This property of water serves as a solvent and extracts water-soluble enzymes and vitamins, minerals, etc. Most other naturally occurring liquids don't have a broad solubility range like water.

The effect of heat and moisture on foods, leading to their collective AFTT is very complex. However, it is not unreasonable to assume that the temperature of the boiling water provides enough heat energy to break and make chemical bonds at some specific points in the food molecules. These processes of the bond rearranging, breaking, and making could eventually lead to forming some final substances. These substances must always form in a specific proportion. These substances collectively characterize the AFTTs of the foods cooked by the methods. These end substances can always be reproduced with the same recipe and the same cooking technique. Because the same reactions are always repeated under the same set of conditions. Such a scenario of chemical and physical changes will be expected to take place on ingredients whenever the ingredients are cooked with the hot water (slow cooking, steaming, boiling, and pressure cooking). See safety **CAUTION** about steam burns on page 182.

Slow Cooking. Slow cooking is done at just below the temperature of boiling water, approximately 93C (200F). This temperature range is below the simmering temperature. The slow cooking is usually done in a stoneware pot. It provides constant heat that surrounds the food unlike other methods that heat from below.

The cooking process is much like steaming in that no mechanical agitation by the escaping steam bubbles occurs during cooking. However, unlike steaming, the hot water, oil, and melted fats surrounding the ingredients penetrate and diffuse gradually into the ingredients. The hot water pressure surrounding the ingredients (hydrostatic pressure) assists the liquid mixture in the penetration. This process assists the reactions, extractions, and transfer of heat to the inner part of the ingredients with smoothness and effectiveness. Consequently, the water-soluble and oil-soluble extracts from the ingredients are retained more in the ingredients and the broth. Thus in slow cooking, loss of moisture and volatile extracts are less than cooking by boiling.

Steaming. Like slow cooking and boiling, steaming is done at about the boiling temperature. Steaming can be used to cook meats and vegetables, and the result is an AFTT similar to those produced by slow cooking and boiling. This similarity occurs because the ingredients are chemically and physically changed by the series of chemical reactions similar to the other methods of cooking with hot water.

Steaming differs from boiling. During steaming the food is enveloped by the steam, which gradually penetrates and cooks evenly. Unlike boiling, the steam molecules bombard food with less aggressiveness (lesser energy) by the emerging vapor bubbles from the boiling water. Because the foods are not immersed in the boiling water, the penetrating steam cannot get assistance from hydrostatic pressure as in other similar cooking methods discussed above. As a result, heat transfer from the steam into the food takes longer to gelatinize meat connective tissues and soften vegetable structures. Thus resulting in longer cooking time. Such steaming provides better control against overcooking and the taste is somewhat smoother than boiling. Because there is no mechanical agitation during steaming, foods molded to particular shapes will retain these shapes better, and foods can be arranged attractively on the steaming bowl for steaming and serving. If you are not in a hurry, steaming may be preferred over boiling.

Boiling. When boiling meats or vegetables, the water itself is heated to 100C (212F). It cannot go any higher. Boiling, then, is nature's automatic thermostat that controls heating at 100C at sea level. But what happens if the heat is increased? Simply put, the agitation of water will increase and evaporation will be hastened. At the boiling point, the liquid water is transformed into steam vapor bubbles at the bottom of the pot nearest to the heat source. As these bubbles build up enough vapor pressure to overcome the atmospheric pressure on the water surface, the bubbles escape into the atmosphere. Thus you observe the boiling phenomena. When the heat is increased, this additional heat energy is used up by the boiling water in converting more liquid water to steam vapor bubbles at a much faster rate. The excess energy is thus used up in speeding the water evaporation rate rather than raising the temperature of the boiling water. Hence the boiling points of liquids are defined as the temperatures at which the pressures of the liquids' vapors are the same as the prevailing atmospheric pressure. The boiling points, then, vary depending on the prevailing atmospheric pressure. Therefore the boiling point of water is stated as 100C (212F) at sea level. The exact temperature of boiling water changes with the prevailing barometric pressure, going up or down as the pressure goes up or down. Thus the boiling point of water will be lower at a lower atmospheric pressure (water boils at about 69C (156F) at the top of Mount Everest, about 5.5 miles above the sea level, where the pressure is about 0.4 atmospheric pressure) and it will be higher at a higher atmospheric pressure (water boils at about 120C or 248F under twice the atmospheric pressure in a pressure cooker). Raising the boiling point by increasing the pressure is the principle behind the pressure cooker, which is discussed in the next section on pressure cooking.

The one aspect common among the techniques that are used in the same temperature range (simmering, slow cooking, boiling, and pressure cooking) is that the food is immersed in water during the cooking. This immersion allows the hot water to transfer the heat from the burner to the foods evenly and effectively, thus allowing the heat from the hot water to cook the foods and extract the water soluble substances from the foods. The extracted substances, then, react among themselves and with substances from elsewhere forming many types of products. These substances are formed in specific proportions, which are collectively responsible for their characteristic AFTT. The extracting and cooking are assisted by the mechanical agitation from the escaping water vapors (boiling bubbles), which exert hydrodynamic pressures on the foods. Thus cooking in boiling water is faster than slow cooking, simmering, and steaming. The mechanical bumping by the boiling bubbles facilitates the cooking. The aggressiveness of mechanical agitation is very subdued in the slow cooking and simmering but more pronounced in the pressure cooking. However, use of an excessive amount of water in boiling pasta, eggs, vegetables, etc. is counterproductive: it wastes effort, energy, time, and water.

Pressure Cooking. This method of cooking with water is done around 100-120C (212-248F) when you want to cook foods that take long hours of cooking, such as preparing soups (beef tongue, ox tail, pig's feet, etc.), stews (beef, mutton, lamb), cooking cereals, rice, and vegetables. Much less expensive cuts of meat are often used by some families with tight budgets. Sometimes, if you are in hurry and would like to prepare your meal with the above ingredients, this method of cooking may be used. Occasionally, I use the pressure cooker for preparing beef brisket curry. Frozen dinners and canned-foods manufacturers use pressurized steam to precook meats, poultry, vegetables, etc. Temperature in the cooker is about 20C (36F) higher than the water boiling in an non-pressurized pot. The higher temperature is attained by creating a steam pressure totalling 2 atmospheric pressure in the cooker (1 atmospheric pressure in the cooker in addition to the ambient pressure at sea level, that is twice the pressure at the sea level). A precisely crafted weight is placed on the pressure release nozzle to create the pressure in the cooker. Higher temperature translates into more aggressive bombardment of water bubbles on the foods, and they are assisted by the steam at twice the pressure of boiling water. Pressure inside the cooker forces penetration of steam vapors inside the foods much more effectively than boiling at sea level. As a consequence, the foods are cooked faster and with more physical destruction to the texture of the foods. Time of cooking becomes very crucial if overcooking is to be avoided. The AFTT of the dish is similar to the previous methods using water as the cooking medium. However, the foods taste much smoother and have softer texture with the pressure cooker.

CAUTION: The pressure cooking must be done with care. It requires more precautions than the other methods of cooking. It is imperative that you study the manufacturer's instructions carefully before you get into pressure cooking. Any do-it-yourself projects, including cooking, are only fun if you do not encounter any form of accidents. Accidents are very counterproductive in every aspect. See also page 182.

Cooking at Higher Temperatures

Next we move on to a higher temperature range, 121-204C (250-400F), where we use baking, broiling, frying, grilling, roasting, and smoking. These techniques do not use water, they are cooked by radiated heat.

To cook at temperatures above 212F, without using pressure cooking or oils, we need to turn to baking, roasting, broiling, grilling, and smoking. In each of these processes, the food is heated in an enclosure enveloped by circulating heated air consisting of a small amount of moisture, and other gaseous substances. One difference between these methods and steaming is the amount of moisture surrounding the foods.

Baking and Roasting. The food is cooked in an enclosed chamber where the heated dry air at a preselected temperature envelopes and circulates around the foods. The foods are cooked by the indirect heating, by convection. These methods are slow because the food is cooked from the outside, gradually cooking through the inside of the food. As the cooking progresses, the temperature gradient is formed beginning at the oven temperature on the outer layer and gradual decreasing the temperature as it gets to the center of the food. That is the reason we use the meat thermometer and judge the doneness of the meat by monitoring the temperature in the center of the meat. For example, when the temperature inside the meat attains 60C (140F) the meat is said to be cooked to rare, 71C (160F) is said to be cooked to medium, and 77C (170F) is said to be cooked to well-done.

As the outer layer of the food approaches the oven temperature, the outer surface gradually gets hardened as the cooking progresses. The hardened surface partially seals its heated natural juices inside the food. As the cooking progresses the meat inside gets cooked similar to a slow cooking. However, if the cooking is prolonged the food loses its moisture, leading to dryness and eventually charred to a carbon mass.

Frying. This method is used to cook meats and vegetables at higher temperatures than those used in boiling. These temperatures can be reached because oils are used in place of water. The oils can be heated up to about 375F before breaking down or burning, depending on the oil used. Typically, the term "cooking oil" includes oils from corn, cottonseed, mustard, olives, peanuts, sesame seeds, soybeans, sunflowers, and so forth.

The cooking process itself starts on the outer surface of the food and works its way to the inside. In frying, when the food is placed in the hot oil moisture and other volatile from the food surface is driven off and the cooking starts. Thus, the outer surface gets cooked before the heat could reach to the inner part of the meat. The surface gets hardened and also hinders the escape of moisture, other volatile, and natural juices. But when they are fried too long, these escape through cracks on the surface. Continued frying can eventually turn foods to carbon, something that cannot happen in the methods that use water as the cooking medium. Because oils cannot hold or retain much heat (low heat retention or capacities) the heat energy is transferred to the food very fast. Therefore, you should not fry too many food pieces in the oil at one time. The temperature of the oil could go down quickly, frying could take longer, and the food could soak up additional oil. During the frying, the heat from the burner is continuously used up in cooking the food rather than heating the oils to their decomposition point.

Frying hazards: Frying is one of the most hazardous cooking processes. Extreme care must be taken to avoid letting water splash or sprinkle the hot oil (dry the food with a paper towel before adding the food to the hot oil). Because the oil can't boil at normal atmospheric pressure, continued heating without anything frying in it will cause the oil to break down and eventually catch fire and burn into soot (carbon particles). Should oil catch fire, do not panic, the best way to extinguish it is to cover the pan first, then turn the burner off, remove it from the heat, and put it on a cold surface. Use a fire extinguisher rated for oil fires or some baking soda to extinguish the fire. Never add water to the pan. The water will spit out the burning oil from the pan and spread the fire all over your kitchen.

Broiling, Grilling, and Smoking. In broiling, grilling, and smoking, the foods are cooked at higher temperatures than boiling and baking. The foods are heated directly by the radiated heat. Direct exposure of the foods to the heat source subjects the foods to intense heating. The way the intense heat hardens the outer surface and cooks the inner layers of the food are quite similar to the ways of hardening and cooking processes in baking and roasting. When the food is thin, such as vegetable leaves, stems, sliced tomatoes, and so forth, they get cooked much faster and get dried or burned. Prolonged heating eventually dries and shrinks the foods as the moisture, juices, and volatile are driven off. Thus, frequent basting with oil and moisture during broiling is a common practice.

Heating temperature during broiling and smoking are manipulated by adjusting the distance between the food and the heat source. Good judgment is required to set the optimum cooking speed and doneness (rare, medium, well-done, etc.). When grilling food wrapped in aluminum foil, a careful watch over the heat is necessary because intense heat can still dry the food as well as change the AFTT.

Smoking is similar to baking, roasting, and broiling except that the AFT of the smoke is included in the envelope surrounding the food. Smoking is sometimes done over a tray of water to impart a smoother flavor, taste, and softer texture to the smoked foods. To make bacon, pastrami, sausages (beef, pork, poultry, etc.), and smoked fish, the meats are treated with some seasoning and flavoring ingredients, namely sugar, salt, spices, and chemical preservatives such as sodium nitrite, sodium nitrate, and so on. After adding these ingredients and preservatives the meats are smoked for a few hours to few days. When the smoke flavors are incorporated into the food, complex chemical reactions are possible because smoke contains many chemicals. Some of these by-products are known to be carcinogens. Moreover, the nitrites and nitrates used as preservatives are generally considered as sources for producing carcinogenic substances in the cured meats. The oxides of nitrogen formed from the chemical preservatives are known to react with fragmented meat proteins, amine, and generate a potent carcinogen called "nitrosamine". Even though each person has her or his own metabolic capacity for carcinogens, the prudent and safest way is to avoid frequent and prolonged consumption of highly smoked foods.

Smoking is also used extensively for curing meat, fish, poultry, seafood, and sausages all over the world. In fact, it is one of the food preparation and preservation techniques almost as old as the human history. Most foods are cured with seasoning ingredients, such as salt, pepper, cayenne pepper, sugar, and so forth. Foods are placed at some distance over the heat and smoke source for a slow curing process. Warm air and smoke are allowed to envelop the food over a few days. During the curing the food tissue cells are allowed to dehydrate and react with the seasoning ingredients and smoke gradually. The dehydrated and smoked food tissues can now inhibit the invasion of airborne microorganisms that promote the decay and spoilage of the food.

Flavor and the Techniques

This section intends to relate the AFT and the cooking techniques. Understanding their relationships will help you develop skill for finding alternate techniques and creating recipes.

It is a basic rule of chemistry that the rate of chemical reactions is affected by temperature. Most chemical reactions get faster with increasing temperature and get slower with decreasing temperature. This basic rule also holds for the reaction of food molecules in our cooking. Thus the reactions of food molecules at the freezer temperature are slower than at the refrigeration temperature. These temperatures are very low for any cooking reaction to take place, and at these temperatures the environment cannot provide enough energy to cause the food molecules to fragment, extract, react, etc. Thus, cooking cannot be done. However, very slow microbiological reactions can take place to spoil the foods over some period of storage at these low temperatures.

The chemical changes that take place in cooking at room temperature and above are extremely complex which makes this a difficult subject. I doubt that anyone really knows the reaction mechanisms for the formation of a multitude of these substances and the substances that are collectively responsible for the overall AFT of the foods developed by the cooking techniques. We can only use a simplified reaction scenario as far as our insight, imagination, intuition, experience, and knowledge can handle for the correlations.

Let us imagine and see how complex are the reactions in our cooking pots. The foods are mostly organic substances and they can contain carbohydrates, proteins, saturated fats, animal fats, vitamins, inorganic minerals, etc. Each of the substances themselves is very complex. During cooking they may react with each other producing many different products. In some cases the food molecules may break down into various fragments, and they may in turn react among themselves and with others forming many complex products with varying proportions. Some fragments would be extracted of their oil and water solubles by the oil and water used in the cooking. The blended flavor of the foods developed by cooking at various temperatures is due to the differences in the way the food molecules are fragmented, reacted, and extracted. The kinds and proportions of these reaction products formed in the cooking are collectively responsible for the AFT of the dish. Because the AFT of a dish can always be reproduced by using the same recipe, the kinds and the proportions of the products formed in the cooking must always be the same. Using this scenario let us look into various cooking techniques and see how they may be related to their AFTs.

AFT of Freezing and Refrigeration Preparations. As indicated in the above subsections, these temperatures are very low for any cooking reaction to take place. Thus preparations done at these temperature ranges involve very little chemical changes, if any, in the foods. Therefore, the AFT developed by these preparations is a blended mixed AFT of the individual ingredients. This AFT has its own characteristics and identity. Moreover, it also has some suggestion of the AFT of the individual ingredient. For instance, the AFT of each component of a vanilla ice cream (milk, cream, sugar, and vanilla flavor) is identifiable when it is eaten. However, there is an additional dimension to the AFT of the ice cream because it is cold and frozen to solid. Similarly, soda pops, beers, and cold drinks also develop additional dimensions to their AFTs for being cold.

The temperature of foods and drinks (hotter or colder than room temperature) has a significant effect on our taste buds when we eat or drink. Sudden changes in the temperature in our mouth (that is, on the gums, tongue, and oral cavity) as we chew, suck, and swallow gives a FT

256

(flavor and taste) to foods that is different from other FT at other temperatures. These physical changes enhance the AFTT of the foods. Just changing the temperature gives us a sensation of change in FT. There is no chemical change involved in the foods per se. The enhancement of FT have to do at least with some reversible physical changes in our taste buds, such as change in the shape and/or size of the taste buds. This change in our taste buds signal our brains to let us experience the sensation of FT enhancements. However, preference for hot or cold food is subjective. For instance, our son Patrick, when he was younger, liked to eat our family's favorite food, rice and "Beef and Turmeric", served cold, whereas the rest of us enjoy the food served hot. He now eats less red meat.

AFT of Room Temperature Preparations.
The room temperature has enough thermal energy to cause some food molecules to react at rates faster than at the freezing and refrigeration temperatures. Therefore, preparations such as marinating, curing, soaking, fermenting, and so forth can take place. These reactions cause chemical changes in the foods. AFT of the ingredients are now changed to the new hybrid AFT (see Hybrid flavor, next paragraph). When the prepared foods are cooked with heat, they develop the hybrid flavors which are different from the hybrid flavors of the foods cooked without the preparations.

Hybrid flavor: The new blended AFT may be described with the words "hybrid flavor". The hybrid flavor is analogous to a child's gene. The child is the product of the parents and carries both the genetic traits of the parents. However, the child has his/her own characteristics and identity which is altogether different from either of the child's parents and yet the child carries the parents' traits. Similarly, the hybrid flavor of a cooked food has its own characteristics and identity; yet the hybrid flavor hints the presence of the AFT of the ingredients in it. There is a specific proportion of the parents' genetic traits in the child. Similarly, the hybridized flavors are also formed by the combination of various substances in a specific proportion. Thus hybridized mixing is different from simple blending or mixing because in simple mixing the proportions of the ingredients can be varied in the mixing.

AFT of Boiling, Simmering, Steaming, etc.
Let us consider boiling a pork chop for one hour. Here we are subjecting the chop to a much higher energy than at the room temperature preparations. This heat affects several physical and chemical changes to the pork chop.

257

Consequently, many kinds of substances are formed during these chemical changes. Each of these substances has its own characteristic AFTT. These AFTT collectively develop a hybrid flavor of the boiled chop. Because we would get the same hybrid flavor when we repeat the boiling with a pork chop, we must conclude that the same substances are formed in the same proportions every time a pork chop is boiled. The remaining techniques - pressure cooking, simmering, slow cooking, and steaming - are also used at the same temperature range. If we repeat cooking a chop using each of these techniques, we would get the same hybrid flavor of the cooked pork chop in every case. We must then conclude that similar reaction scenarios take place with each of these techniques, producing similar substances in the similar proportions. Thus the collective AFTT developed by each technique will also lead to a similar hybrid flavor of the boiled chop. When we rationalize these observations (AFTT) we would conclude that different techniques, at the same temperature range, would develop the similar AFTT with a given recipe. Thus the same core hybrid flavor must be commonly developed by the techniques with the same recipe.

AFT of Baking, Roasting, Smoking, etc. Let us use the same pork chop and bake or roast it at 250-350F for one hour. Here we are subjecting the chop to a higher temperature range than at the boiling temperature in hot air environment. Thus we expect the chop to have similar reaction scenarios, but the molecules would be reacting with higher energy, more aggressively and with a faster rate than at the boiling temperature. Consequently, although the chop was cooked only for the same amount of time as in the boiling, we would observe hardening, browning, and crusts formation on the meat's outer surface. The inner layers would be protected, at least partially, by its hardened surface and cooked in its own moisture and juices. The hybrid AFTT of the chop would now consist of two main components. One of the components would be from the inner layers, which would be similar to the hybrid flavor of the meat cooked at the slow cooking temperature. The other component would be from the combination of the browned hardened meat flavor and the crispy crusts flavor. These components would collectively characterize the hybrid AFTT of the chop cooked at the temperature range. Here we may conclude that the same chop cooked for the same time at the temperature range develops its characteristic hybrid AFTT, which would consist of the hybrid AFTT developed by the effect of the roasting temperature and the core hybrid AFTT of the boiling temperature.

Similarly, in smoking the pork chop the cooking process would be very similar to the reaction scenarios of the boiling, baking, and roasting but the scenario would also include the reaction of the smoke with the substances formed in the cooking. Therefore, its characteristic hybrid flavor would include the complex flavors of the smoke integrated with the hybrid AFTT of baking and roasting.

AFT of Broiling, Grilling, Frying, etc. When the chop is subjected to direct heating, as in broiling and grilling in the temperature range 350-450F, it is heated to a more intense heating than the previous techniques. Basically the reaction scenario would be very similar to the baking and roasting, except the outer surface would react very fast to harden, brown, and burn. At this temperature range neither organic nor biological molecules would survive too long. The chop would be cooked to the same extent as roasting in a much shorter time. In fact, it would be thoroughly charred if it is cooked for one hour as with the previous techniques. Thus, the chop would be turned over every 1-2 minutes or so to cook the chop to the desired doneness and to avoid burning it to a carbon mass. The hybrid flavors developed by these techniques would consist of the hybrid flavor of its outer surface layer (which would be the hybrid flavor of the toasted nutty flavor of the browned and burnt crust flavors) and the hybrid flavor of its inner layers. Thus these techniques would develop its hybrid flavor very similar to the hybrid flavors developed in the roasting and baking.

To compare the AFTT of a fried pork chop with the other hybrid flavors, the chop is fried without its batter at about 375F. The chop is well immersed in the hot oil during the frying. Thus the heat of the oil expels moisture and volatile, and it extracts the oil solubles from the meat. As these substances are removed, the cooking of the meat progresses rapidly. If the chop is not removed in time from the frying, it would be fried to crisp crunchy texture and eventually burnt to a carbon mass. To compare its hybrid AFTT with the other hybrids, the chop would be fried only to the beginning of the crust formation on the surface. The chop would then have the AFT of the oil and the crispy crusts on top of the core hybrid AFTT of the inner layers of the meat. The core hybrid AFTT is practically the same with the core hybrid AFTT developed by the other techniques of boiling, baking, and roasting However, because the oil would also extract the oil soluble substances from the chop, the remaining hybrid flavor of the chop would be somewhat different from the chop cooked with the other cooking techniques.

Techniques versus AFT. The cooking techniques may be grouped as shown in Table 10 below for comparing the basic hybrid flavors developed by them.

TABLE 10. Grouping of Techniques that Develop Similar AFT

Preparing Techniques

Group 1	Group 2
chilling	curing
freezing	raising dough
	fermentation
	marination
	mixing
	pickling
	soaking
	sprouting

Cooking Techniques

Group 3	Group 4	Group 5
boiling	baking	broiling
pouching	roasting	frying
pressure cooking	smoking	grilling
simmering		
slow cooking		
steaming		

Groups 1 and 2 are some of the preparing techniques, primarily used for developing preliminary FT for use with the cooking techniques listed in Groups 3, 4, and 5. For example, meats, fish, poultry, etc. are marinated and grilled to prepare shish kabob. Salted fish are soaked in water and cooked with the techniques in Groups 3, 4, and 5, and so forth.

Each cooking technique in Groups 3, 4, and 5 can simulate the hybrid flavors of the other members of the same group. For example, the boiling technique in Group 3 can simulate the hybrid flavors develop by the other techniques (simmering, steaming, and pressure cooking) from the same group.

Water is used in the Group 3 techniques, they cannot be used for simulating the hybrid flavors of Groups 4 and 5 by themselves alone. Because the substances that change into the brown crusts on the surface of the foods are formed at temperatures above the boiling and the crusts are soluble in hot water.

However, the techniques in Groups 4 and 5, except frying, can simulate the hybrid flavors and the textures of the Group 3 techniques. For example, a beef stew dish may be prepared by one of the techniques in Group 3, such as simmering. The same dish may also be prepared by baking (Group 4 technique) the beef stew ingredients in a tightly covered pot. You can prepare the dish either way. So you may choose either method, Group 3 or 4, to prepare the stew depending on your preference or circumstances. For instance, during hot summer days you may find it necessary to use simmering for making the stew to avoid heating your kitchen and additional expenses to your air-conditioning bill.

Corn can be cooked wrapped in its own husks (husks tied together at the top and presoaked in water) and cooked to the texture and the hybrid flavor of the boiled or the steamed corn by baking or grilling techniques. Similarly, potato, meat, and poultry can be wrapped and sealed in an aluminum foil and baked, grilled, or broiled. Baking, roasting, broiling, smoking, and so forth over a tray of water can simulate the results of the foods cooked by the techniques in Group 3. Thus Group 4 and 5 methods may be used to simulate the effects of Group 3 techniques, but not the other way around using any one of the Group 3 techniques by themselves. Groups 4 and 5 techniques produce very similar hybrid flavors and textures, hence the techniques are interchangeable.

The frying technique in Group 5 is unique. That is because the hybrid flavor obtained in frying is dominated by the flavor of the brown crispy crusts and the oil which are easily identifiable as the fried foods. However, we can still obtain AFT close to the hybrid flavor of the frying by roasting meat in its own fat, and by basting the foods with oil during or after broiling, grilling, toasting, smoking, roasting, and baking.

Combined Techniques. In principle, all the basic cooking techniques that use heat in the cooking can be used as a stand-alone, one-step cooking technique. However, some can be laborious (such as charcoal grilling), some take a longer time to cook (such as steaming or roasting), and some require safe technique (such as pressure cooking and frying).

261

Most home cooking uses the simplest, one-step technique. Such technique mixes all the ingredients and cooks them together using one of the basic cooking techniques, such as boiling, baking, frying, and so on. Examples are preparing a traditional beef vegetable soup, meat and seafood stews, roast beef, and so forth. In the case of making bread, cookies, pizza, and so on, they can be prepared only with the baking technique.

I have stated earlier in the above subsection " Techniques versus AFT" that Group 3 techniques cannot simulate the effects of Group 4 and 5 just by themselves. However, a Group 3 technique (simmering) in combination with a Group 5 technique (sauteing) can simulate the hybrid flavor of the frying. For example, you mix meat with water and oil and simmer until the ingredients are partially or totally cooked. Then evaporate any residual water until the ingredients sizzle in the oil. The sizzling is allowed to self-saute on low heat setting until the ingredients attain the frying hybrid flavor. This combination technique (simmer-saute) is used extensively in most recipes given in this cookbook.

Another example that employs at least two basic techniques in combination to create many elaborate and complex dishes, such as an Asian steam fish (or poultry or seafood or meats) dish. First, the fish is coated with corn starch (or flour) and black pepper. The fish is then fried in oil until it is crisp and browned outside. The browned fish is then steamed for about 10 minutes with partially sauteed scallion, tomato, and onion. After steaming, a CIs mixture (spices, soy sauce, soybean paste, corn starch, and rice wine) is thickened in oil and water, then poured over the steamed fish. The dish is garnished with diced scallion or cilantro.

The latter two techniques are accomplishing the hybrid flavors of steaming and frying. These two techniques can neither simulate the other hybrid flavor by themselves. But in such combination, they accomplish the unusual tasks. See safety **CAUTION** on page 182.

GLOSSARY

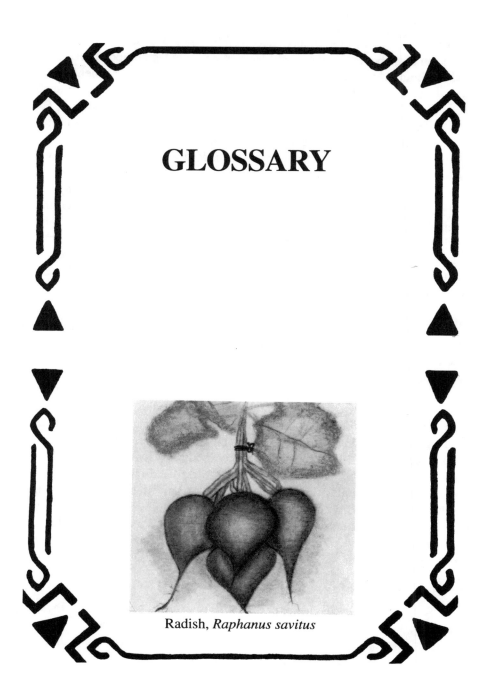

Radish, *Raphanus savitus*

Seasoning Ingredients

Most of the Asian ingredients used in this cookbook are described and listed in alphabetical order. Each description includes composition, AFT, uses, ethnic origin, and availability. Stripped recipes for experimenting on small scale and preparing for the four servings are included for each ingredient. They are intended for use with the Example Recipes Ex 7, Ex 8, Ex 9, and Ex 10 described on pages 227 through 229. Further experimenting may use the ingredients in the recipes (referenced with their Recipe #s) listed at the end of each description. The explorations would require either replacing only the seasoning ingredient used in the referenced recipe with the experimenting ingredient or simply adding the experimenting ingredient to the recipe. Other remaining ingredients and their proportions and the cooking procedure would remain the same. The recipe numbers for the adaptations are omitted for the trivial ingredients. The stripped recipes are excluded in the descriptions of the ingredients that are unsuitable for the experimenting; instead, recipe number(s) are cited at the end of the descriptions that illustrate their uses.

Bamboo Shoots. There are four basic types used in Asian cooking. They are bamboo shoots in water, sour or pickled bamboo shoots, dried bamboo shoots, and braised bamboo shoots in oil. Bamboo shoots in water are made of boiled whole or sliced bamboo shoots. They are then packaged in the boiled water. Their taste is very mild and neutral with a subtle bamboo flavor. Sour or pickled bamboo shoots are made by fermenting boiled bamboo shoots in brine, vinegar or cooked rice. They are packaged in brine. They taste sour, salty, and pungent. Dried bamboo shoots are either made from the bamboo shoots in water or the pickled bamboo shoots. The bamboo shoots are mostly used either as a primary or secondary vegetable for making variety of stir fries and soups. The dishes are prepared with fish, meat, poultry, seafood, and shrimp. There are many excellent brands processed in Hong Kong, People's Republic of China, Thailand, and Taiwan. They are readily available in most Asian grocery stores. See below for description of the braised bamboo shoots in oil.

	For experimenting	For 4 servings
Meat	4-oz	24-oz
Bamboo shoots	1-2 Tablespoons, diced	1-2 cups, diced

See Recipe# 95, 128, 134, and 202.

Bean Curds. It is also known as tofu. There are six basic kinds used in Asian cooking. They are fresh bean curd, pickled tofu in rice wine and its hot version spiked with the red pepper, pickled tofu with red rice soaked in rice wine and its hot version spiked with red pepper, and fried tofu. All the ingredients are made from the fresh bean curd. It is processed from pureed soybean by filtering the water from the puree through a cloth bag and molding the soybean residues into fresh soybean curd or cake (bean curd). It has a mild and neutral subtle AFT to it. It is used for preparing soups and stir fries. Plain pickled tofu in rice wine and its hot version are primarily used as relishes. They may also be used as a basic flavoring ingredient in many steamed, stir fried, and stewed dishes. But, the pickled tofu with red rice and its hot version are exclusively for cooking use only. They are not used as relishes. They are used for making stews and stir fries. The red rice pickled tofu instills a heavy, robust, salty, and satisfying flavor to the dishes. The fried tofu is used for making soups and stir fries. All these tofu ingredients are excellent with fish, meat, poultry, seafood, and shrimp. The fresh tofu is either locally made or processed in nearby metropolitan large cities. The fried tofu is processed and packaged in the U.S. There are many excellent pickled tofu brands processed in Hong Kong, People's Republic of China, and Taiwan. Some red rice pickled tofu are packaged in earthenware pots. They are all readily available in most Chinese, Korean, Thai, and Vietnamese grocery stores.

	For experimenting	For 4 servings
Meat	4-oz	24-oz
Bean curd, fresh	1/4 of a cake, diced	1-2 cakes, diced
Bean curd, pickled	1/2 of (1"x 1") cube	2-3 (1"x 1") cubes

See Recipe# 1, 175, and 191.

Black Beans. Black bean is the basic ingredient in making a variety of Chinese, Japanese, Korean, and Vietnamese seasoning and flavoring ingredients, such as soy sauce, black bean sauce, etc. The beans are steam cooked, salted, fermented, and preserved in many forms. There are three general kinds: Dried fermented black beans, black bean sauce, and black beans in oil. There are many variations to these basic kinds. They taste salty with a hint of fermented tartness. They are used as a main seasoning ingredient in many Southeast Asian cooking. They are excellent for stir frying, steaming, and marinating fish, meat, poultry, and shrimp. There are many excellent brands. Our family favorites are processed in Hong

Kong, People's Republic of China, and Taiwan. They are readily available in most Chinese, Korean, Thai, and Vietnamese grocery stores.

	For experimenting 4-oz	For 4 servings 24-oz
Meat	4-oz	24-oz
Black beans	1-2 teaspoons, diced	1-2 Tablespoons, diced

See Recipe# 37, 40, 68, 86, 175, and 188.

Black Bean/Garlic/Red Pepper. Black bean is cooked and seasoned with garlic and crushed red pepper and then preserved in soybean oil. It tastes salty, spicy, hot, and pungent. It tastes great with simmer-sauted beef, chicken, shrimp, and pork. It's also used as relish. They are mostly manufactured in Hong Kong, People's Republic of China, Philippines, Thailand, and Taiwan. They are readily available in Chinese, Korean, Thai, and Vietnamese grocery stores.

	For experimenting	For 4 servings
Meat	4-oz	24-oz
Black bean/Garlic/Red pepper	1-2 teaspoons, diced	1-2 Tablespoons, diced

See Recipe# 15, 37, 80, 87, and 122.

Black Bean in Soybean Oil. See Black Beans above.

Braised Bamboo Shoots. Contains cooked sliced bamboo shoots seasoned with salt, spices, and red pepper. It is preserved in red pepper oil. It is hot but very tasty with simmer-sauteed pork. It's also used as relish. They are mostly manufactured in Hong Kong, People's Republic of China, Thailand, and Taiwan. Numerous brands are readily available in the Chinese, Korean, Thai, and Vietnamese grocery stores.

	For experimenting	For 4 servings
Meat	4-oz	24-oz
Bamboo shoots	1/2 Tablespoon	1 cup

See Recipe# 95.

Catsup, Tomato, Burmese. The tomato sauce is one of the favorite sauces of most Burmese people. It is like the American tomato catsup. However, the sauce is a staple food and is a part of the Burmese culture. Some Burmese authors romanticize the food in some classic Burmese

poetries and stories. Basic ingredients used in the sauce includes tomato, onion. garlic, crushed red pepper, unrefined cold pressed peanut or sesame oil, fish sauce, fresh cayenne pepper, and fresh cilantro. There are numerous variations to the sauce. One of the popular variations uses a fermented salted fish, such as red snapper, catfish, shad, sardine, mackerel, and so forth. Dried shrimp and shrimp paste are also among the common ingredients used in conjunction with the salted fermented fish. A popular variation among the Burmese tomato catsup is the use of tamarind which gives tartness and a mild ripened fruit sweetness to the sauce. Use of vinegar in the sauce is rare.
See Recipe# 77, 79, 86, 90, and 93.

Chinese Preserved Vegetable. It contains Chinese radish bud, chili powder (cayenne pepper), salt, and spices. It is hot and salty. It is very good with simmer-sauteed beef and pork. The vegetable is used for preparing steamed dishes with meat, poultry, fish, seafood, and shrimp. Slice the vegetable and soak in water for 1 hour before use for a milder concoction. They are manufactured only in the People's Republic of China, and Taiwan. They are readily available in Chinese, Thai, and Vietnamese grocery stores.

	For experimenting	For 4 servings
Meat	4-oz	24-oz
Preserved Vegetable	1-2 Tablespoons, sliced	1 cup, sliced

Curry Leaves. The herb, fresh and dried, is commonly used in Asian cooking to season and flavor many vegetarian and non-vegetarian dishes. However, it is central to the South Indian provincial cooking. It is a key ingredient in authentic Madras curry mixes. It has a characteristic AFT. It is more subtle and milder than the bay leaf. Some Burmese dishes use the herbs as a featured flavor, like the South Indian cooking, in fish, beef, lamb, goat, and lentil soup dishes. The fresh herb is now available more frequently than before only in the Indian/Pakistani grocery stores. The dried leaves are, however, readily available in the stores.

	For experimenting	For 4 servings
Meat	4-oz	24-oz
Curry leaves	2-3 leaves	5-8 leaves

See Recipe# 173, 195, 201, and 207.

Curry Paste. It is made of basic Indian/Pakistani curry ingredients blended with hot cayenne pepper, salt, sugar, and oil. The curry paste is similar to the spaghetti sauce mix which is ready and simple to cook with egg, meat, poultry, and shrimp for authentic and flavorful curries. There are many brands imported from India, Japan, Pakistan, and Thailand. Our favorite brand is a Japanese S&B Golden Curry Mix. The S&B pastes (mild, spicy, and extra hot) are readily available in most Chinese, Korean, Thai, and Vietnamese grocery stores. The other pastes are mostly available in the Indian/Pakistani grocery stores.

	For experimenting	For 4 servings
Meat	4-oz	24-32 oz
Curry paste	2 teaspoons	2-4 Tablespoons

See Recipe# 22.

Curry Powder Mix, Madras. It is a basic seasoning ingredient for cooking vegetarian and non-vegetarian curry dishes. There are numerous variations to the formulation. However, all formulations contain the basic curry ingredients: cardamon, cinnamon, cloves, coriander, cumin, red pepper, and turmeric. The commercial curry mixes are all spicy, hot, and pungent. There are many ways of preparing the curried dishes. However, most curry preparations use the curry mix as one of the basic seasoning ingredients along with onion, ginger, garlic, and oil. There are numerous brands manufactured in Canada, India, Japan, Malaysia, Pakistan, Thailand, United Kingdom, and the U.S. They are all excellent brands and are available in your local supermarkets, departmental stores, specialty gourmet stores, and the Asian grocery stores.

	For experimenting	For 4 servings
Meat	4-oz	24-32 oz
Curry powder	1/2 teaspoon	1-3 Tablespoons

See Recipe# 7, 9, 13, 176, and 202.

Fish Sauce. It is a salty and fishy liquid byproduct collected during making of the shrimp paste. Miniature shrimp variety is used for the making. The shrimp is ground with salt and stored in large jute cloth bags. The bags are stored under heavy objects for several days. During the storage the liquid products, fish sauce, seep out of the bags. The remaining solid shrimp mass is dyed with a purplish colored food dye and used as the shrimp paste. Fish sauce is used for flavoring and seasoning Asian soups, stews, sauces, and stir fries. They are salty with a fishy odor. It imparts a rich flavorful body to the dishes. The sauce is also commonly served as a table sauce on the family and restaurant dining tables. Most are manufactured in Hong Kong, Indonesia, People's Republic of China, Malaysia, the Philippines, Taiwan, Thailand, and Vietnam. They are readily available in the Asian grocery stores.

	For experimenting	For 4 servings
Meat	4-oz	24-32 oz
Fish sauce	1/4-1/2 teaspoon	1/2-1 Tablespoon

See Recipe# 24, 77, 78, 90, 92, and 93.

Garam Masala. It is commonly used as a secondary seasoning curry mix. It is a lesser complex formulation than the curry powder mixes. The basic ingredients used in a garam masala are toasted and contain peppercorn, cardamon, cinnamon, cloves, coriander, and cumin. There are many variations to the basic formulation. Garam masala is generally used as a garnishing ingredient in meat, poultry, lentil, and vegetable dishes. It is also used commonly in making Indian/Pakistani pastries and marinades. There are several imported and domestic brands. They are readily available mostly in the Indian/Pakistani grocery stores.

	For experimenting	For 4 servings
Meat	4-oz	24-32 oz
Garam masala	1/2 teaspoon	1-3 Tablespoons

See Recipe# 21, 25, 26, 42, 176, 184 and 205.

Hoisan Sauce. A basic Chinese seasoning mix used extensively in seasoning Chinese sausage and barbecue roast beef, chicken, duck, pork, and pork ribs. It is also a popular sauce to be served with the Chinese pancakes. It is a paste made of soya bean, garlic, flour, sugar, vinegar, sesame seeds, cayenne pepper, and spices. It tastes salty, mildly tart, and slightly hot. It tastes great with simmer-sauted beef, chicken, pork, and fish. There are many brands manufactured in Hong Kong, People's Republic of China, Taiwan, and the U.S. They are readily available in most Chinese, Thai, and Vietnamese grocery stores.

	For experimenting	For 4 servings
Meat	4-oz	24-32 oz
Hoisan sauce	1/2 teaspoon	1-3 Tablespoons

269

See Recipe# 4 and 114.

Kim Chee. It is a Korean national condiment. It is a pickled mustard leaves (bok choy), seasoned with garlic, red pepper, and a shrimp sauce. There are also several other vegetables, daikon/daikon leaves, and cucumber etc. are used for making the Kim Chee. Freshly made Kim Chee are very spicy, pungent, and hot. Although the Kim Chee can be stored refrigerated for months they develop sour taste with the length of the storage. But, they instill robust and satisfying flavors to the meat dishes. Most Asians use Kim Chee as a relish. Our family uses the Kim Chee after rinsing part of its hot flavor with water. They are excellent pickled vegetables for use as relishes and as vegetables for preparing hot, sour, pungent, and salty soups, stews, stir fries, and steamed dishes. Most of the Kim Chee is made in the U.S. and is available in Korean, Thai, and Vietnamese grocery stores. Some supermarkets in large metropolitan cities also carry the ingredient.

	For experimenting	For 4 servings
Meat	4-oz	24-oz
Kim Chee	1 Tablespoon, sliced	1-2 cups, sliced

See Recipe# 140.

Lentils. Chana, Mung, Pink lentil, Toor, and Urad (dhal, dhall, dal): The word dahl is an Indian/Pakistani generic word for the lentils. They are commonly used among the many varieties of the pea family. The dahl dishes are one of the basic dishes in Indian/Pakistani menus. They are used as gravies, sauces, or soups in both vegetarian and non-vegetarian menus. The texture of the dishes vary from very dilute liquid soups to thick pastes. They are seasoned with the herbs and spices used in the curry mixes, such as cardamon, cinnamon, clove, coriander, cumin, ginger, vegetable oil, onion, red pepper, and turmeric. Their AFTs range from mild to spicy, hot, sour, and pungent. The lentils are also used as secondary ingredients in meat, chicken, shrimp, and vegetable curried dishes. The lentils are commonly available in Indian/Pakistani, Thai, and Vietnamese grocery stores.
See Recipe# 173, 179, 193, 200, and 207.

Meat Masala. This is a specialized curry mix blended for use in preparing meat curries. It may be used as a stand alone seasoning mix or in combination with a curry mix and garam masala. The curry ingredients used in this formulation are basically the same as the basic curry mixes with some variation to the types and proportions of the herbs and spices (cardamon, cinnamon, clove, coriander, cumin, ginger, vegetable oil, onion, red pepper, and turmeric). It is generally hot and spicy. Our family uses the M.D.H. brand for preparing beef curries in combination with one of the Madras curry mixes and garam masala. The masala is manufactured mostly in India/Pakistan. This ingredient is available only in Indian/Pakistani grocery stores.

	For experimenting	For 4 servings
Meat	4-oz	24-32 oz
Meat masala	1/2 teaspoon	1-3 Tablespoons

See Recipe# 9 and 21.

Mushroom, Dried, Chinese. The mushroom is prepared by treating mushroom with soybean based spices and dried. It is commonly used in preparing Chinese meat dishes (soups, stews, stir fries, and steamed foods). They are readily available in Chinese, Korean, Thai, and Vietnamese grocery stores.

	For experimenting	For 4 servings
Meat	4-oz	24-oz
Mushroom, dried	1-2 teaspoons, diced	1-2 Tablespoons, diced

See Recipe# 128.

Mustard Green, Preserved. There are three basic kinds of pickled mustard green or leaves. The most common one is the pickled one. It is pickled in vinegar, salt, and sugar. Most Southeast Asians use cooked rice, in place of the vinegar, for the fermentation. It is salty and sour. There are several variations to the Chinese pickling. They include preserving the pickled vegetable in sweetened wine, and red pepper. The pickled vegetable is extensively used for serving as a relish and preparing Chinese and Southeast Asian meat, poultry, seafood, and shrimp soups, steamed dishes, and stews. In most large metropolitan US cities you may also see the pickled mustard green brewed locally. There are numerous brands available in the market. Most are manufactured in Hong Kong, People's Republic of China, Taiwan, Thailand, and the US. They are readily available in Chinese, Thai, and Vietnamese grocery stores.

	For experimenting	For 4 servings
Meat	4-oz	24-oz
Mustard green preserved	1 Tablespoon, diced	1-2 cups, sliced

See Recipe# 31, 128, 134, 191, and 202.

Noodles, Instant, Oriental. These noodles are partially cooked, flavored with seasoning ingredients, such as extractive of beef, chicken, pork, shrimp, and mushroom, then dehydrated in vacuum. They are very convenient and simple to prepare. You may use the noodle for your lunch, dinner, snack, and any other time when you are hungry. The noodles are packaged with seasoning ingredients and sesame oil bags. However, most Asians use additional vegetables in cooking the noodle. There are many brands imported from Japan, Korea, Taiwan, Thailand, and Malaysia. Instant noodles made in the U.S. are also very good. They are readily available in most supermarkets and Asian grocery stores.
See Recipe# 14, 19, and 147.

Oyster Flavored Sauce. This sauce is a basic seasoning ingredient used in Chinese cooking. It is an ingredient as basic as the soy sauce. It is sometimes used as a substitute for soy sauce in preparing stir fries and stews. It contains oyster extractive, sugar, MSG, corn starch, and caramel color. It tastes similar to the soy sauce but flavored with robust oyster/caramel flavors. There are several brands in the market. Most are manufactured in Hong Kong, People's Republic of China, Taiwan, and Thailand. It is available in Chinese, Thai, and Vietnamese grocery stores.

	For experimenting	For 4 servings
Meat	4-oz	24-32 oz
Oyster sauce	1/2 teaspoon	1-3 Tablespoons

See Recipe# 108 and 147.

Pickles (Indian/Pakistani). There are many types of pickles made of mango, mixed vegetables, garlic, eggplant, turmeric root, chili pepper, tamarind, just to name a few. They are commonly used as relishes and served with main meals. The vegetables are first preserved in salt and dried. Then, the dried vegetables are seasoned with basic curry herbs and spices, such as red pepper, cumin, coriander, fenugreek, etc. and preserved in oil. They are hot, sour, pungent, and salty. Their spiciness ranges from spicy and sweet to spicy and extra extra hot. Most are manufactured in India/Pakistan and the U.S. There are many name brands available in all Indian/Pakistani and some other Asian grocery stores.

	For experimenting	For 4 servings
Meat	4-oz	24-32 oz
Mango pickle sauce	1/2 teaspoon	1-3 Tablespoons

See Recipe# 112.

Radish with Red Pepper, Preserved. Contains turnips, chili, salt, sugar, and salad oil. It is hot, salty, pungent, and sour. Super with simmer-sauteed beef, chicken, pork, and shrimp. It is also commonly used as a relish. Most are manufactured in Hong Kong, People's Republic of China, Thailand, Taiwan, and the U.S. There are several brands readily available in Chinese, Thai, and Vietnamese grocery stores.

	For experimenting	For 4 servings
Meat	4-oz	24-32 oz
Radish/Red pepper	2 teaspoons	1/2-1 cup

See Recipe# 15, 37, 80, 87, and 122.

Rice Wine. In Chinese cooking rice wine is used mostly for flavoring stir fries, soups, and stews. It is also used commonly in marinating meat and poultry for roasting. It contains alcohol, sugar, salt, and spices. There are several brands mostly made in Hong Kong, People's Republic of China, and Taiwan. They are available in most Asian grocery stores.

	For experimenting	For 4 servings
Meat	4-oz	24-32 oz
Rice wine	1 teaspoon	1/2-1 Tablespoon

Salted Fish. Salt water fish (mackerel, red snapper, and croaker fish) are usually used for making the Chinese salted fish. The fish is treated with salt, dried, and preserved in peanut oil. They are mostly used in Asian cooking except for the Indian and Pakistani meals. These ingredients are very salty and similar to the taste and flavor of the Spanish anchovy. Western cheeses are not among the ingredients used in the Asian cooking; the salted fish, shrimp paste, and fish sauce are used instead. Although the salted fish and the cheeses are used differently in preparing the Asian and Western dishes they both instill similar saltiness and robust flavors to the dishes. The salted fish is cooked quite differently among the Asians. Chinese would use the salted fish in some steamed pork dishes. Whereas, the remaining Asians Burmese, Cambodian, Filipino, Laotian, Malaysian, and Thai use the salted fish in many different ways and it is one of the ingredients used practically in everyday meal. The Southeast Asian make their salted fish with both the salt and fresh water fish. The salted fish is not preserved in oil like the Chinese fish is. Instead, they are dried or pickled. The Southeast Asian used the fish for making vegetable sour soups, tomato stews, fried salted fish with turmeric, dried shrimp, shrimp paste, crushed red pepper, garlic, and onion. Most are manufactured in Hong Kong, People's Republic of China, Malaysia, the Philippines, Taiwan, and Thailand. The salted fish is available only in the Chinese, Thai, and Vietnamese grocery stores.

	For experimenting	For 4 servings
Meat	4-oz	24-32 oz
Salted fish	1/4 teaspoon, diced	1 section, whole

See Recipe# 77.

Sambar Mix, Instant. Instant Sambar powder contains a mixture of lentils, tamarind+ and herbs/spices (asafoetida, cumin, turmeric, curry leaves, red pepper, and several other ingredients). Asafoetida+ is a gum resin with an unusual AFT. The mix is used for making a traditional and popular South Indian vegetarian dish. It is served with a South Indian pancake "dosa" and also as a main course soup. AFT of the soup is typical South Indian. The dish is spicy, hot, and tart. The basic vegetables used in making the soup includes, among others, unripe banana, bitter gourd (Carilla fruit), bottle gourd+ (White gourd), cayenne pepper, coriander leaves (Cilantro, Spanish name), drum-stick+, eggplant (Brinjal), okra+ (Lady's Finger), taro+, tomato, and snake gourd+. The soup is garnished with black mustard seeds, curry-leaf+ (Curry-leaf), and dried red pepper fried in mustard oil. It is one of our family's favorites. There are at least three name brands manufactured in India. They are readily available in most Indian/Pakistani grocery stores.
See Recipe# 173.
+See page 276 for the published literature names.

Shallot/Garlic/Ginger in Oil. Contains minced and cooked shallot, garlic, and ginger. Spiced and preserved in vegetable oil. It tastes salty, sweet, and slightly tart. Very good with simmer-sauteed beef, chicken, pork, fish, and shrimp. It is also commonly used as a relish. There are

274

several brands manufactured in People's Republic of China, and Taiwan. They are readily in the Chinese, Thai, and Vietnamese grocery stores.

	For experimenting	For 4 servings
Meat	4-oz	24-32 oz
Shallot/Garlic/Ginger	1 teaspoon	1-2 Tablespoons

See Recipe# 15, 37, 80, 87, and 122.

Shrimp Paste. It is also known as shrimp Sauce. There are two basic versions, fine and coarse textured. They are very salty and have fishy odor similar to the taste and flavor of the Spanish anchovy. The sauce is used in cooking quite differently among the Asians. Chinese use the sauce in some steamed pork dishes. Whereas, the remaining Southeast Asians use the sauce in many different ways and it is used practically in everyday meal. The Asians used the paste for making vegetable sour soups, tomato stews, and fried shrimp paste with dried shrimp, crushed or whole red pepper, turmeric, garlic, and onion. The paste is not used in Indian and Pakistani cooking. Most are manufactured in Hong Kong, Indonesia, People's Republic of China, Malaysia, the Philippines, Taiwan, Thailand, and Vietnam. They are available in Chinese, Thai, and Vietnamese grocery stores.

	For experimenting	For 4 servings
Meat	4-oz	24-32 oz
Shrimp paste	1/8 teaspoon	1/4-1 teaspoon

See Recipe# 77, 80, and 90.

Soy Sauces. There are five basic types of the sauce. Most commonly used in Asian cooking are the light and the dark soy sauces. They are used as flavoring ingredients in soups, stir fries, stews, and marinades. They are used in preparing many Chinese preserved foods. The dark variety is preferred when dark colored sauces are desired. There is a viscous black variety which is mostly used for coloring sauces. Another kind, soybean paste, is widely used as coloring and flavoring stir fries, soups, and stews. Less commonly used variety is the black soy sauce mixed with vinegar. It is used for making dark sweet and sour sauce and preparing pig's feet dishes. The light variety brewed in the U.S. and Japan are readily available in most supermarkets. The remaining varieties are manufactured in Hong Kong, Korea, People's Republic of China, Taiwan, and Thailand. They are readily available in Asian grocery stores.

275

	For experimenting	For 4 servings
Meat	4-oz	24-32 oz
Soy sauce, light	1 teaspoon	1 Tablespoon

Tofu, Fresh. see Bean Curds
Tofu, Pickled in Rice Wine. see Bean Curds
Tofu, Hot Pickled in Rice Wine. see Bean Curds
Tofu, Pickled in Rice Wine/Red Rice. see Bean Curds
Tofu, Hot Pickled in Rice Wine/Red Rice. see Bean Curds

Tofu Sauce. It contains soybean paste, tofu, red pepper, bamboo shoot, and mushroom and preserved in vegetable oil. It is hot, spicy, sour, salty, and pungent. Excellent with simmer-sauteed pork, beef, chicken, shrimp, fish, and vegetables. It is processed only in Taiwan and is available in Chinese, Thai, and Vietnamese grocery stores.

	For experimenting	For 4 servings
Meat	4-oz	24-32 oz
Tofu sauce	1-2 teaspoons	1-2 Tablespoons

See Recipe# 15, 37, 80, 87, and 122.

+Several different ethnic names (Chinese, Indian, Korean, Thai, and Vietnamese) are used for the herbs/spices/vegetables in the Asian grocery stores. Published literature names of some of the ingredients are shown below. See reference below for the other names.

English Name	Burmese Name	Botanical Name
Asafoetida	Shein-go	*Ferula foetida*
Bottle Gourd	Bu-thee	*Lagenaria vulgaris*
Curry-leaf Tree	Pyindaw-thein	*Murraya koenigii*
Drum-stick	Danda-lun	*Moringa pterygosperma*
Okra (Laday's Finger)	Yon-padi	*Hibiscus esculantus*
Snake Gourd	Pe-lin-mwe	*Trichosanthes anguina*
Tamarind Tree	magyi	*Tamarindus indica*
Taro	Pein-u	*Colocacia antiquorum*

Reference: "Some Medicinal and Useful Plants, Both Indigenous and Exotic, of Burma", Khin, U San and Myat, U Tha, First Edition November 1970, Published by Khin Khin Aye, No. 55, 120th Street, Rangoon, Burma.

INDEX

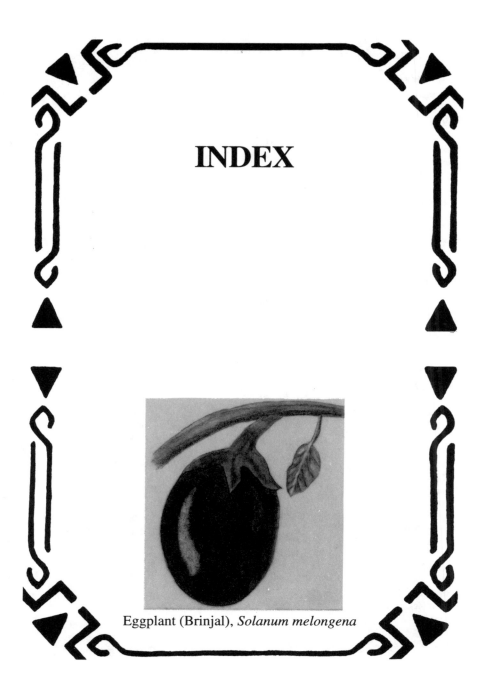

Eggplant (Brinjal), *Solanum melongena*

279

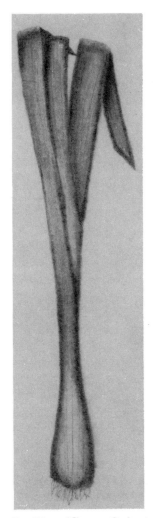

Scallion (Green Onion),
Ascalonia, caepa